A Return to Ancient Wisdom

From Her Enchanting Childhood in the Highlands of Guatemala,
To Corporate Executive with Global Multinationals,
To Honoring the Call of Her Spiritual Truth ...

A Return to
Ancient Wisdom

Beatriz M. Orive

A Return to Ancient Wisdom

First Printing: 2016
Printed in the United States of America

Lived and Written by: Beatriz M. Orive
Edited by: Roberta Binder, RobertaEdits.com
Book Cover Design by: Lotus Design, Deanna Estes, LotusDesign.biz
Book Design by: Lotus Design, Deanna Estes, LotusDesign.biz

ISBN-13: 978-0-9976493-2-1
ISBN-10: 0-9976493-2-1

Note: The names of people and companies have been changed, throughout this book, out of respect and to protect the identity of all involved.

Disclaimer: The modalities and ceremonies in this book are meant to provide overviews. Actual practices require years of dedicated training and guided experience.

Additional copies of this title can be ordered through:
www.AwakeningTheSoul.net

Dedication

My eternal gratitude and appreciation goes to my parents, especially my mother, who gave me the solid foundation of love and inner strength to stand upon for all my trials and tribulations. My mom taught me how to face challenges and emerge humbly, acknowledging the lessons and blessings of the teachers. She also showed me how to live life fully each and very moment, with full knowing that only my intent stood between my dreams and my reality. She taught me how to see the magic in life and to always carry forth a passion for the possible. My dad celebrated the triumphs in my life and cried with me during painful situations. His love of nature allowed me to always be in awe of and have reverence for all that exists in our beautiful Earth. I hope he knows how those moments have, even today, given me the power to move forward. They both gave me treasures that I will always carry throughout my soul's existence.

From my heart to yours!

Table of Contents

Prologue

THE ADVENTURE YOU ARE ABOUT TO EMBARK UPON MAY be your own. Although this book is about my path of spiritual awakening, the intent is for it to serve as an example that when you have the courage to search for your own Truth you will ultimately find that window into stillness. This window opens continuously as opportunities flood our lives, those glimpses of absolute peace and wholeness that we capture if even for seconds. Anyone can enter this world, and my story shows that the moment you say, 'Yes!' the treasures of your soul are waiting for you.

The book is organized into three sections, each one denoting a major passage in my life. It starts with the innocence of my incredible childhood and then moves into the 'domestication phase' of education and career. The first section sets the stage for a typical overachiever's life, driven by expectations and pathways to success that others had laid out. Once there, the realization that happiness and joy isn't about following someone else's path begins to open a chasm within my own life. The second section contains the progression of my spiritual journey, beginning with the search for that special something that would help me fill the void. That void is an empty feeling inside that cannot be filled with anything external, yet permeates everything inside and out. Only the connection to our soul begins to satiate it, little by little. We all have calls to search for our own Truth throughout our lives. The big questions are:

- Do we listen?

- Do we have the courage to reach for the magnificence of who we truly are?

- Or is it more comfortable to continue 'doing' that which we are accustomed to and which allows us to belong, yet never truly satisfies us?

The third section delves into my spiritual practice, which allows me to participate in the boundless present.

Within each section are my spiritual experiences in *italics*, a progression of amazing occurrences that took me into quietude and expanded my own perception of what is possible. You will witness the major shifts that have brought me to this amazing stage of stillness, all stemming from honoring the search for my Truth. As we live and love we realize that happiness is not that ephemeral moment of laughter or a wonderful trip. Rather, it is the ability to be quiet enough to notice the continuous miracles of life. That stillness helps us realize that we are steeped in magic at all times if we just happen to pay attention.

One of the greatest lessons throughout my spiritual path has been to honor my personal ethics and integrity. As I was awakening my intention was to study with people that exhibited those traits. In my experience as a corporate executive I saw the other side of it where people taking advantage of others and being manipulative was the norm, all for the sake of a false power. I am sure all of us have witnessed some form of this. And we need to keep searching, for deep inside each one of us is a universal impeccability that we begin to access as the ego drops away and as we awaken to the totality of our being. Do not compromise for that will only bring experiences that will mirror behaviors that lack honesty. Did I find those spiritual teachers? Somewhat! Each one had wonderful insights and lessons for me to learn; yet the teacher I kept looking for was *inside of me*. I now honor her in my everyday life and as I consciously connect to the wonderment of my soul, I am free … I am whole.

I hope this book brings you to the realization that the 'ultimate joy' is within each and every one of us, especially if you are willing to release all the layers that have kept your own inner jewel hidden for so long. I share with you a Tibetan prayer that has guided me:

May I be filled with loving-kindness, may I be well,
may I be peaceful and at ease, may I be happy.

The Beginning

The Cornerstones

"Let us remember that within us there is
a palace of immense significance."
—Teresa of Avila

BORN IN GUATEMALA THE FALL OF 1961, I WAS TO BE THE
only girl amongst three children. Even though I was in the middle,
the fact that I was the only daughter allowed me to have the vision
of the firstborn. My parents were very well educated, both attending college in the United States. My father was born in Guatemala
from a very dominant French descent mother and a loving but strict
father of Basque ancestry. He was the traditional Latin American
man: hard working, family-oriented, and intimately involved with
us as we were growing up. He was adventurous, athletic and very
handsome. My mother was born in El Salvador from a German
descent mother and a Basque blooded father. She was a very loving
person that carried a luminous light reserved for highly advanced
souls, and everyone that engaged with her was mesmerized. She
had the spirit of a revolutionary, breaking patterns of the typical
Latin American woman from the moment she was born.

My mother believed in equality for men and women, and raised
my two brothers and me with that view. Whatever the boys had
access to so did I. This was a significant departure from the cultural expectations in Guatemala. She had graduated college at

the age of nineteen, managing several coffee farms for her father by the age of twenty-one. She was dearly loved and respected by all the farm workers, almost venerated. At the forefront of the intellectual groups in both Guatemala and El Salvador, she was comfortable being a minority amongst a group of leading male scholars. She loved to open doors for others, whether that was in the arts, economics, or supporting education for less privileged children. My mother also loved defying the norm, and her light and beauty allowed her to bring down walls that had been in place for many centuries in that culture. She did not confront people, but rather they magically became her allies.

My father was a farmer; his love for animals and the land was evident in our upbringing. Even though a very dominant mother had raised him, he did not support women in leadership roles. Women were supposed to support their husbands and take care of their children, as was the fundamental culture in Latin American societies. However, in marrying my mother, he would have to compromise and consider that a woman did not have to be dominant to be a leader. This would set the basis for my upbringing, a silent clash between what was expected of a woman in our culture and the endless possibilities for a woman capable of dreaming a new paradigm that defied the established. Although my father was not too enthused by total equality he was always supportive of equal education. *I often wonder if he knew he had signed up for two female rebels within our family!*

My two brothers are also very unique yet different from each other. The oldest one is three years older than me and is more driven by the intellect than the heart. He is brilliant and studied to be a lawyer, first in Guatemala and then a post-graduate degree in the United States. His career has been mostly geared to international trade and diplomacy. He has strived to be an advocate on behalf of and to have a positive impact on Guatemala, and is well respected within the professional trade circles worldwide.

Within the family he has been a wealth of information, defending his viewpoint more intellectually than passionately. My early memories are of an older brother delighting in scaring us by wearing monster masks. We share a love of music, cultures, soccer, and specially Lake Atitlán in Guatemala!

My younger brother is just a year younger than I am and carries his heart on his sleeve. He is a very social being, engaging with people at every chance. He is also incredibly passionate about his loved ones and about specific topics that hold interest for him, never afraid to show emotion. Quite involved as a parent, he travels to sports and educational events where his children participate. Even today you can still find him inventing games to play with his own and other's children. His professional focus is on the land and he studied agricultural business in the United States. He is a farmer just like my father, and has an incredible magnetism with animals. When I think back to my childhood I remember him the most as we were so close in age that we did many things together. We supported each other unconditionally even though we were very different in our approach to life. I loved to silently rock the boat; he liked to be a part of it, but was rather thunderous. Today we share a love and appreciation for nature, animals and scientific discoveries. We also compare memories of our parents and our upbringing with vivid stories, usually chuckling as we reminisce.

Guatemala is an absolutely breathtaking country! The Sierra Madre Mountains split in three distinct ranges. They cover a large portion of the country with magnificent mountains and many volcanoes, several of which remain active. The altitude ranges from sea level and tropical rainforest to majestic mountains reaching over 11,000 feet. The diversity in biospheres makes for amazing glimpses of flora and fauna throughout the country. The tropical rainforest accounts for about one third of the country, and it is here where the giant Mayan pyramids and complexes reside. The Maya descendants, however, live in the highlands. The capital city is at around 5,000 feet and the weather is spring-like all year long, with temperatures ranging between high 50s to mid 70s Fahrenheit. The major change in the climate stems from the rainy versus dry season, each one lasting roughly six months.

As a child I remember weekend outings with my family. My parents took us to see ceremonies in Mayan towns throughout the country. They both felt that we needed to learn about our own country before traveling abroad, a sentiment that was not widespread amongst our friends and peers. My mother was fascinated by the Maya people and given that Guatemala's population had over 70% of Mayan ancestry, we were taught to respect and appreciate their uniqueness. Each town of Maya descendants was so colorful and so distinctive, not only in their dress, but also in their ceremonies. They bartered amongst themselves and with neighboring towns, exchanging fruits, vegetables, and animals. Those who owned a plot of land worked it with fervor. Girls helped their mother in gathering, weaving and cooking, while boys helped their father in the fields, planting, harvesting and cutting wood for their clay cooking ovens. Their participation in the economy and political arenas was minimal, their school attendance negligible. They did not see the need of learning to read or write when their old traditions satisfied their heart and soul, so they continued as uninterrupted as possible. One of the most amazing things I remember is that the children were always smiling. The adults were amiable and very engaging. This is something I noticed in my early teens and I always felt my schoolmates were missing the true magic of their own cradle.

Guatemala City was very different from the beautiful Mayan towns and their inhabitants. It was a typical 'western' city, with all the hustle and bustle of a large metropolis and the impersonal and competitive nature that goes with that. Although the Maya descendants were the majority of the population in Guatemala when I was growing up, their ways were not our ways. Many of the 'mestizos' (mixture of European with Maya) and direct European descendants did not honor the ancestors of our land. In fact, most people I grew up with would rather travel internationally than nationally if they had a holiday and could afford it. There was a certain disdain towards the Maya people from most mestizos and European descendants regardless of their socioeconomic level. Even though they had paradise in the beauty of their country they were not taught to appreciate it.

I recall one of my grandparents scolded my mom and asked her why she was so adamant about taking her grandchildren to all those 'Indian towns.' Thank God my mom adored the Maya people so much that she had taken the time to thoroughly learn about them. She ignored my grandmother and the society around us, and, together with my dad, was determined to teach us about the 'real Guatemala.' They were firm in their belief that 'you must know your own country before you can appreciate others' and that Guatemala had so much cultural value that it would be an injustice for us not to know our motherland.

During our trips to the highlands we had picnics and sleepovers in the distant mountain towns. We often went to Lake Atitlán, which remains to this day, one of my favorite places on Earth. Three massive volcanoes and twelve small Maya towns surround this volcanic lake. Each of the towns is named after an Apostle.

My childhood memories also included visiting the farm, a large ranch where we engaged with horses and rode a giant bull-looking steer. The Pacific and Atlantic Ocean beaches were beautiful too; the Atlantic with its light colored sand and turquoise waters, in stark contrast to the Pacific's black volcanic sand and deep blue sea. Most of our family outings involved being out in nature. I loved running wild and merging with my surroundings. It gave me a feeling of boundless freedom, allowing me to dream awake.

In utter contrast to the beautiful Maya people and the magnificent countryside was a tremendously unstable political environment.

The country's leadership changed continuously. Presidents were either overthrown through coup d'états or forced to resign in a less dramatic way. When I was barely two years old, Coronel Peralta Azurdia installed himself as President after a coup d'état on General Ydigoras Fuentes. Coronel Azurdia was in power for about three years until the population demanded democratic elections, subsequently choosing Mr. Mendez Montenegro. He remained in power the usual four years and was followed by another democratically elected candidate, General Arana Osorio.

After his four years General Laugerud Garcia was installed in Presidency due to fraud in the 1974 democratic elections. General Laugerud Garcia survived two coup d'états. This unrest continued for the next ten years with diverse military factions battling civilian political parties to install their leader as President of the country. If the President was a civilian, he knew he had to have the backing of the military. However, the military was divided in factions so you never knew when another surprise event would influence the change in leadership.

This leadership crisis was magnified by the guerilla warfare that had been ongoing since the early 1960s. It was most evident in the rural parts of the country where leftist guerrilla groups continuously battled the military. The 'capitalist' countries supported the military, while the 'socialist' ones supported the guerrilla insurgency. Neither seemed to consider the effect their bloody war was having on the Maya population of Guatemala, even though the guerrilla groups maintained that this 'quasi civil war' was in the name of indigenous rights. Both factions recruited soldiers from diverse Maya groups, many times by force. Violation of human rights was rampant!

A large part of my childhood was plagued with insane violence and unstable governments. My experience with guerilla warfare was that it seemed and felt foreign. I remember being stopped by guerrilla groups when traveling to the countryside on many occasions. You never knew what they would do for it largely depended on their leader. They were not a cohesive force, with many factions operating individually. Invariably they would ask us to get out of the car and join other people for a speech. Amazingly the speech was given in several languages yet none of them were Mayan dialects! Many of the leaders I encountered were foreign: Cuban, Nicaraguan, and Russian. They would also search your car and take whatever they felt like, be that food, clothing or anything else that called to them. Whether it was the military or the guerrilla stopping you for a search you never felt safe. Your rights as a person were non-existent with either group!

One of the most intense reactions I had to organized religion developed as a result of the guerilla warfare, with many Catholic priests and nuns involved in one way or another. Millions of innocent people were killed as they blindly followed religious leaders who spoke in the name of God. Men were killed in large numbers, especially those of Maya descent, leaving entire families hungry and destitute. And still priests asked for a contribution to the church. Experiences like this contributed to my desire to seek a more direct connection with God.

The Catholic religion was and still is the dominant faith in Guatemala. The Conquistadors brought the religion with them and the Maya people were deemed 'civilized' once they followed the guidelines of the church. The majority of today's Catholic population sees them as pagan because they venerate the many forces of nature and a multitude of 'gods,' sometimes while at the church. In travels with my parents, we witnessed many Maya ceremonies and I was always taught to respect their traditions.

My mother had quite a few challenges with me related to religion. When I was five years old I asked her where the women were in the Catholic Church. She just opened her eyes in bewilderment, and said: "Good question. They are not part of the leadership. The nuns stay in their convents, many of them in seclusion." On several occasions I asked her why I needed a priest to speak to

God. "Can't I talk to God directly?" I would ask. Her response was that I could reach God however it felt right in my heart.

That option wasn't that simple however for Catholic religion was so rampant it was part of the 'social acceptance protocol.' We were raised loosely Catholic until our first communion at age eleven. My father was not religious at all, only attending church on major dates such as Christmas. Noticing my rebellion to blindly accepting a faith whose rules didn't make sense to me, my mother allowed me to explore my own spirituality after my first communion.

I did not believe in a God that would punish its children or that had a list of 'sins' we had to repent from. Rather, I believed in an all-loving God, genderless and compassionate, who welcomed us to the Garden of Eden. All of these experiences would greatly influence my search for the Divine later on.

The Farm

The farm I spent a significant part of my early years at was a cattle ranch. One of the most exciting things to witness was the newborn calves. I would put my boots on, ask for my horse to be saddled and off to maternity I went. This was the section of the farm designated for cows that were close to giving birth. Once born and for a few minutes while they were still sorting their feet trying to get up, calves looked steeped in pleasure as their mothers licked them dry. Their big eyes would gaze at me sweetly and innocently. A few hours later they would get up, their moms at their side. They trembled a bit as they took their first step, then quickly became braver and took a few more steps. Then they would start running in spurts. In no time they would begin to play. I must have been about six years old the first time I witnessed this and thought, "What a miracle!"

A few years later, I was allowed to witness the branding of calves. I wished I had never seen it because I felt as though it was happening to me. The poor little calves just a few months old would be pinned to the ground against their will by one of the cowboys. They would squeal and kick when the hot iron approached them, and then buck as it burnt their skin. I would kneel down and pet the calf's head and cheek, saying words of healing and hoping to alleviate some soreness. I remembered my father saying, "What kind of a cowgirl are you? This is necessary so that they don't get lost or stolen." I didn't care. The animal was in pain and I was there to help it.

We spent many weeks of our three-month school holidays at the farm. I learned to ride horses at three years old and was allowed to ride with the cowboys when I turned eight. The cowboys were a happy bunch, making jokes about each other the entire time we rode. Their language and awareness was different: the way they spoke to the cattle, their keen eye that could perceive any subtle movement within their periphery and their communication with each other. It was evident they had developed a sixth sense.

They taught me to yodel so the cattle would walk together. I learned to talk to animals in different tones. When an animal strayed I would call it; if it didn't return I used my horse to retrieve it. Vultures had to be driven away when newborn calves were around. If the sun was scorching the cowboys knew how to stay cool. Many trees were fruit bearing and they taught me to identify the ones that were poisonous. They also showed me how to use a slingshot to bring the fruit down. In essence they taught me how to commune with Mother Earth and see nature in a completely different way.

I relished the 7:00 a.m. bell and waited for the horn to be blown so I could jump out of bed to meet up with the cowboys. My boots, hat and water jug were ready. We went far, riding a few hours each time. A morning's work included herding cattle to greener pastures, distributing salt to them, healing those that had wounds, repairing fences, and anything else that arose. Returning home for lunch was followed by a mandatory 'siesta,' everyone stretching lazily on their hammocks, caressed by the afternoon breeze.

With so much youthful energy, I couldn't siesta so I looked for interesting animals to play with. The farmhouse was over one hundred years old, with thick walls, long corridors and large rooms. The kitchen was a separate building from the main house as was the bathroom. There were always fascinating things in the kitchen, ranging from little turtles and parrots (caught by cowboys and brought to the main house for nourishment) to large iguanas that had approached with curiosity. It was a world of wonderment for me. If no animals were around, I listened to the stories of the girls in the kitchen—a life so different to mine. It was no doubt my after-lunch entertainment venue!

On one occasion someone brought a young deer, a 'Bambi.' We had a small, natural and protected jungle within the farm boundary, where hunting was not allowed. However, every now and then hunters would sneak in and poach. This little one's mother had been shot and killed, and the fawn was orphaned. We nursed and loved our 'Bambi,' and when the time came to go back to the city for school we convinced my mom and dad to let us bring the deer to the city. We had a garden and it could stay there. "At least it would have love," we said. The fawn didn't know what had happened with its environment, but it adapted within a couple of weeks. Eventually it grew so large it plowed through doors to open them. It was then that we had to give the deer away to the zoo. The zoo! I was so saddened by this that I went to my bedroom with my puppy Sissy, closed the door and bawled my eyes out.

While at the farm we got to ride a huge 1,300 lb. domesticated steer called 'Negro Bonito' (Beautiful Black). I was barely four years old when I first rode him. His size and sweet demeanor fascinated me. We also raised a monkey, a few parrots and an iguana.

Early Mystical Experiences

Throughout my childhood themes of the unknown and unexplained mysteries were my favorite. Not scary stories, just those that were puzzling. Many years later, as an adult, I asked my mom if I exhibited any 'out of the ordinary' abilities while growing up. She said, "No, I don't recall any otherworldly gifts yet you were always very curious and an absolute rebel. You were quiet in your rebellion and many times your father and I didn't know you were doing your own thing. You always thought there were 'other' explanations for things that happened ... other than those given to you. There was also no need to 'belong' for you. You would do your own thing whether other people followed or not. You seemed always so entertained and creative." She finished by rolling her eyes in wonderment.

Nevertheless there were a few experiences from my early years that marked my life and which now I would definitely put into the 'mystical' category.

I was around two years old when I found myself looking into the eyes of a beautiful angel. I marveled at her wings, which were white and soft and perfect. Her hair was golden and shiny, and every time she turned she left a trail of sparkles. Her eyes were deep blue and when I looked into them I floated to a place of utmost peace and love. I gathered this is where I had most recently come from. I seemed to have the ability to talk to her although I could barely construct sentences then. She understood everything I said to her, as though she was in my head. I felt comforted, loved and safe with her by my side. One day I said to her, "I want to go back. I made a mistake."

She gently replied, "Don't worry sweet one, I will take care of you. You cannot go back now. It is not time yet. It will all be OK."
This reassured me, yet the feeling that I probably should not be

here stayed with me. Ever since I was a child I believed I didn't really want to come to Earth; that I was pushed from Heaven.

A few years after starting my awakening path I began to see trails of sparkles when turning suddenly to my side or back. I know she is with me, as are others …

When I was about nine years old I was given my own room. For the first few nights I resisted going to sleep while thinking about all the things I could do now that I had my own room. I could leave the light on all night if I wanted, or read a fun book, or open my window and stare at the stars, or just dream awake. I was in love with stars and somehow I knew them and could visit them by just staring intently. On one of those nights I decided it was time to star dream.

I opened my curtains and froze in my tracks. Right in front of me was extremely bright lights, blinding yet attracting. I stared at them for a few minutes and they rotated and changed brightness with lightning speed. This was no star. The hue of the lights was different from anything I had ever seen. I quietly and quickly went to get my dad. He came back and saw the same lights. He snapped the blinds closed and said, "I don't want you mentioning this to anyone. People will think you are crazy." He made me give him my word yet the experience was too intense for me to just 'forget it.' When he left I opened the curtains again. The lights were still there although a little further away. Suddenly the object made a sharp turn and disappeared. I used to wonder if 'they' had come to visit me, and what would have happened if I had gone outside to meet 'them.' Since that time a part of me has felt comforted knowing that I have wise beings watching over me.

A couple of years later when I was 11 years old I joined the CISV (Children's International Summer Village). This consisted of a group of young adolescents who traveled to a different city in the world, with the intention of meeting other kids the same age and learning about their traditions and customs. You represented your country and showed other kids various aspects of your culture. Each delegation had four kids, all 11 years old, and a chaperone that was usually in the early 20s. Our group was scheduled to go to Belgium, but before reaching our destination we traveled around Europe. One of our stops was Holland, and as with every major tour we were loaded onto a bus to see the most important sites in Amsterdam.

As we reached one of the neighborhoods my stomach muscles tightened. I didn't know what was happening and decided that I must have indigestion. We walked toward a four story, narrow house that made me feel sicker by the minute. Something important in history must have happened or so I wanted to think. I told my chaperone, "I can't go in this house. I know this house and something is wrong." The other three kids in my delegation always had perfect behavior. They never steered away from the group, never questioned anything and were always compliant. They began to surround me and said, "Describe that house before we go in." Something took over me and I began to describe the house in detail. I saw spiraling stairs, a narrow bathroom on the first floor, somber, dark windows, and a bedroom on the top floor. I knew this house. They went inside the house and saw exactly what I described. Breathing hard they ran out and taunted me, "You are a witch!" My chaperone embraced me and said, "Don't listen to them. You are obviously having an experience that is unique to you." Her words nurtured and appeased me. I couldn't wait to share this with my mom!

When I returned to Guatemala I told my mom about the occurrence and began to cry. It was the first time I had ever experienced such an unusual déjà vu. She held me and said, "Well, we will try to understand what you experienced in Holland." With that reassurance I relaxed and went to play outside. A few days later she had a present for me. I remember my eyes widening as I slowly read the title: *Reincarnation* and opened it. I couldn't wait to start reading it! Afterwards I knew with all my being that I had lived in Holland in a previous lifetime and that the house I saw was a catalyst for me to know the truth about souls … that we have been in this plane several lifetimes for different reasons and with different human characteristics. A million possibilities opened for me with that experience and I was so grateful to my mom for being open and supportive, even though this went against her beliefs and upbringing. That book on reincarnation altered my view of life. It was a wonderful turning point, which lead to my eventual awakening!

The Maya People: My Land's Heritage

As I mentioned before my parents took us to different towns in the Maya Highlands since we were young, and we witnessed a variety of ceremonies. They were all unique and each town celebrated something on a given weekend. My mother, who was born and raised in El Salvador, had migrated to Guatemala after marrying my father. She was in awe of the Maya people and studied avidly about their culture and traditions. She then taught us what each ceremony meant when we arrived in the various towns, including relating the corresponding legends. My siblings and I looked forward to these outings.

Since my early childhood I searched for 'magic' in every Maya town we visited. It had all stemmed from an experience I had at a very young age and it would become a theme throughout my exploration of the Maya people. I found it, several times …

As we arrived in one town my mom remembers me disappearing amongst the town people only to reappear a few moments later. I was about five or six years old. She learned to trust me and knew that I would come back to where she was, safely. With this trust I earned the ability to go a little bit further each time. One time I was gone for about 15 minutes and when I came back she noted I was vividly agitated. She asked me what had happened and why I was so excited. I answered, "Mom, I just saw 'magic.'" She smiled and we continued to walk towards the plaza where the town's ceremony would take place. 'Magic' was the unexplained, the mystery, in a context of awe.

San Juan Sacatepéquez is one of the Maya towns engraved in my mind, for it was there that I had a major recollection of witnessing 'magic.' We had just entered the town with my parents and brothers, arriving slightly before the ceremony was to commence. As many people ran around town gathering the last pieces necessary for the celebration my eyes glanced across the horizon. I wanted to capture the whole scene ... beautiful Maya women in golden yellow skirts moving quickly with smart, small steps ... children running around playing with their handmade tops ... tourists gathering. Yet I knew there was more, much more for me to see and experience.

While everyone was waiting I set out to explore the town. Although I was young I walked around as though I knew where I was going. I weaved in and out of the streets and looked inside the open houses. One house in particular drew my attention, as there was a lot of smoke coming out of it: the windows, the door, and the cracks in the thatched roof. I trotted cautiously towards it, determined to go inside. It was hard for me to see and my eyes had to adjust to the dim light. I was motioned to sit in one corner. I don't think it was customary for 'chancles' to be accepted into their private rituals ('chancle' is a Maya slang term for people of European ancestry). But maybe because I was a child I was allowed in, or perhaps the man leading it knew something about me I didn't know about myself at that time.

In any case I could see a person lying on the floor, visibly sick. The man who had motioned for me to come in and sit down was chanting and moving sprightly around the sick person; he seemed to be in charge. He was holding a bundle of leaves and sweeping it above the sick person's body. His words got louder and echoed as he kept sweeping. He grabbed several small containers, each one emitting smoke and unusual smells. He fanned the smoke around the person lying on the floor, 'cleansing' the air around him. Then he chanted more words I could not understand and flailed his hands in the air. Rarely did he touch the person on the floor.

Then he beckoned the relatives of the sick person to come forth, giving them instructions. Within a very short time the person who was gravely ill got up and walked out with his relatives. It was as though he had just come to visit. The man in charge then stared at me and I took this as my cue to leave. I started running with all my strength the moment I stepped out of the house, towards the central plaza. On the way there I literally ran into my family. Out of breath I took a hold of my mom's hand. She asked where had I been. I exclaimed, "Mom, I just saw 'magic' again." She smiled knowingly and quietly replied, "I'm glad you are back."

My heart would not stop pounding that entire day and probably for a few days after. The excitement rose again within me just remembering what I had witnessed. Later in my life I realized that what I was seeing in these amazing experiences were shamanic rituals ... medicine men and women tending to their patients and doing 'magic' to heal them. I witnessed patients entering the healing houses ill and in pain, and then leaving feeling well. This was my interpretation of 'magic' then, and in a peculiar way it is so even today.

Santiago Atitlán is one of twelve towns around Lake Atitlán, known for its artists and sculptors. It is also of a different Maya heritage than the majority of the towns around the lake, which are predominantly Cakchiquel. The Cakchiqueles are one of the largest groups of Maya descendants still in Guatemala today. Santiago is Tzutuhil, a small group who in the past were in direct conflict with the Cakchiqueles. You felt the difference in these Maya descendants, as they were not so friendly in their interaction with westerners. They seemed reluctant to engage and much more proud than people from other towns. I was always curious as to why they behaved so differently. Most Maya people I had met were humble and sweet, and it always struck me as strange that this particular group was such an exception. After docking in Santiago we headed towards the central plaza. On our way we could see primitivist art being exhibited outside of the houses.

A small girl approached me and asked, "Do you want to see our Maximon?" My mom said to her, "We have already seen it." The little girl said, "No, this is OUR Maximon, not the tourist one." That was enough to peek my interest. I glanced at my mom and she nodded, so I ran after the little girl. Although she had clearly stated it was close by I realized we had different perceptions of distance when we were still walking a half an hour later. We had walked several kilometers by the time we finally descended a third hill. Right in front of us was a humble Maya complex with three houses. She pointed to the one on the right and I followed her in.

There were several wooden benches set up for the attendees. I soon realized the people gathered there were to engage in a specific ritual. I sat down and observed. Again there was a lot of smoke. It was from the copal incense and it smelled great to me! The atmosphere lulled me. The Maximon, or St. Simon as we would call it in Spanish, was a doll with a serious appearance and adorned with a hat and lots of handkerchiefs and ceremonial scarves. The person who approached the doll brought 150 proof alcohol and a cigarette. He then drank and smoked WITH the doll. He placed a cigarette in the doll's mouth. The ashes would fall as though a real person were smoking. The drinking was the same and you could hear the alcohol falling underneath the doll after it 'drank.' This mesmerized me. How could a doll smoke and drink? The prayers from the person in front of Maximon were loud and commanding in tone, almost screaming at the doll.

These people appeared to demand certain things from the doll in exchange for the gift of cigarettes and alcohol they brought, and would even pat or hit the doll on its knees. Although I didn't understand I soaked it all in. I was transported into a different more magical reality. I got up from my bench after observing a couple of people 'negotiating' with Maximon and ran out towards the central plaza, again in search of my family. I found them quickly, and again my mom just smiled, as she perceived my excitement.

When I relayed the story to her, she explained that Maximon was the symbol they used to appease the gods they prayed to, so that bad things would not happen to them or to their families. Later I learned that each town has its own Maximon, and although they might look different the symbolism is the same.

A few years later we went to a Maya town called Zunil. My mom had just explained to us that this is the town where we would see the hanging of the Judas. It was Holy Week. Even though I was brought up Catholic the syncretism of the Maya was far more intriguing and colorful to me. They had led the Spanish

Conquistadors to believe that they worshiped the cross, and the Spaniards thought that meant they had become Christians and thus had finally converted them. What they didn't know was that the symbol of the cross was already worshiped by the Maya long before the Spaniards arrived; it stood for the four directions, and each of the directions had a meaning and a 'guardian.' The Maya descendants today will walk into a Catholic Church and pray to both the Catholic God and saints as well as to their own gods and spirit helpers.

We were seated in the central plaza and I felt a mixture of anticipation and fright. I thought, "Judas was a bad guy to Jesus, so if they 'hang the Judas' does this mean they will actually kill him?" Then the action started. A group of townspeople went to the town jail to get Judas. He was found guilty and therefore would be punished. There was a pole with ropes in the central plaza. The man they were dragging was presented to the people, given a murky drink and then tied up with ropes to secure him during his hanging. The people began to swing him around a pole and as he gathered speed he rose up the pole. At one point he was horizontal to the ground. I kept wondering if he was suffering so I asked my mom. She said, "No, this man has volunteered to be the Judas for this ritual in order to honor the town and its families. He is tied in such a way that it doesn't harm him although it is not comfortable. Also, he is being given 'aguardiente' constantly so he will feel no discomfort." I would later find out that 'aguardiente' was the locally distilled alcohol, more potent than a kick from a cow. I was aghast. To this day I remember how disoriented Judas was during his hanging!

Lake Atitlán:
Where Magic Meets Beauty

Lake Atitlán, located in the highlands of Guatemala, has been and still is my most sacred sanctuary. Ever since I was very young I sat and looked at its magnificent beauty for hours, thoroughly entertained. It is the most breathtaking and majestic body of water in the world! A perfect merging of feminine and masculine, always helping me feel balanced and tranquil. The cloud patterns, the wind, the sun and the moon, the stars ... they all seem to dance here. Its volcanoes call me, each one in a different tone and with a different feeling. The waves have a different rhythm and the twelve Maya towns around it add the color and uniqueness that characterizes it to me. The lake is never the same. Of the hundreds of times I've been to my sanctuary I cannot say I have seen the same landscape twice. It seemingly changes as our lives change. And each time I realize again just how alive it is!

The horizon of this lake is the kind you read about: a place where faeries and devas live and create beauty, where souls find respite from the everyday world and reconnect with their primal essence, a place where we speak to our angels and to the Divine. My first memory of being in this beautiful and majestic place was when I was about three years old. I looked over at the three volcanoes feeling they were guardians looking over me, protecting me as if they were God's angels. My first intention was to learn the names of the volcanoes around the lake: San Pedro, standing firmly by itself right in front of me ... Atitlán, the roundest of them all and the keeper of the balance in the middle of the three; just like my place within my family ... Tolimán, rougher, sharper and more masculine than the other two.

Later I found out that the towns that stood at their feet ... at their 'skirts,' like the locals say, named the volcanoes. So the San Pedro volcano had the town of San Pedro at its skirts, the

Atitlán volcano had the town of Santiago Atitlán and Tolimán had San Lucas Tolimán. When I was five I went to my friend's house near Santa Catarina. There I learned that there were 12 Maya towns flanking the shores of the entire lake, many of them with the names of the Catholic Apostles (San Pedro, San Lucas, San Antonio, San Pablo, San Andrés …). Every time I arrived at the lake I stood incredulous that Great Spirit could have created such beauty. Just the mention of Lake Atitlán brought a tingling to my body, as though its essence reverberated inside of me. I felt I belonged with this lake!

Going to school in the city was the 'in-between' time for me … in between the times we would be at the lake. Every trip to this breathless paradise taught me magical things that I could not quite understand; yet somehow I knew it was the true definition of 'home' for me. Its deep blue water, imposing landscapes and picturesque people are unrivaled. Whenever I have been in its presence I have felt the sense of being held. No matter how many times I have glanced at the horizon I have always felt captivated. My older brother shared the same wonderment about this lake that I did, and together we would dream of having a place to call our own within the shores of Lake Atitlán. The rest of the family admired the lake, but they did not have the absolute reverence that he and I had. We always jumped at the opportunity of being in the lake's presence.

When I was in my early teens my father told us he had rented a lake house from friends. I could hardly contain my excitement and wanted to go there that same day! I remember the first trip to that house as though it was yesterday. There was no road to the house so we drove to San Lucas and then traveled by boat. We had so much stuff to make the house livable that you could barely see our heads poking out from above the mounds. When we arrived a guardian named Goyo received us. He was an elder of San Antonio and fourth generation in his lineage. Goyo was also part of the town council. He had special rights afforded only to those in the 'cofradia.' He would teach me so much about this lake in the next ten years.

One time Goyo hurried down the mountain calling my name, "Biatriz, Biatriz." I poked my head out the door of the main house and saw him practically rolling down the hill. "Cangrejos, Biatriz," he managed to repeat. The crab fisherman was right in front of our house and Goyo was asking if I was interested in buying some. I went down to the water's edge with Goyo so we could talk to the fisherman. He had a bathing suit and a snorkel, plus a friend who paddled the 'cayuco' (a small wooden kayak). He also had a stick of 'ocote' (tree resin) in his hand. The fisherman lit it above the water's surface, took a deep breath and then went underwater with it, trying to use the first glimmer of it to see the crabs hiding in the rocks at the edge of the lake. He would temporarily disappear and then rise up with a crab in his hand. He searched for the 'cayuco' and delicately placed the crab in the green moss they had collected. As he came up and placed the crab on the boat, I asked, "Vende cangrejo?" (Do you sell crab?) He said, "Si." So we agreed on a price. Then I turned to Goyo and without me saying anything he pulled a bag from under his wool skirt. He was grinning because he had anticipated my desire to buy crabs. We piled fifteen small crabs in the bag.

Happy with my new find I ran upstairs to show my family the loot I just purchased. My parents looked at me as though I was crazy, but my youngest brother was excited and joined me. Goyo was still with us, and as we prepared to make a "sopa revividora" (a revitalizing crab soup), he told us how to differentiate the male crabs from the female. If female he showed us where to look for the crab's eggs. After a few hours the soup was ready and the aroma permeated the entire house. Everyone was congregating in the kitchen, anxious to try the aromatic soup. It was fabulous!

A Young Florence Nightingale

In disparity to the joyful and loving family environment I grew up in were my mother's health challenges. When I was barely one year old she had a major accident that resulted in a severe spinal injury. She was pregnant with my younger brother at the time. There was calcification around the medulla, and it manifested as major nerve pain that sometimes led to temporary paralysis of selected areas (arm, neck, back). The pain was severe and she was always courageous in confronting it. Operating the spine was out of the question for, at that time, the chances of paralysis resulting from surgery were above 90%. She was prescribed intense pain medication that dimmed her light and presence considerably.

From as early as I can remember she had to be in traction for her neck. I would go and lay on her side just to keep her company. I recall feeling helpless and impotent. She could not speak to me while she was in traction, but I still remember her large eyes transmitting such powerlessness. The pain medication was naturally causing side effects, from severe migraines to stomach ulcers. It was then that I was first confronted with the spiral effect of prescription pills. The whole scenario brought about an intense desire to help her feel better. *Was the healer born then?* I have often wondered.

Since the age of seven I was trained to take care of her and given significant responsibilities. For example, I was in charge of paying school for the three of us. By age eight I was already trained to answer her phone calls, make appointments, and resolve house issues. I did it with eagerness as if doing so was going to help my mom feel better. Her significant health challenges did not greatly limit our family time or outings to the Maya land, however, and there were long periods where she felt well and was not medicated. Given her incredible aura it was when we enjoyed our family adventures the most.

The Years Beyond Childhood and Into Teenager

As I grew older into my preteens life got more serious. Because we were living in a country plagued by guerilla warfare we had to learn how to handle guns and rifles in order to be able to defend ourselves. Initially my father taught us how to shoot metal and paper targets. Some people shot alligators and iguanas, and the condition was that whatever you shot you ate. My younger brother and I learned to shoot when I was eleven and he was ten years old. He was excited to learn and jumped in front of me to handle the weapons first. When it was my turn I trembled as I held the gun in my hand. There was something about this whole experience that I abhorred.

When using the rifle I aimed at the target and hit it, but was never able to aim it at an animal. I remember long nights awake wondering if I would ever be able to aim a weapon at a person. When I expressed my doubts to my parents they both said, "Hopefully you will never have to use it. But don't worry, if you ever have to you will know when and how. If one of us is being attacked, I'm sure you will use it in defense." I could not say anything, but I really didn't know if I could actually pull the trigger. Even today I wonder if I could point a weapon at a human being or an animal and shoot. There is a reverence to all life that I feel I understood even then.

This was a challenging part of my life. I was forced to exit the beautiful and magical world that my parents had woven for me and enter the merciless reality of tough, tribal rules. I began to realize women weren't allowed to participate in life freely. We were seen as vulnerable, and the dangerous political environment confined us further. The farm had lost its enchantment as well because I didn't feel free there anymore. Rules had to be obeyed, and were strictly laid out even though many of them did not make sense.

Fears of 'what could happen to a girl at this age' and 'what a girl at this age should be doing' dictated the limits that were imposed. Early adolescence was life changing to say the least!

I was really looking forward to turning 15 years old. I thought that my independence would begin, and this Latin American girl would finally be allowed to go out and party with her friends. However, my father was overprotective and although my 14-year-old brother was allowed to go out with his friends, I was told that as a girl I would have to wait until I was 16. This devastated me because for the longest time my dream had been to reach 15 so that I could come and go freely again. My mom saw how distraught I became and suggested I go to El Salvador to visit my cousins. I agreed and packed quickly. I knew this was my chance to fly free for the next six weeks! So I arranged to spend one week with each of my four favorite cousins and two with my awesome grandmother. My dream of being free to go out and enjoy myself with friends was finally coming true. My cousins in El Salvador had been going out for a few years now, so they taught me the ropes of partying. I loved the warmth of the people in this country!

One night, as I was sleeping over at one of my cousin's house, I began to hear noises and feel movement. I opened my eyes and turned the flashlight on, but found nothing unusual. The next morning I told my cousin Sonia about the noises I had heard and she calmly said, "It must have been my sister. She travels while she sleeps, you know." I did not understand what she was saying so I decided to go ask her sister. She told me about traveling 'outside of her body' during dreamtime and being able to see others sleeping. She had seen me wake up and turn a light on. Mind you I had not said anything to anyone other than Sonia. Her sister told me she was able to go anywhere she wanted by just thinking about it. I thought this was awesome and added it to my 'bucket list.'

Upon returning to Guatemala my freedom evaporated once again. I could not understand why women were so constrained.

I would soon discover that this was the way in Latin America, not just Guatemala. My younger brother and I would talk about issues like this and I welcomed a different perspective. However, he could not fully understand it because he did not have to live it. I could only dream of someday having the freedom that boys had.

When I turned 16 I was finally allowed to go out. The only rule was that I had to be with friends that my parents knew well. I also got my driver's license, which was another passport to freedom. Nevertheless I was not allowed to take the car out on my own until I turned 17 because it wasn't 'safe' for women. Once I did and began my senior year in high school I celebrated finally being able to drive alone!

My teenage years were an awakening period, but mostly to the reality around me. It was at this time that my spiritual curiosity began its pull and I avidly read every Carlos Castaneda book I could find.

Sports

I learned about sports at the farm. Returning to the house after a hard day's work we would run and play with all of the workers' children. I always played with the girls, and to gather them I had to go from house to house asking each child's mom if their daughters could come out and play with me. If they weren't playing in the fields with me they had to help with household chores. In addition parents of adolescent girls were concerned that their daughters would go too far with potential boyfriends. We played tag, hide and seek and other local games; we were not allowed to play soccer though, and there was concern that if we played with boys they could hurt us. But I loved to run.

During my teenage years I began to participate more seriously in sports, both at school and at the national level. When I turned

15 my physical education teacher asked if I wanted to compete with other schools in track and field. I gladly said, 'Yes!' Our school had not been able to compete openly with other schools in the city because attending such events was considered dangerous. The political instability had touched many areas of our lives. But track and field gave me the opportunity to meet people from other schools, to learn about how they were raised, and to eat 'street food' such as tostadas with guacamole and salsa.

When I was not training for track and field I played co-ed basketball at the American School. During one of those days the principal's wife approached me and asked if I wanted to play on a women's basketball team in the major league. The major league is equivalent to a professional league, but women didn't get paid. I remember thinking: 'there is a major league for women in Guatemala?' She seemed to have read my thoughts and began to tell me more about it.

I told her I had to ask my parents and she said she would be glad to talk to them on my behalf. It definitely helped that she was the wife of the school's principal. Since I was only 15 she promised my parents to personally take care of me, and would drive me from school to basketball practice daily. It was so very exciting to join her team! I was at least five years younger than any other team member. They protected me, taught me the tricks of the trade and also some very tough life lessons about not belonging to their social class. I could not understand the weariness some members of the team showed towards me, especially since I had just met them. Later I would come to understand the unfair aspects of the social class system and how discrimination works both ways. I endured prejudice from some team members even though it had nothing to do with me as a person or as a soul!

From 15 to 18, I played several sports, winning National and Central American Championships in badminton, basketball, volleyball and squash. After a few years my father said that I had to choose two sports or I would burn out fast. He picked badminton for me because he enjoyed us playing mixed doubles together. I obliged and picked basketball as my second one.

Sports taught me so much about how life could be outside the confines of my protected home environment. I learned about social classes and social conscience, about team spirit and team playing, about losing and winning, and about the discipline required to get anywhere. It was a microenvironment of the real world I would later find out, and it prepared me remarkably well for what was to come. They also gave me the self-confidence to make personal choices, including if and where I wanted to 'belong.'

As a college freshman, I played on the Varsity basketball team. This was 1980, also the time of the Olympics to be held in Moscow. Years later I would find out that Guatemala's Olympic committee had called my home, inviting me to be part of the country's badminton and basketball teams. My parents had not told me about the telegrams asking me to participate in the Olympics on behalf of my country because they feared I would leave school to pursue an Olympic dream. In the end I wouldn't have gone anyway for these were the Olympics that were boycotted by most of the Western world. However, it was a choice I wish I had made on my own.

In the mid 2000s as I was organizing letters and other papers stored in my old bedroom at my parent's house, I found an essay written when I was 16 years old. My friend, Ana, was with me and she asked me to read it out loud. In the assignment we were instructed to pick two themes that we would expand upon after reading an assigned book. My themes were: 'social classes should be abolished' and 'never sacrifice love for money.' As soon as I finished reading Ana started laughing. I asked her what was so humorous and she said, "Isn't it interesting how those two themes have been so prevalent in your life? You must have been born with them because neither one of us was taught that growing up." When I look back, of course I have to agree with her. Social

classes were carefully segregated in Guatemala and discrimination occurred even if you were born in the higher classes. No one
could climb the social ladder so you were stuck where you were
born. I always viewed this as unfair. The theme about love and
money ... I think that is an obvious one for those willing to lead
their lives from their hearts rather than sell their souls for the
sake of material goods!

Higher Education—
Developing the Mind

*"The intuitive mind is a sacred gift and the rational mind
is a faithful servant. We have created a society that
honors the servant and has forgotten the gift."*
—Albert Einstein

WHEN I TURNED 18 I WENT TO COLLEGE IN THE UNITED
States. We had been told since we were toddlers that we were
going away to university in the States because education was
paramount. "What you have in your head no one can take away,"
my parents would repeatedly say. Both of them and their families
had lived through rough periods of political land reform where
government powers would arbitrarily take land as they pleased.
Confiscated land would become their property and was seldom
redistributed. It was always farms that were productive. In addition colleges at home were usually on strike, and education in the
United States was perceived to be the absolute best. So I worked
hard to get excellent grades and off to college I went.

My mother was my advisor for college as there was no one at
the American School assigned to help with university applications.
Since both of my parents had gone to college in the northeast of
the United States they unanimously decided that this was the best

place for me as well. After researching with her it was my dad's turn to take me to see the schools that had made it to our top ten list. Considering all things important to me at the time I ended up enrolling at Lehigh University in Bethlehem, Pennsylvania. It was academically outstanding and small enough that I wouldn't just become a number. I also knew that a big part of studying abroad was immersing myself in the American culture, and appreciated that Lehigh had few foreign students. In addition, the location was close to the schools my friends would be attending.

Higher Education

Upon arriving at Lehigh, I decided to double major in mathematics and computer science. The latter was a field that was exploding in the mid 80s and I thought it would be interesting, so I selected it. This lasted only a couple of semesters for the environment was somewhat strange for me. Some of my classmates loved playing games with other students' computer homework assignments and messing them up. In addition the computer science coursework was just not motivating me so I switched my major to Business and Economics.

I had already taken advanced placement mathematics and science classes in high school, so I had plenty of time during my freshman year to pursue other interests outside of school. I learned how to snow ski, met friends from Guatemala while I visited New York City, Washington, D.C. and Boston, went to rock concerts (which I had never done before because bands never made it to Guatemala), and also played Varsity sports. I even had time to pursue another one of my passions: Spanish Literature. This was mostly independent study and I would read the masterpieces of all my favorite authors: Jorge Luis Borges, Pablo Neruda, Miguel Angel Asturias, Octavio Paz, and Mario Vargas Llosa. I wrote essays about them, compared their works to their lives, and immersed myself in a magnificent world of narrated illusion. I loved the balance between the numbers and the words, the linear and the abstract. This dichotomy continues in my life today as I continuously bridge the ordinary and non-ordinary realities, the visible and the invisible worlds.

By my sophomore year I had liquidated my life savings and purchased a VW Rabbit. Bethlehem was a small town and with so many incredible cities around me the temptation was too big. My chariot was to complement my education, taking me to see the multifaceted northeast. I was thrilled to have entered a world of absolute freedom without limitations of safety or danger! Conquering the world outside college was becoming far more interesting to me until one day I was summoned by the dean of admissions to his office. One of my classes had mandatory attendance and even though the teacher would put us all to sleep, performance during tests and homework were irrelevant if you did not attend class. My parents' only requirement had been that I maintain a 3.5 (out of 4) average, which I had exceeded up until then. It took a chat with Mr McGeady for me to gain enough perspective and straighten my priorities. The thought of my freedom disappearing was earth shattering and he seemed to sense this. I will always remember Mr McGeady as someone very special during those college years; he nurtured me and always nudged me softly back to my path.

My senior year went fast and by the last semester I had decided to stay in the United States for a bit longer. I was finally FREE like I had never been before! Even small things such as being able to go to the supermarket at 10:00 pm, by myself, were fantastic! I did not have to answer to anyone. I also noticed that women in the United States could get jobs by simply being intellectually capable. I thought this was sooooo cool!

Once I graduated college I decided I wanted to get some work experience before furthering my education. After six months of interviews and over two hundred resumes sent I realized that most companies were not willing to sponsor a recent college graduate for a temporary work permit. It soon became evident the doors were not going to open until I furthered my education. So I decided to speak to my parents about it and see if they could help me financially. Scholarships to foreign students at the Graduate business level were not common then. My parents responded that if I got into one of the top ten MBA schools in the United States they would find a way to help me. *"Oh my God," I thought. "I should have applied myself more to get into those top schools."*

But my resolve was strong, so I pursued it further. Marketing and Strategy had become my passion. I researched the top business schools in the nation that included such programs and promptly applied. The top rated school in Marketing was the Kellogg Graduate School of Management (Northwestern's Graduate School of Business) and I was elated to be accepted. Even though the Chicago area winters were brutal, the program and the teaching staff were outstanding. So I enrolled there for the next two years and studied like never before.

Graduate school was a different experience. My classmates were very sharp and extremely competitive. Their only objective was to get a great paying job. My objective was to experience working in the United States for a couple of years. This would give me the freedom to decide what I wanted to do and where I wanted to live. I realized that 'freedom' had always been a huge consideration for me in major life decisions. I studied hard and focused, using 'freedom' as my main motivation. After all I had been well trained to be a perfectionist and an overachiever!

It was at Kellogg that I met one of the most influential people in my life. He was my professor of management policy and, later, my career advisor. His name was Professor Lavengood. His disheveled hair made him look like Einstein; he was brilliant and had a genius wit. In his management policy classes he had us do case studies and compare our recommendations with the philosophies of Socrates, Aristotle and Plato. His classes were challenging, creative and exhilarating. He taught me that the same principles of ethics and values that applied then are relevant now and would be tomorrow. As my advisor, he pointed me in the right direction with such simplicity yet always allowing me to make my own choices. Amazing person that Mr. Lavengood!

The world at Kellogg propelled me into the high-powered and high-stress arena of global business. Corporate interviews, recruiter dinners, open company forums; all of them had their own protocol and language. You needed lots of self-confidence to even attend these events because you had to approach total strangers and boldly ask them to employ you. Small talk and the usual company lingo accompanied each conversation and I quickly understood it was a big game with many anxious players. The whole scene of hundreds of company interviews and lectures was overwhelming, but part of the game.

Having finished my MBA majoring in Marketing, Finance and International Business, I interviewed with numerous companies in different arenas. There was a lot of diversity for me to choose from and I would soon have to make a decision. On one occasion I had several interviews with a major Investment Banking firm from Wall Street, the possibility of an offer was very close. I visited the company's headquarters and met with a host of people. During my last round of interviews, however, I encountered a group of people who were more interested in telling me how wonderful they each were and how imperative it was to get out and party hard. I loved going out but it seemed inappropriate to visit that subject during interviews. The environment did not feel right for me. I had also found the financial world too aggressive and impersonal.

I had prayed for job offers that would take me far from the freezing cold of the Midwest, either to California or to the South. I loved Chicago and its suburbs, but the wind was wicked and the gray skies depressing. I couldn't help but think that if Chicago had been located a few latitudes lower it would have been one of the most ideal cities for me. But the Universe had plans of more freezing weather as the two job offers that I was seriously considering were both in the Midwest. One of them was with the largest packaged goods company located in Ohio and the other one a major appliance manufacturer headquartered in Michigan. Although the packaged goods offer was an impressive company, they had taken the liberty of planning my career for the next five years, without my input. The appliance giant, on the other hand, would give me at least a 50% say in my next move within an accelerated management program; in addition they had ambitious plans to significantly expand internationally and this was tremendously appealing to me. Again I went for the choice that gave me the most freedom and respect, which was the appliance company. In the process I learned to embrace the amazing aspects of the Midwest, like the strong sense of family, the fact that people were open, honest and welcoming, and I admired that it was the industrial backbone of the country.

Florence Nightingale Grows Up

As I moved into my adulthood, so did the caretaker role of 'Young Florence Nightingale.' Coming home the summer after my sophomore year I found my mother doubled up in pain on her bed. I approached and inquired what was going on; she held her stomach, but couldn't coherently explain what was happening. The pain was so severe that she asked me to call an ambulance. My father was at the farm and there were no telephones there. He called once a day via radio, but we had no time to waste. My younger brother was at the farm with him; my older brother was away.

I called the ambulance and jumped in with her as we headed to the emergency ward at the local private hospital. The moment we arrived I asked for them to call her general doctor. He happened to be unavailable in surgery at another hospital. The emergency doctor that saw her told me she had internal bleeding in the stomach area and that they would have to do exploratory surgery immediately in order to find out what was going on. Since I was the only family member with her I was faced with the decision to authorize open surgery or not. I don't know that I was fully aware of all the risks involved, but seeing that my mother was almost unconscious from loosing blood I consented. At the same time I asked a family friend to radio my father and let him know. They were unable to get a hold of him until several hours later.

My father arrived at the hospital a few hours after my mother came out of surgery. Doctors had found a stomach ulcer that was bleeding and were confident that with dietary changes she would make a full recovery. I breathed a sigh of relief. However, my father was very upset with me for authorizing the surgery, telling me the risks of her being adversely affected had been very high. But I knew in my heart that it had been the right thing to do, and at that point the only choice. This episode taught me that you have to trust your instincts when making serious life and death decisions, especially when uncertainty is high.

After my mom came home from the hospital I noticed she was not herself. She was sad and her light was dim. The people that worked for my parents at the house told me this had started right after my younger brother left for college the year before. It seemed she was going through the 'empty nest syndrome.' The kids were gone and her mother role had significantly changed. My father was gone half the week at the farm. In an effort to reinvent herself, she obtained a Harvard led MBA from the local private university and graduated with the highest honors in the school's history. She started a management consulting company with two other colleagues and as it developed into a successful business, one of the partners became ethically challenged. Disillusioned she departed the consulting world and entered a severe depression that would last over 20 years, almost until her death. She went to psychotherapy the entire time, many years with a psychiatrist and several with a therapist. Yet only glimpses of her emerged every now and then.

This experience would catapult me into an intense search to try to help her come out into the light. For many years I studied diverse approaches to overcome depression. I would plan outings with her and when we were together I would witness her temporary revival. Later in my own spiritual quest I would explore energy medicine methods such as soul retrieval, feeling soul loss had greatly contributed to her continuing depression. Some approaches would work in amazing ways and she would feel well for several months. But it was a continuous rollercoaster. Today, I wonder if all these medical and psychological challenges weren't part of an agreement she and I made in order to nudge me into the path of Energy Medicine.

There were many situations since my early 20s when I was called into family emergencies, mostly related to my mother. During my junior year in college I was summoned to meet my parents in Houston's Methodist Hospital, where my mom would finally have spinal surgery. The odds of success were now much higher and she had decided to try to address her severe spinal injury. However, uncertainty was high as she would be one of the first patients to undergo such a surgery. The procedure was successful, but so many years of atrophied muscles had already handicapped her severely. She had to have physical therapy every day, while severe painkillers and muscle relaxants continued being prescribed. The pills would create serious side effects and dependency throughout her life.

My mom loved the attention she received while she was ill. The entire family would hover and love on her. This is when I first became aware of the victim archetype, something she and

I would discuss at length. This is not to take away from the tremendous pain and suffering she was undergoing, but hopefully provided her with some understanding of 'actions' and 'results.' We have all felt victimized at times in our lives yet a few hold on to the perception that 'things are always done to them' or 'that things always happen to them.' Continuous illnesses are part of the victim archetype as well. During my own healing process I had to find the gift in the 'victim' in order to shed it completely. What I understood was that victims are able and willing to receive love and attention. I also realized that I had unconsciously decided to go in the opposite direction, becoming self-sufficient and a giver. *Was being able to receive part of what my mom was meant to teach me?* I continue to ponder this question.

An Overachiever's 'Traditional' Career

"When I let go of what I am, I become what I might be."
—Lao Tzu

MY CAREER PATH IN CORPORATE AMERICA WAS PROBABLY one of my most intense and eye-opening experiences to this day. My dream of becoming successful was based on the definition I grew up with—from society and from my family: a nice house, good income and a stable job with a strong company. This was the definition of success my parents and grandparents had ... generations that were part of a war or post war period in which stability (particularly financial) was the primary objective. So I went right into the thick of the material world, trained to participate in a mechanized environment that had very little room for change or innovation. Some of the experiences that follow will seem intense and at times unfair, but my intention in sharing them is to highlight a choice we will forever face: either becoming stronger and truer to ourselves given the hardships we face, or move further away from who we are as we compromise ourselves and our ethics in lieu of acceptance.

I joined the first major Multinational Corporation at 25 years old, right after graduating from Kellogg. I chose to live in Indiana rather than in Southwest Michigan for I wanted to be close to Chicago and all the many cultural experiences it offered. In addition, I knew that this region in Michigan endured tremendously intense winters with continuous gray skies due to the extreme lake effect. If Chicago was already very cold for me, my emotional and physical wellbeing were bound to suffer in this frozen tundra. The only drawback to my decision of living in Indiana was that I would be driving 150 miles round trip every day in what is known as the 'snow belt' of the United States, plus changing time zones on my way there and back.

My first position was as a *Distribution Analyst* for a top brand of appliances in the United States, where I would learn about warehousing, forecasting and logistics. I started my career with a dynamic group of people. My boss, Anthony, was a kind-hearted man. He patiently explained how things were done at Corporate and why I couldn't just immediately change something that wasn't working. It did not make sense, but I complied. Mona, Logistics Manager in that department, took me under her wing. With over 30 years of corporate experience and still pure of heart she taught me the ropes of do's and don'ts in business with the utmost kindness. To this day the memory of Mona brings a smile to my face. My greatest lesson in this assignment was that what humans feel and their intuition were much more accurate than computerized forecasting models. Mona was always more precise in her forecasting of products, models and colors than the complex computer program developed by a very expensive, top-ten consulting company. She was truly amazing!

After a year of feeling comfortable with the department and developing friendships with several co-workers it was time to select my next assignment. The Corporation was about to acquire a significant portion of a global appliance company, and the people within their ranks who were able to speak a second language and understood other cultures could be counted with the fingers in one hand. So I was enlisted to participate in a new international division as *Global Product Development Manager*. Although I did not have an engineering background, I had to manage the development of appliances in four continents and 15 manufacturing facilities. This was a fascinating experience because I learned about the different 'home habits' of people around the world. It was also very challenging as I was in the middle of internal staff (sales, engineering and manufacturing) and external customers (consumers, distributors).

One of the most culturally interesting experiences I had involved meeting our distributors from Saudi Arabia. Since I was a woman I could not be invited to their home offices because women typically did not work in the business environment. I was told many of their male employees would quit if I entered their building to discuss business. So we agreed to meet in neutral territory. Our Middle Eastern clients made one more request. I had to take a 'male assistant' with me to our meeting. So I asked a close friend of mine to accompany me. Although I am respectful of all cultures and a social anthropologist at heart, I could not understand why women were treated so demeaningly even when going to neutral land. These were the late 1980s and it seemed worse than what I had grown up with in Latin America. I thought that if we were meeting in unbiased territory then regional prejudices should not have been present. Oh how naïve I was! We gathered in a meeting room at a hotel in Switzerland: the clients, my friend posing as my 'male assistant' and I. Our clients wore dark glasses so we couldn't 'read' their eyes during the negotiation; this was apparently typical behavior in their region. They began to talk about a special cooking appliance they wanted, their chairs tilted towards my 'male assistant,' their conversation directed solely to him. I would answer most of their questions, yet they continued to address him. In spite of the fact that they knew I was the decision-maker on these types of projects they never acknowledged me.

As we were leaving one of the clients asked how long their 'request' would take. This was the first time he addressed me directly. I turned to him and responded, "How much respect would you give to a request made by people who didn't show respect for you as a human being?" He hesitated, surprised, then apologized. I think this was the first time his prejudices got in the way of his business objective and he had to make a quick decision as to which was more important to him. I left the meeting shocked by the whole experience. My good friend who acted as my 'male assistant' was still aghast. He could not believe the behavior he had just witnessed from them! I believe it was the first time in his life that he witnessed what a woman in the Global Business World had to endure. This job taught me so much about cultures, about living habits and traditions around the world, and about different areas of expertise within a corporation.

After 18 months of product development it was time for a new challenge. The next position I moved into was *Sales and Marketing Manager for Mexico*. The Corporation had a joint venture with a Mexican company and managing the relationship had always been a challenge for them. Before I was granted the position the International Division's top management had to decide if it was in their best interest for a woman to take over the Mexico account. The joint venture partner had never 'allowed' women into their Board Meetings, and the Corporation did not want to rock the cultural boat. They felt I was the right person for the job, and even though it was already the early 1990s my move was postponed until they had the blessings of their joint venture partner. Once approved, I spent one to two weeks per month in Monterrey, Mexico. This was the beginning of another adventure in Corporate Business, working in one of the strongest patriarchal societies in the world.

The gentlemen I had to mostly deal with in Mexico were the Director of Marketing and the Director of Sales. The former was an American expatriate. He was omniscient and his attitude was that he was there to teach his 'Mexican counterparts.' The latter was a Mexican 'Omar Sharif,' dressed like a dandy and as charismatic as could be, more interested in his popularity and in being admired than in his job. They were both my clients yet they did not speak to each other. Given my assignment I had to work closely with both of them yet they remained in their separate boxes. The head of Sales was very smart and knew how to operate within his culture, his charismatic personality motivating his team of sales managers to strive to meet his lofty goals. And they did! So much so that Mexico became the #1 account in all the international markets of the Corporation.

In every company there is always a 'political group' that agrees with their boss and does everything just to 'belong.' This 'yes group' was not happy that Mexico had become the top account in the Corporation's International Division, and since I was not a part of the 'political group' they declared a silent war on me. I had always refused to participate in political games so I chose not to engage. This meant I was also ousted from their social gatherings. What a blessing! At that time I was the only female in management within the International Division at the headquarters location. As is usually the case there was always an 'angel' ready to protect those with pure intentions. Both the President and the Vice President of the International Division supported and protected me completely from being affected by the numerous political dramas. Later, I would become this 'advocate' resource for others in the corporate world.

On one of my trips to Mexico, while visiting local accounts with the salespeople, the news of my upcoming transfer arrived. The local sales team found out first, and as we had become very close during the months of my tenure, they were saddened by the news. Several of them were traveling with me and said, "We have just found out you are moving to Miami as *Marketing Manager for Latin America*. We are happy for you, but very sad to see you go. As a farewell we would like to invite you to go to any place in Mexico that you may have dreamt about. Two of us will accompany you for the remainder of this trip." With tears in my eyes I thanked them. What a beautiful gesture! I chose Oaxaca, a beautiful state in Mexico that had been calling me for a while. The trip was fabulous and the company incredibly sweet. My experience with Mexico and its people was great, thanks to this group of loving, genuine people who had been my 'customers' for almost two years. And on to Miami I went!

I returned to the Midwest to define the details of my new job and imminent relocation, and to pack my belongings. By mid-1991, I was heading to South Florida. I had mixed feelings about this for even though I wanted to be in a sunny area I had never lived in the heat of the tropics. Guatemala's altitude was 5,000 feet and the weather was spring-like throughout the year. Coming from the cold of the Midwest, Miami was sure to be a drastic contrast. At least I would be closer to Guatemala—my family and friends, I reasoned. The time for Miami was ripe. Latin American countries that had been closed for imports were now opening their borders and the Corporation wanted to be one of the first companies to capitalize on this. Miami was rapidly becoming the doorway to the Americas, developing as a mini-hub for Fortune 200 companies looking to do business in Latin America.

I decided to rent an apartment close to the beach in Aventura for my first year. This would allow me to become familiar with the area before deciding where to purchase my first house. Hurricane Andrew would have a say in this for it surprised me a few months after arriving. Although I had already lived through an earthquake in Guatemala this was totally different. People were advised ahead of time that a major natural disaster was coming and you could feel, and experience, the fear in them and around you. Earthquakes were a total surprise so people just reacted with kindness and compassion towards each other afterwards.

In South Florida the fear had prompted odd and aggressive behaviors from people. You had to be careful when parking at the supermarket or home supply store because people would practically crash your car to take your spot. While at the grocery store people took items out of your cart and put them in theirs, especially water. I was evacuated from my 16th floor apartment forty-eight hours before the hurricane hit. Interesting to be put in a position to consider what I would take with me. Those items close to my heart came first, like photographs and family mementos. Once I left my place I went to stay with friends that lived about 20 miles west of Ft. Lauderdale. One of the greatest impacts such an immense natural disaster had on me was deciding to search for a house inland, away from the beach. I ended up finding my first home closer to the Everglades and further from traffic, crowds and possible evacuations. The wildlife was incredible, especially the birds! In October of 1992, after turning 31, I purchased my first home.

While all this was going on I had a big surprise at work. A few months after my arrival in Miami I would learn that the American expatriate who had been in Mexico and had been so mean was going to be my boss! He had four department heads reporting to him: finance, logistics, sales, and I represented marketing. Henry was quick to assign the office search, selection and setup (including design) to me because in his words: "This is a woman's job." So I learned commercial real estate, architecture and design of open spaces, furniture contracts and selection, as well as coordinating deliveries of furniture and equipment. The whole office was assembled within a couple of months including hiring new employees.

I tried my best to comply with Henry's numerous requests and inappropriate comments, but each time he pushed the envelope further. Within a year I was doing two jobs: part of his and mine! Our office was split between two countries; half of the people were in Miami and half in Brazil. Henry was to divide his time between the two offices, but after just a couple of trips to Brazil he decided he was tired of traveling and assigned me to be the one to travel between both offices. Mind you this was an international office that served 22 countries so traveling was definitely part of the package. I did what he assigned me to do and traveled at least two weeks of every month, acquiring amazing training in leadership and human resources. Shortly thereafter I was assigned with the responsibility of developing the strategic plan for the region. Although I was already doing two jobs this was a great opportunity to learn, so I fully embraced it.

The reward system that was established in the Miami office, and one which is common in many Corporate America settings, was to recognize only those who were 'Yes' people. These were people who always agreed with their boss and who sacrificed their own principles and creativity for the sake of belonging. When there are many of these individuals in a given organization mediocrity ensues. On the other hand if you used your brain and suggested improvements you were dismissed and chastised for 'disrupting the team.' Needless to say I was a system buster and this was to become one of the greatest challenges throughout my corporate career.

After a couple of years I was getting tired of the political environment at the office and of what I perceived as injustices, when a small light came shining through. Our region had just gotten a new President named Derek, and Henry reported to him. Derek was an amazing man and he would make quite a difference in my life. One of his first endeavors was for the company to take the leadership in Latin America and he assigned Henry to develop the strategic blueprint for this to happen. The project was quickly passed on to me except, Henry did not tell anyone he had done this. When it was time to present to the corporation's CEO and to Derek, Henry asked me to go with him, but to remain silent during the presentation.

He got up and began presenting. As Derek and the CEO started asking questions it became evident by the minute that Henry did not have a full grasp of the background information that supported the strategic recommendations. So Derek turned to me and said, "Beatriz, we would like to hear from you. Can you answer these questions?" I began to respond slowly, tiptoeing so as not to step on my boss's toes. I think Derek had his suspicions and this whole scene made it obvious to him. He proceeded to congratulate me in front of the CEO and of Henry; then the CEO did as well. I couldn't help but feel compassion for Henry who had trapped himself in his own political web. If one waits long enough without engaging in these games the dense energy usually comes back to the initiator.

Derek immediately assigned a Human Resources Director to our Miami office. This was the beginning of a positive change. The Human Resources Director was appalled at the stories of unfair treatment he heard from almost everyone in that office and started to understand why the environment was so tense. After being there for a few months he began reviewing everything, including unfair appraisals. A call to order was in the air.

During my third year in the Miami office I found out that I had been promoted to *Director of Marketing and Strategy* 14 months before, but Henry had decided not to tell me nor give me the promotion. Derek had ordered my promotion from manager to director within a few months of being assigned President of Latin America. When I found out and confronted my boss he became cynical in order to avoid answering; in fact, he was quite nasty. I left his office without responding, gathered my things and left, allowing my emotions to run the gamut before making a final decision. If I decided to quit my greatest concern was for the people. I had become their protector; the only one who stood between Henry's abuse and the office staff.

I came back Monday, talked to the Human Resources Director and expressed my desire to terminate my job. He tried to talk me out of it telling me to be patient, but I knew deep inside that my assignment here was finished. I was worn out and needed to take care of myself. Within one week of my decision Derek and the Vice President of the region flew to Miami, asking me to stay. They even offered me the General Manager and VP position that Henry had! I told them that I would consider taking the job for two years, provided they allowed me to change some of the department heads that would be reporting to me. There were a couple of 'Yes' people in key positions and in order to make a turnaround I knew we needed strong leadership. The issue in the Miami office was clearly a 'people' issue. They said to me, "You will have to stay with the people in those positions for one year, and then we will see." Realizing the turnaround would be practically impossible I declined and thanked them for their confidence in me.

Later I realized how many gifts this job had given me. On a professional level it had taught me how to manage a multi-country division, how to develop strategies for an entire region that could be implemented locally, and how to manage remote offices and manufacturing facilities. It also taught me to manage personnel from diverse cultural and professional backgrounds, the legal and accounting do's and don'ts of most Latin American countries, the setup of new offices including hiring personnel, forecasting and data extrapolations to determine market potential, and the ability to make fast decisions to resolve daily fires.

On the personal side I learned about the cultures and peoples of the 22 plus countries that we were responsible for. I also learned to speak Portuguese, getting to know Brazil intimately and being able to communicate more effectively. I traveled to incredible locations that showed me the magnificence of Mother Earth, in the process earning enough airline miles to travel for the next several years for free! As a cultural anthropologist and strategic thinker, learning about the idiosyncrasies and colloquialisms of Latin American countries was fascinating. I learned to separate my work from my personal life without letting the former affect the latter; most importantly, I reaffirmed the belief to never ever betray my personal ethics. It was time for me to thank the Universe for the blessings and move on to what I loved. Later I would realize that this was one of the most valuable experiences that best prepared me for what was to come in my career.

There was another major issue influencing my decision to quit my job with the initial Multinational Corporation. I was in my early 30s and had just learned that my father had been diagnosed with leukemia. He had always been the strong one, the healthy one that had always been there to take care of my mom. When I had kidney stones he was the one to fly from Guatemala to Chicago to be with me during surgery. So that was a significant blow to my own stability as the net that had always held me suddenly became fragile. It was my turn to support him and I would become his primary liaison with doctors during his bout with leukemia. It didn't take long for me to see the effect chemotherapy had on him, diminishing his absolute presence. This would prove to be tremendous motivation for me to go into Energy Medicine a few years later, in a quest to find an alternative to western medicine that would help him heal.

I was 32 years old and my father's illness had given me a wake up call. Clearly titles, money and recognition had not made me happy. The crazy life of travel, meetings and hotels had become tiring. I wanted to enjoy life more and be more spontaneous. So I decided it was time for me to work with one of my passions: the Maya people of Guatemala. I went about establishing my own company called The Mayan Link, with the objective of connecting Mayan textile co-ops with wholesalers in the United States. It proved to be a very challenging dream and a massive cultural test. The Maya people felt that it was a privilege for a customer to get whatever they made and the whole concept of customer satisfaction had no context or meaning to them. The wholesalers and buyers in the United States were amazed that their requests were usually 'altered' in the process. On one occasion they received blue bags instead of the red ones they had requested. When I contacted the co-op to inquire they innocently said, "We couldn't get red thread and blue thread was abundant so we made them blue." It was clearly a cultural dilemma. Eventually I decided to get involved in helping the Maya cooperatives with small business management concepts, and those who were willing to learn were able to maintain clear communication with international wholesalers.

Another humanitarian initiative which I was briefly involved with was in the arena of 'appropriate technology.' I went as a volunteer with a group called "De Hermano a Hermano" (from brother to brother), visiting towns decimated by guerilla warfare where men were few yet women and children abounded. The men had either been recruited by the army or by the guerilla and many had never returned. Their families didn't know what had happened to them and if they attempted to find out it would put them in danger. If there were no men in the village this meant there was no one to work the fields and therefore a limited food supply. We took food and medicines to them. Additionally, engineers would teach them how to produce electricity out of waste and how to reduce the amount of wood they consumed in their clay ovens by placing clay 'bumps' inside the burners—making the air recirculate more and thus use less wood.

It was thrilling for me to see the faces of the women and children upon our arrival, and how incredulous many of them were that we would bring help without wanting something from them. They had felt so wounded by the war and by the 'white people' (anyone from non-Mayan descent) that it was hard for them to trust anyone. With time they began to have faith in us and became very hospitable. On one occasion they had a banquet prepared for us upon arrival. We knew how much effort this had required, especially for a town that barely had food. The concept of reciprocity was very strong among the Maya people. They even shared their 'boj' with us, which was their home brewed alcohol. Fruit was buried for some time and then brought out and mashed until it became liquid. This was offered only on very special occasions. The whole experience was magical for me and for the first time in a long time I felt renewed and exhilarated. It was also a big lesson. In all my years at work in Corporate America I had never felt as fulfilled and accomplished as I had in such a short time with the Maya people.

Barely over a year had passed since I left the Corporate world. It was September and a visiting friend asked if I would ever return to Corporate America. My answer was, "Not if I can avoid it." He went on to press and asked, "If you HAD to go back what industries would you consider?" Thinking about it for a little while I responded, "Maybe the toy industry because it would be fun to research and market toys ... and maybe the technology industry because it would move fast and have lots of inventions." Little did I know the energy I had just sent out!

On the same date, in December—only three months later, I got a call from two corporations. The former was a leader in the toy industry, while the latter was a leader in the technology industry. The coincidences were too amazing and I thought maybe it was a message from the Universe for me to prepare to return to what I considered 'modern day hell.' I decided to call each company back and promptly schedule interviews. I didn't want to ever think back and feel I missed an opportunity.

The interview process began in January and my first ones with toy company were via telephone. They wanted a Director of Marketing for Latin America, but located in Southern California. I asked them if knowing their consumers and proximity to the territory was more important, or if product and manufacturing processes had a greater priority. This would tell me if they were a consumer-oriented company and thus put emphasis, decision-making and investment dollars in the given region, or if they were a product-oriented company and had an inward focus, concentrating more on product development. It seemed very bizarre to me that they would want to locate a Latin America region position in Southern California instead of South Florida. After all I had learned that companies that were serious about their consumers and the respective markets would try to be closest to them. This meant that South Florida was the best U.S. location to address Latin America and its consumers. If their priority was Mexico I could understand the California location. The consensus from the four interviews I had was pretty clear: they had an inward focus. I declined to be flown to Southern California for more interviews, citing the fact that I firmly believed Latin America had to be addressed from a location closer to the region rather than from their headquarters. They were shocked!

A week later I received a call from the second corporation for their Latin American Division, calling to schedule four interviews. The available position was Director of Marketing and Strategy for Latin America, with offices located in Boca Raton, Florida. My thought was that since this Corporation was a corporate giant it would take at least two months before they could make a decision and therefore an offer. So I felt confident that I had time to prepare for it would be many moons before they would ever call me back, if they even did. Within two days from the first four interviews, their Human Resources head called, asking to schedule another set of four interviews. I began to get nervous. Corporate America was not supposed to move this fast and I didn't feel ready to return that quickly.

I doubled up on my meditation time to see if I was missing something. Obviously I was resisting rather than listening for I was meant to go back to yet another Corporate experience, this time with a Fortune 50 company, even if for a short period. The magic words they said were, "We need you to start Marketing from scratch. We have lost touch with our consumers over the last 20 years. You will have to develop the whole division's strategic plan as well as the marketing strategy, plus staff the department." I loved startups. They had me hooked! And so I returned to Corporate America once again.

My full time job began four weeks after the first set of interviews! This was much faster than I had anticipated. I guess one year had helped me forget what the environment was really like, but I was soon introduced to it again. This time it was much more intense than my first experience. A technology company had you 'connected' in more than one way: the pager was linked to the cell phone, linked to your e-mail, linked to your house phone ... until you became their technology slave. Weekends or not you were linked and available, and the expectation was that you would jump at the call of your boss.

Our division's boss was 'special' in every sense of the word. Lucinda did not speak Spanish, knew very little about the Latin American culture, and seemed to care even less about the employees or the customers. The day I arrived at the office she said to me, "Beyatriz get ready for us to travel together. We will be in Chile and Argentina for the next two weeks. I want to start introducing you to our people." I thought, 'Two weeks in those two countries ... that is crazy! They account for less than 6% of the region's business.' I knew something was not quite right. I sighed in relief when I found out a few days later that there would be another person traveling with us: the Sales Director for the Southern Cone. I had spoken to him enough to feel more comfortable.

Shortly after telling me about our trip Lucinda asked me to write my bio. She wanted to send it to our distributors and clients. She gave me hers to read and after going through all the accolades she gave herself I felt ill. I knew you did not do this in Latin America; the focus had to be on our distributors and clients. We should have been the ones asking for their bios to learn more about them. Her approach was clearly backwards and very egocentric. I told her

I would rather not send mine for I did not think it was appropriate. She understood that it wasn't appropriate for me to send my bio because only hers should be sent, as she was the 'jefe.' She then asked me to translate hers to Spanish. Once done Lucinda sent it to the country sales managers for Argentina and Chile, and ordered them to send it to each and every client we had in those countries. They followed her request only to get comments from our clients about how inappropriate this was.

So off we went, first to Chile. We arrived in Santiago and right off the bat we ran into another Corporate Vice President. Lucinda found out this executive had a press conference in a few hours and did everything possible to include herself in the possibility of short-lived fame! Since she did not speak Spanish she dragged me into the event with her. I was so embarrassed to translate many of the things she said!

That evening we went out to dinner with the local sales manager and the regional sales director. While at the restaurant we discussed our plans for our week in Chile, consisting of four visits to customers and many visits to tourist attractions. There were several strange things here: we would visit only four customers and she would allow a maximum of one hour per customer. The whole trip could have been completed in a couple of days at most since Chile accounted for less than two percent of the region's total sales. The customers were obviously not the main reason for our visit and most of them felt insulted by her actions and requests. After we finished each of our numerous activities we had to 'debrief' with her at the hotel bar while she sipped a cocktail. Lucinda would then ask us very personal questions, many that I declined to answer. Then we would go to dinner as a group. At no time were we to leave her alone. The only time she could be alone was when it was time to sleep.

A day later Lucinda told me that she had scheduled me for dinner with the marketing manager of one of our customers. I had no option, but to go. Halfway through the dinner I realized this was a setup. This gentleman was not even employed in the technology industry yet my boss thought it would be fun for me to go out on a blind date. The guy she arranged for me to go out with was completely inappropriate in his behavior and I had to make a quick escape. I marched into the hotel furious. I went straight to her room and banged on her door. Lucinda came out with a mischievous smile thinking the setup had been such a fun idea. Once she heard what had happened she shut the door and said I was ungrateful. Imagine that!

We then flew to Buenos Aires, Argentina. Upon our arrival in Argentina we were transported in the company car to our hotel. Lucinda had picked an exclusive hotel in Buenos Aires: the Alvear Plaza Hotel. Buenos Aires was known to be one of the most expensive cities in the world at that time. We arrived at noon and our rooms were not ready. She had a fit! She told them she was a very high executive with a very important American Corporation and that with just her word the entire company would never stay at their hotel again. They tried to explain nicely that most hotels in the world have a 3:00 p.m. or later check-in time, but she did not want to hear it. She demanded to talk to the hotel manager and since he only spoke Spanish, proceeded to make a scene. We quickly dragged her to lunch and when we returned to check-in our rooms were ready. There was a small issue though as the hotel staff had assumed that the man in our group was the boss. Our regional sales director got a very nice room, nicer than my boss's! She was irate with the hotel staff and demanded the rooms be exchanged. The regional sales director and I had a good chuckle.

Thank goodness I had friends in Buenos Aires and decided to call them and avoid any other tourist plans Lucinda had made for us. This helped me regain sanity temporarily. The day of our return had finally arrived. I had spent too much time on this trip and I couldn't wait to get home. All I kept thinking was, "how did I get into this?" The regional sales director was happy that someone else in the group had some sanity, as was I about him. Together we were able to put up with the absurdity of those two long weeks.

Coming back to the office was almost scary for you never knew what she would do next. One of Lucinda's last whims involved installing a glass door at the Latin America headquarters office in order to clearly divide the executive level from the managerial level. I couldn't begin to imagine a division between levels within the same office! Her boss denied her request and she was very upset. Many things happened in the following months, including her leaving the company. In that short amount of time Lucinda taught me a lot about what not to do!

A couple of weeks later the acting Vice President of our Division came into my office. He was a soft and brilliant man, and one I had come to admire tremendously. He would prove to be like Derek was for me at my initial Corporate experience, a bastion of truth and support amidst a sea of sharks. His name was Barry. We had been without a boss for several months and I had so many questions for him. After patiently answering them he said, "Can I talk to you now?" I felt embarrassed and nodded. He calmly proceeded to say, "We would like to name you Acting Vice President and General Manager of this Division, and wondered if you would accept. I've met with the Human Resources Executive Vice President of the company and with a few other executives and our decision was unanimous. We believe you can do the job!" I could not speak. He said, "This is the quietest I've ever seen you Beatriz." I still could not speak. He told me that I would continue to be in charge of the marketing and strategy areas, and that I would have to double up for a while. So now I had twice the work and couldn't help but wonder how I would ever be able to pull this off. I felt honored, but I also realized how much work was involved. This feeling was all too familiar!

I stayed for another year in that division until I felt totally drained. A trip to Hong Kong to meet with other regional Vice Presidents and General Managers was the last straw. First it took me twice as long to get to Hong Kong and back than the duration of the entire meeting. Second not one of my counterparts seemed really interested in their regions or their consumers; they all knew these were temporary assignments. I realized that with few exceptions I had reached a level where politics were very intense and ego battles harmful.

I decided to ask Barry's secretary for a meeting. She wrote me down for the next day and asked if there was anything she could help me with. She was also an amazing person! Once I entered Barry's office I could tell he had something up his sleeve. I think he had guessed what I was there to do and had prepared himself well. When I told him that I was leaving and cited several personal reasons, he offered me a promotion. I declined. He was amazed and said, "You are the first person to resign after a promotion has been offered. I won't accept your resignation and hope you will work on a temporary assignment with us so that we can allow time for your personal issues to get resolved." I was confused, but knew there had to be a good reason for this to happen.

It was 1996 and I realized that this temporary assignment would be a great blessing. My father had just moved up a stage in his leukemia and things were not looking good. The company had just offered to give me work for two weeks a month. So the part time job would not only allow me to take care of personal matters with my family, but also give me the freedom to start my own consulting company. It was not planned, however I was finally able to be free again. This work was enough for me to pay my bills.

I had just turned 35 and was so tired from the whole corporate fast track that I needed a few months to recover. It confirmed once more that titles, money and ego were not part of my happiness; I knew this was my last time in this environment. I relished the peaceful times with nature and my inner world. I had been forced to limit my spiritual practice during this employment stint, for the only moment I had outside of work was for sleeping. It was time to come back to my spirituality with greater commitment. So I decided that one week of every month would be dedicated to my spiritual search for that 'something missing.' At roughly the same time my friend Maggie said that she would be thrilled if I would consider joining her market research company. They were lacking expertise in the areas of strategy consulting and international business. It was tempting, but first and foremost was my dedication to my spiritual path. This time it was clear to me!

After a few months of getting my life back in order and feeling centered, I called Maggie. She and her business partner asked me to consider joining them as a full partner, but instead we agreed that I would work as an independent consultant for one week per month. It had become apparent to me that I did not want to be employed by someone else, rather be the steward of my own time. This was the only way I could commit to my spiritual path without being pushed into work schedules and responsibilities that would distract me. I realized that a part of me had been taught to be overly responsible, particularly to assignments given to me by someone else. So I started my own consulting company called *Marketing Solutions*.

Marketing Solutions was very active for almost seven years. It was a virtual company managed out of my home office, located in south Florida. During the first couple of years two thirds of the work was from my own clients and the rest from Maggie's company. Most of my clients had been co-workers or bosses who had changed companies and were now at the Vice President and President levels. Maggie's organization was small and had a couple of large clients; her objective was for me to help them grow as much as possible, especially in the strategy and international arenas. My objective was to pursue my spiritual path with greater dedication, as I had decided to concentrate on Shamanism and Energy Medicine.

My projects were in different industries and diverse in nature. Some of them involved startup companies or ventures, others dealt with developing the first strategic plans or marketing plans ever done by the company, and still others dealt with drastically turning a company or division around before its competitors would swallow it. Some months I would travel only domestically while others I would be in Europe or Latin America.

While in Mexico, with a particular client, changes in their management structure demanded I work with about four different management groups. Interestingly the last group was part of the first Corporation I worked with, as they had purchased the remaining percentage in the joint venture I had originally managed more than ten years before. The majority of the top executives were American and did not speak Spanish. My presentations to the company had to be both in English and Spanish; English for the top executives and Spanish for the rest of the company. This proved invaluable in the startup of **Awakening the Soul** a few years later—my newly formed spiritual school and healing center—for everything had to be done in both languages in order to address the U.S. and Latin American audiences. *Life is a wonderful puzzle whose pieces fit perfectly together, isn't it?*

Throughout the next seven years I would marvel at how the moment I was done with an assignment the phone would ring and a client would call with another project. For the most part projects were massive and would take two to three months. I was never idle or without work for more than a few days in seven years! Travel was intense, sometimes two to three weeks per month depending on the project. However, for the most part I was able to follow my intention of taking one-week per month to delve into the depths of my inner world. The more I would step into who I truly was the more it lured me. And the more I touched that stillness, that realm of absolute inner peace and joy, the more addictive it became. My passion was in the spiritual world and it became harder and harder to stay in the business world.

In late 2002, a maturing Florence Nightingale would be called to action again. I had just entered my 40s and my mom had had a massive heart attack. My dad called for me to come to Guatemala immediately, telling me she was dying. I arrived the next day and found her hooked up to several machines. She was dithering between life and death. By then I had been practicing Energy Medicine for about eight years and my mom had participated on many occasions. While she was in Intensive Care I began doing energy work on her; she would help me by distributing the energy throughout her system. Two days later five of the six machines were removed and she was able to travel. We called an air ambulance and headed to the Cleveland Clinic in Ohio, for her condition was so rare that it could only be addressed there. She was due to have 'manual' heart surgery two days later. After running several tests to make sure she was ready they discovered a bleeding ulcer and the operation had to be postponed for another two weeks; the ulcer needed to heal. The surgery finally happened in late December of 2002 and she was miraculously stabilized from a heart condition that most don't survive. A very close call to death of one of my most beloved souls on Earth would force me ponder what was important in life yet again.

By the beginning of 2003 the clock of my 'real life' was ticking and I could feel it would be the year to make major changes. In March I finally made the decision that in a few months I would quit Corporate America and business consulting altogether. I advised my clients and Maggie well in advance so that they could make contingency plans. July would be my last month of full time work. Business had become extremely boring to me and I had to exert an inhuman effort to do my job. The world of spirituality held so much daily magic that anything else was just not satisfying enough for me. *Why would anyone forgo the extraordinary for routine and safety?* I was about to happily explore that option.

By May I had finished the projects for my clients and had just one remaining venture with a client of Maggie's. It was supposed to be an exciting startup venture for an office furniture company. I worked closely with the group that led this new venture that if successful would revolutionize small offices spaces. I knew most of the players involved and both Maggie and I thought the woman in charge of the overall project was sharp and had integrity. We looked forward to working with her.

On the other hand, I could have known that my guides and angels had other plans, as this would be the last project I would ever want to be involved in within Corporate America. The woman that Maggie and I had so much faith in proved to be exactly the opposite of what we thought. She destroyed the initiatives and morale of each team member one by one, and rejected the impartial consumer research results that didn't endorse her own specific agenda. She flatly refused ours and others' recommendations, which resulted in her failing miserably with the company's top management at approval meetings. Each time she failed she blamed Maggie and me for not giving her the right advice. What I could not understand was if this was 'her pet project' why was she sabotaging it? The politics became so toxic that I suggested to Maggie we withdraw from the whole project; her company's reputation was in jeopardy. Maggie decided to continue attempting to straighten out the situation, but the more she tried the worse it became. After another month the project was cancelled. I realized that this whole drama was played out so that I would be able to close the door on the corporate business world once and for all. I had experienced this tough arena many times, but this particular incident left such a bad taste in my mouth that the thought of ever returning was out of the question. It was already July so I decided it was the perfect time for me to publicly announce my retirement from the corporate world. As I would soon find out it was all in Divine and Perfect Order.

Maggie and I had spoken about me staying on one week per month until December. My exit would be gradual and I could pay my bills while developing my new spiritual company. During that one week I would be doing analysis or anything that would not require client contact, for we had decided that it would be unprofessional to attempt to take care of customers only one week per month. So I planned my last trip to Michigan to say farewell to Maggie and company. I loved everyone in that office. We had grown together. I had witnessed most of them being hired, had worked closely with each and every one of them, and always felt honored to be in their company.

A few days before my travel date I got a surprising e-mail changing plans, saying we would be traveling to Evanston for a Board Meeting. I was part of their Board of Directors and usually the meetings were held close to their offices. I had hoped to have enough time with all the employees to say my farewells during this trip. However, I ended up being in the office only one out of the four days! My personal ethics were challenged by those I perceived to be my friends. The trip turned out to be a tough one for me, with many realizations, some major disappointments, and broken agreements. I tried very hard not to take anything personal.

Returning to my house I meditated for a few days, allowing my heart to heal. All signs were telling me to leave the business world completely. Staying one week per month doing work that went against my core could jeopardize my new venture. I would have to give up the safety net of knowing my financial obligations would be taken care of. It was time to jump with both feet and move on, honoring the clarity of the message I had received. When I made this decision it was as though a heavy load was lifted off my back. I felt light and free for the first time since I had started working! As an interesting side note Evanston is the city in Illinois where the Kellogg Graduate School of Management is located. By returning there it was obvious that I was concluding a major cycle in my life, for that is where my business career had started. Unconsciously a part of me knew a major chapter of my life was closing the moment I got the e-mail telling me I would travel to Evanston.

An interesting pattern had begun to emerge between my parent's intense health challenges and my life. On the one hand their experiences had undoubtedly propelled me into pursuing Energy Medicine as part of my spiritual practice. I was seeking an alternative to western medicine that would help them heal. On the other hand it seemed that every major transition in my life had been preceded by a significant health event of one of my parents. Just as I allowed myself to be swallowed by responsibility once more and fall into extreme patterns of lack of self-care that threatened my own sanity, their emergency situations forced me to reevaluate life once more and straighten the ship. Was this a soul agreement between us? The almost death of my mom would prove to be the final push I needed to commit to my spiritual path and soul mission. I was finished with Corporate America. It was time to start making a conscious difference in this world! *After all it is who we **become** that changes the world, not just what we **do**.*

The more whole-heartedly I moved into Shamanism the stronger the signals I received supporting this major life transition. Or maybe I had more stillness and was therefore more 'in-tune' to notice. In any case one of the groups that completely supported me through this time was the animal kingdom. It was fully engaged with me, encouraging and confirming that jumping into my mission without reservations was the right thing to **do**.

*First there were **spiders** everywhere, telling me that I was too scattered and needed to focus. I needed to set time apart to weave my web ... my new endeavor into the spiritual arena. Then **lizards** appeared in numbers indicating that I was to move into a new state of consciousness and needed to 'detach'* *(like their tails do) from others who were preventing me from going fully into my mission. Lizards also told me others could not see, hear or feel like I did, so there was no reason for me to wait for them to validate anything. Both spiders and lizards confirmed that the decision to leave the business world as soon as possible and enter the spiritual teaching/healing world was perfect.*

*Then the **golden eagle** approached, coming right onto the lawn inside my garden! It grabbed its prey and stayed for about fifteen minutes inside the fence. It had booted legs with white fur and an open fan-like tail (dark brown). Its back was dark brown and its chest golden. So what does the golden eagle mean? According to Ted Andrews in Animal Speak the golden eagle represents 'illumination of Spirit, healing and creation'! It symbolizes the balance of being in the Earth, but not of it, of resurrection and alchemy, of mystical powers awakening, and of greater sight and perception. I would learn to move between the worlds, touch all life through healing, and become the mediator and bearer of a new creative force within the world. The golden eagle was telling me to accept a powerful new dimension and a heightened sense of responsibility for my spiritual growth.*

*Next came the **giant blue heron**, one that would become a strong power animal for me. This beautiful and elegant creature would teach me 'aggressive self-determination and self-reliance.' It symbolized balance and mastery of many diverse skills, and represented an ability to progress and evolve. It implied the exploration of other dimensions on Earth, which enabled one to follow our own path. It brought an innate wisdom that helped me maneuver through life by following only my internal wisdom.*

*Finally the **mockingbirds** came and told me to 'find my sacred song' (mission) and teach others how to hear their 'true song.' In other words they were saying that I needed to look for new opportunities to sing my song, therefore following my own* *path. I needed to learn to take what I could and apply my creative imagination and intuition so that I could sing it in the manner and tone most harmonious to me in my life. Mockingbirds are masters of language both spoken and unspoken, with an uncanny ability to read the language of the body and to teach the secrets of all communication to others. This was exactly what* **Awakening the Soul** *would be all about!*

It was clearly time to make the radical transition from Corporate America to founding a Mystery School. A Mystery School is where people study the sacred. But before doing so I would spend a few weeks with my parents in Guatemala. My father had had another emergency situation stemming from his leukemia, this time with complications severely affecting his lungs and therefore his breathing capacity. After a very delicate thoracic surgery he was able to return home for recovery.

I dreamt of visiting Lake Atitlán during this trip if only for a couple of days. I knew it would help me reset before the upcoming life changes. I did not know if it would be possible and much would depend on how my parents were doing. But my younger brother seemed to have intuited my dream and had a surprise planned for me. As soon as I landed he told me to get ready to depart early the next morning. He had spoken to my parents that he would only take me away for a couple of days.

He picked me up at 7:00 a.m. and wouldn't tell me where we were heading. Yet my soul felt that I was going 'home.' As we got the first glimpse of the lake my heart began to beat faster. I thanked him with my eyes and continued looking at the curves of the mountains surrounding Lake Atitlán. We headed towards San Lucas for he decided we would take the boat to the lake house. As we navigated towards the house we perceived a strong South Wind enveloping the lake. In slow motion the lake became completely blanketed with a thick fog. The other side of the lake was invisible within a few minutes and we couldn't even see the bay next to us! It was as though we stepped into a mystical place of kings and queens from medieval times. After lunch he turned to me and said, "Remember your dream of spending a day and night alone at the lake?" I nodded. "Well this is your chance. No one in our family will know. I have to go to the farm, spend the night there and return tomorrow morning. Is this OK with you?" I could hardly answer from excitement. He knew it and packed his small bag, then went to the boat. We knew this lake like the palm of our hand so in spite of the fog I was certain that he would be able to get around it.

I heard the roar of the motor as he left. As it got softer and more distant I realized I was in a dance with my sanctuary, ALL BY MYSELF! The fog continued to get thicker except for the bay I was in. It remained clear enough for me to feel that this was all being staged for me to watch. I felt as though I was in Heaven. I became part of the fog. Slowly the bottom part of the fog lifted and I could see the other side of the lake right next to the water. The volcanoes and mountains were still covered. I went to sleep on the deck until the dew and the cold forced me to go inside. It was an incredible experience and one I thanked my brother for from the bottom of my heart. I was more than ready to face what came!

The Quest
for Truth

The Spiritual Life—
How It All Began

*"Those that danced were thought quite insane
by those who could not hear the music."*
—Angela Monet

IT WAS THE LATE 1980s AND THE SPIRITUAL ARENA HAD not yet opened. At age 27, I had a nice corporate job and career, a comfortable place to live, and was traveling the world. I was 'successful' in significant areas of my life and that were meant to bring about happiness ... or so I had been told. Yet I was not happy deep inside. So my quest to fill that 'something missing' began. Those of us seeking fulfillment and inner peace were seen as strange and non-conformist, and sometimes as atheists—if we didn't subscribe to an organized religion. The ability to find our own path was not supported by our culture, meaning we had to venture out on our own.

I decided to begin by studying a little of each religion that piqued my interest. I was greatly intrigued by Hinduism and Buddhism for both of them placed 'individual spirituality' at the center of their teachings. These religions were not about 'controlling' the group or following rules based on the fear of punishment. Nor were they about instilling guilt. The focus is on becoming the best person you can be by following your OWN soul's calling, and about finding the inner guidance that connects you to the Divine. They were also about taking responsibility for your actions and thoughts. I fell in love with the story of Buddha and its similarities to the story of Jesus. I began to realize that these were Masters sent by the Divine to help us realize we are amazing souls, and that we are unlimited in our potential to love and to create. As religions began to take shape rules and interpretations clouded the real messages from such Masters.

So with the intent of reconnecting to the Source, I embarked on my own quest of discovery. I was thirsty for knowledge of the TRUTH ... my truth. 'New Age' books were just starting to come out and the offering was small, yet it was one of the few options. I remember going to Barnes & Noble or Borders and finding one small aisle with selected esoteric books. As I stood there waiting for a book to call me I could feel the eyes of bookstore personnel and customers watching my every move. I guess it wasn't common to see someone interested in these subjects then; the spiritual revolution was just beginning in the late 80s. I was a 'New Age' person to them because of my choice in books, and at that time it meant I was 'different.' For the next several years I devoured books on diverse subjects: regressions to early life and to past lives, conscious management of energies, quantum physics, energy medicine, shamanism, different ways of reaching altered states of consciousness naturally, speaking to angels, tapping into the collective unconscious, psychic and medium phenomena, psychonavigation, soul companions and soul contracts, and numerous accounts of others sharing their own spiritual awakening stories. With each story I felt motivated to search deeper in order to find my Higher Self, to tap into that source of absolute wisdom we all have inside. I also explored ancient civilizations like the Maya and the Inka, and researched lost continents like Lemuria (also known as Tulea or Mu) and Atlantis. It was all so fascinating yet interestingly very familiar.

In the decade of the 90s the spiritual revolution went beyond the 'early adopter' group and permeated into the 'early masses.' This meant that a significant portion of the population was beginning to pay attention to the questions emerging from within; perhaps also feeling something was missing in their lives. The model of success and happiness we had been raised with no longer worked and a cultural search for internal fulfillment began. New authors were also surfacing. Some of my favorites were: Carolyn Myss, Deepak Chopra, Joan Borysenko, Paulo Coelho, Brian Weiss, Carlos Castaneda, and Jean Houston. I was averaging about one book per week plus attending lectures at local esoteric bookstores.

One of the greatest treasures I found was an author depicting the female as a Goddess. Women were no longer responsible for getting us kicked out of the Garden of Eden nor were they put down as sinners or prostitutes. Instead women were resilient, creative, nurturing, loving, and experiencing life fully through their senses. I also discovered we were each male and female inside, and the ability to balance both energies made the journey even more fascinating. This gave me hope as a woman in this world!

Seminars and workshops from many different spiritual practices were sprouting in the late 1990s and early 2000s, and it was hard selecting from the many offerings. They were all fascinating in the stage of awakening I was in, piquing my curiosity immensely and showing me a world I didn't even know existed. Some of my favorite teachers at the time were: Carolyn Myss, Alberto Villoldo and Jean Houston.

Any book I read or seminar I attended that was lead by Carolyn, Alberto or Jean was outstanding and I craved more. Carolyn explained the management of energies with a simplicity that was breathless. Alberto was so engaging and a true visionary into how shamanism applied to our everyday life. Jean Houston was a brilliant prophet, self-confident yet humble. I felt she lived what she taught and preached. The passion I felt for spiritual subjects was immeasurable. The Universe was calling me and I wanted to explore its depths with fervor. And little by little the void inside began to fill.

After searching for about seven years and studying with a variety of extraordinary teachers I found myself being called to two areas: Shamanism and Energy Medicine. They flowed naturally to me and I could not get enough! Shamanism is one of the oldest spiritual disciplines on Earth; some say over one hundred thousand years old. It is not a religion, but rather a way of life, a discipline ... an attitude. It hinges on harmony and respect of nature, and the realization that we All are One. It is the knowledge that we can create and witness miracles on a daily basis by paying attention and noticing ... in the moment. In shamanism you 'dream your world and your future into reality,' and the past no longer defines who you are. It is also based on the mythology that we are part of and living in the Garden of Eden. Many think that shamanism is limited to 'witch doctors' from indigenous civilizations. But it is much more than that. The time has come to update that definition!

Being one of the most intangible spiritual disciplines that exist my mind had to learn to engage in a totally different way with shamanism. My perception of reality shifted completely as I became entrenched in a world that was usually not visible and many times indescribable. There have been so many direct experiences I have had in shamanism that I cannot put into words; the written language is too limited for this and trying to describe them subtracts from what was experienced. At the essence of this practice is an active engagement with nature and animals, the understanding that we come from and can journey to the cosmos and its stars, magical practices such as invisibility, the brush with realms void of space and time, rituals that acknowledge and honor the whole of Creation, meaningful rites of passage, and above all, a direct communication with Great Spirit or God.

Modern day shamans are those who have mastered life in both the first and third worlds, thereby becoming a bridge between these two. They strive to unite the positives of leading economic and industrial nations with the practices of those who seek harmony with their natural surroundings. The bridge is about people striving to connect the purity of their hearts with the clarity of their minds. It is about those who are driven by possibilities rather than fears, who share information rather than hide it. Shamans are trained to travel to other dimensions or realities with the intention of bringing forth something that will positively affect the current human reality ... to heal it. They do it without judgment of the situation and without the expectation of receiving anything in return; they simply want to help others share in the web of infinity and beauty. Shamans negotiate directly with God (Great Spirit) on behalf of those who need assistance. They have worked hard to open their channels and in most cases are able to receive messages from Light Beings, Angels, Ascended Masters, and even our departed loved ones.

Shamanism engages your soul and spirit before engaging the mind and body. It allows you to gain a clearer perspective of your place within the Universe. It is also a practice of power, especially in managing power. My shamanic teachers used to say, "There is nothing a shaman can't do. There is always a way. You have to be creative." I love this! Shamanism is a discipline for rebels, I thought. In addition it invites our inner child to participate for we can weave a sense of playfulness into the equation of spirituality. This helped me feel connected to my childhood and to the 'magic' I had witnessed among the Maya people. It was a bridge back to my beginnings yet at the same time allowed for integration with what was to come.

Some people believe that shamanism and sorcery is one and the same. While the training for both black (sorcery) and white magic (shamanism) is the same, the difference is in the 'intent' of the person. Shaman have purity of intent and unconditional love, wanting to effect a positive change in this ordinary reality;

meanwhile, sorcerers want power for power's sake. This premise of amassing power is evident in our organizations today—whether they are business, government, or school; they all exhibit 'sorcery-type' behaviors in one way or another. Anytime *we want to win and have someone else lose* we are seeking our power. We must all look deep within to assess what our intentions are in any given situation. If we touch our heart and our intention stems from that perspective we will be walking a path of light ... the path of the shaman.

Energy Medicine is fascinating and goes hand in hand with shamanism. There wasn't a subject in school or college that ever made as much sense to me as energy medicine does, with its explanation of the chakra system and how energy is the source of everything. I love the premise that we are responsible for our own well being depending on how we manage the energy within and around us. The power is ours and things don't just happen to us. We don't need to give our power away for someone else to tell us what is going on and fix us, or to blame others for what has happened to us. We just need to pay attention to our thoughts, attitudes and beliefs, and resolve to change them in order to heal. That revelation in itself was liberating and a radical new concept!

Energy medicine also stimulated my intellectual side by exposing me to new ways of understanding the events and people in my life, the choices I had made, and ultimately the lessons of my life. It taught me that the physical body was interrelated and dependent upon the energetic, emotional and mental bodies. They worked together! I soon began to perceive the world in a totally different way, realizing the interconnectedness of everything in the Universe. I finally understood with greater depth the phrase that we are "spiritual beings having a human experience." Energy is the source of everything and therefore the continuity; it doesn't begin or end. The world was suddenly becoming much clearer!

My first experiences in shamanism were rooted in unconditional love. There was no trickery, no attempt of protecting information or knowledge, no need for gurus, and above all a spontaneity that was just amazing! I learned to listen to my spirit guides and my power animals while incorporating Jesus and the Archangels (especially Michael) to my own mythology. I became aware of the Mother Goddess and her immense love for us. Trusting my intuition and inner guidance is now at the core of my being. *How could I not love and embrace shamanism? Weren't the seeds planted at Lake Atitlán when I was a mere child?*

In 1995 I met Dana, a Lakota elder who became my first teacher in the practice of shamanism. She was in her mid-fifties, robust and unkempt, yet full of vitality and with a childlike innocence. The main premise of her teachings was that everything had to be done with purity of intent and with absolute love. In the fall of that year we traveled to Guatemala with Dana and two other friends of mine. I was on a supply trip for The Mayan Link, the company I had formed to help build a bridge between the US clothing wholesalers and the Maya textile cooperatives. Once in Guatemala many beautiful things began to happen. For instance there was a loving exchange of soul messages between people regardless of language. The Maya descendants of today do not speak Spanish as their first language. They speak Mayan dialects—of which there are twenty-one recognized dialects and uncounted additional ones—and a rough Spanish as their second language. Out of the four of us, only I spoke Spanish. Yet the same phenomenon started happening in each town we went into. Within a few minutes of us being there children would begin to follow our footsteps. Then the women would gather around us. They would approach, take their necklaces off and put them over our head and around our necks, no words spoken. By the time we reached the car we had an entourage following us. They would wave excitedly and the children would run next to the car for as far as they could. I had never witnessed such beautiful encounters, even during my first eighteen years of life there!

Our base while in Guatemala was my parent's small country house in Lake Atitlán. It took about three hours by car from Guatemala City to Panajachel (a town known to locals as Pana) and then we had to veer off onto a dirt road for roughly ten more kilometers. Since we were going to be there four full days we decided to celebrate our journey by doing a different ceremony each day.

The first one we did was for Peace on Earth, the second one to Thank Mother Earth for putting up with our abuses while still feeding and holding us, another one to Thank the Corn Goddess for our food, and the last one for the Healing of All People. Even Jose, the guardian of the lake house, joined us. The energy was magnificent!

The second day we traveled towards Totonicapán, a town about two hours northwest of Lake Atitlán. Our intention was to visit a nearby town that had a very peculiar Mayan cooperative. Andres, the head of a larger textile cooperative in Totonicapán, would be our guide. My friends wanted to see how the locals wove the thread and worked the looms, and were also hoping to talk to some of them. We picked Andres up at ten in the morning. When we arrived he came running out to greet us. We hugged, happy to see each other. I introduced my friends and translated Spanish to English and back. Then we headed to the town of weavers. After a few kilometers Andres asked me to turn right. When I looked over to the right there was only a cliff. I inquired if maybe he meant left but he again pointed to the right, and just then a small dirt road appeared. It was barely wide enough for the car to fit, a wall on one side and a cliff on the other. As soon as we turned onto the road Dana began to hyperventilate. She turned to me agitatedly and asked, "Do you know what happened in the valley below? There was a significant event that ended the Maya civilization during the Spanish Conquest. I see the initials T.U. and you were here. Maybe you were even that person," she said.

I did not know what had happened so I asked Andres to tell me the history of the area. He replied, "We had the last battle of the Maya with the Conquistadors where Tecun Uman finally fell. A spear from a Spanish Conquistador killed him and in the end the Quetzal bird posed itself on his wounded chest. This is why the Quetzal has a red belly." I practically stopped breathing! The T.U. initials that Dana had seen stood for Tecun Uman, the last leader of the Maya people. This had certainly been an important valley in Maya history!

We finally got to the town where the weavers lived and to our surprise they were all men! This is the first time in my whole Guatemala experience where all the weavers were men. We were taken to the weaving rooms where we watched them prepare the thread, sort it and then set it up on the giant foot looms. Then they began to sing, setting their intent for the weaving. It was an incredible sight!

After the demonstration finished we were invited to have coffee and pastries in the center of town. It was a very small town and the center consisted of five houses built closely together. A few elders greeted us as though they had not seen 'white people' for centuries. In time Dana and I were motioned to follow one of the elders. We entered a house and saw an elder lady beckoning us to come in. She took us into a back room where we sat in silence for a long time, just the three of us. The aroma of the copal incense was exceptionally strong and she seemed to change faces as the room filled with smoke. There was an intricate conversation going on between the three of us yet no one spoke out loud. After quite a while she escorted us out of the room. This woman was the town's 'eldest wise person' and she rarely came out to see people, much less 'white people.' They were as surprised by the event as we were! At that moment the energy shifted and we became part of their tribe. We felt loved and welcomed on a much deeper level. Our friends who had remained outside couldn't wait to hear what had happened. It was time for us to return to the lake house. We drove Andres back to Totonicapán and then began our journey back.

We encountered severe thunderstorms. I became concerned that the rainstorms could have damaged the road back to the house as it wasn't uncommon for it to get washed away. Once past Panajachel we entered the dirt road again. After a few kilometers a strange odor began permeating the car. I got out and to my surprise saw that one of the tires was leaking. That explained the foul smell! There were no gas stations, mechanics, or a place to fix the tire! We were far from our lake house and I realized how dangerous it would be for four women to walk that road.

As I got back into the car Dana asked me what was wrong. I told her, letting her know that I was worried. She said to me, "Don't worry Bea. I will ask Michael (Archangel Michael) to take care of it. It will be alright." They had no idea how potentially dangerous this was. I decided to surrender and let her do her thing; there was no other option. I kept driving, feeling the tire pulling the car to one side. Then we came upon a large crevasse on the road, caused by a waterfall that had grown from the heavy volume of rainwater. Several cars and trucks were stuck, some even losing their front chassis in the hole. I had my brother's SUV and after potentially ruining one of his tires I didn't want to risk any more damage. Again Dana jumped in and said, "Bea just keep going. They'll take care of it! Just trust and go forward." I hesitated for a moment, but then moved forward towards the large gap on the road. We passed as though there had been a bridge there for us! I kept inching forward while wondering about the tire. As soon as we got to the house I went around to the other side of the car to check the tire. To my utter surprise it was completely inflated!

A couple of days later as we were driving back to the city we came upon a gas station and stopped to check the tire. It was perfect! The whole trip had been an amazing experience of trust and surrender, and one that would change my life forever. I wanted more of this kind of life, rich with miracles and ecstatic experiences, trusting in the Divine. The 'void' inside continued to fill.

And this is how the never-ending quest began, the overriding pull into a mystical path where spiritual focus became the top priority. I started by deepening my understanding of shamanism across cultures, attending workshops with different teachers. Energy medicine was a natural by-product of the shamanic path. You heal yourself first and foremost before delving into the mystical teachings, thereby allowing the Divine messages to come through unfiltered.

A Gathering of Shamans

One of the first workshops I attended was held in upstate New York at the campus of a well-known institution of spiritual teachings. It was a weeklong gathering of Latin American shamans where participants would experience diverse shamanic ceremonies and healings. There were shamans from Guatemala, Ecuador, Peru and Brazil ... about eleven in total. My friend Annie and I had agreed to meet there. We couldn't wait to get a sampling of the different sacred practices available throughout Latin America as seen through the eyes of powerful Medicine men and women.

The word 'Xaman' is said to have originated in Siberia over 100,000 years ago. There are many interpretations for what a shaman does and how they are perceived. However, during the first day there I heard an explanation that has resonated with me ever since:

A shaman is defined as a person who
journeys into other worlds or dimensions
to gather power and energy, in order to
effect a positive change for the larger
community and for other people.

The workshop started with a couple of evening ceremonies intent on paving the road for the week ahead. One of the rituals would be attempted for the first time in many decades. It was supposed to give us a taste of 'psychonavigation,' but there was uncertainty as to whether it would work. Kathy, an attendee of the seminar, had seven clay kettles given to her by her close friend Edmund. He was an avid anthropologist who had traveled throughout the world and was fascinated by shamanic practices. Before dying of cancer, he decided to gift the kettles to one of his most promising students. As he gave them to Kathy he told her, "This is a forgotten ceremony. I got these kettles from a close friend in Peru and the Inka used them as a psychonavigation tool. The ceremony seems to have become a lost art as I never found out how they were used. Maybe you will be able to revive the ceremony some day." The seven kettles had been carefully stored in a special case, padded and protected to insure their safety. Kathy had decided to travel with the kettles and bring them to the Gathering of Latin American Shamans just in case anyone knew how to use them. It just so happened that the only Inka shaman in the group had witnessed this ceremony as a child and remembered enough to attempt to recreate it. No doubt she was being guided by the Universe and by our Inka ancestors!

It was time for the second ritual of the evening. The 'Coca Ceremony' that preceded it had set the stage, leaving an environment of magical mysticism amongst the group. There was an overriding feeling of peace yet there was also a sense of anticipation in the air. I couldn't wait to figure out what 'psychonavigation' was all about. After all I could barely pronounce the word!

The ceremony began with us gathered around in a circle. The seven kettles had been placed in a straight line right in the middle of the circle. A shaman was positioned in front of each kettle. One at a time, from left to right, each shaman began blowing into his or her clay kettle. The sound emitted was incredibly profound! Each of the seven kettles was tuned ¼ of a note apart from the other. I began to feel the cells inside my body resonate to each sound, developing an internal vibration I had never felt before. The sounds were awaking my cellular body, the part of my soul that had traveled freely so many times. Slowly I forgot I had a physical body. The sounds lifted me and I felt myself being taken away from the physical reality. My surroundings became blurry and visions began. I rubbed my eyes in disbelief, but the visions only got clearer. In one of them I was the 'guardian of the trees and of the forests.' The more the shamans blew into the kettles the more rapidly I revolved around each tree and through the entire forest and then the world's forests, all simultaneously; I had become a luminous spark! The faster I spun the greater the spirals of light.

It was magical how the trees spoke to me. They were saying, "Remember, just remember … you have been the guardian of the trees many times …" I could also feel their pulse beating faster as I circled them, excitedly reveling in the light. There was no separateness between the trees, the forests and myself. We were all one, feeling more than seeing.

In another vision I had a 'tunnel' of light in my hands and realized I could pass people who I shared a heart connection with through the tunnel. The tunnel of light would transmute anything that was weighing them down. As I thought of each person and was granted their permission I passed them through the tunnel and felt their hearts surrender into the light. The glow within each was immense. I was able to do this with my entire family, close friends, and anyone I felt a strong heart bond with. The whole experience was unbelievable!

As the kettles began to wind down I felt myself floating in another realm. I could barely hear them anymore. Suddenly I felt someone embracing me and with soft words began to say,

"Bea, come back. I am here to hold you. It is time to come back."
Gradually I began to return to ordinary reality. When my eyes
opened I saw my dear friend Annie holding me in the middle
of the lawn; everyone from the ceremony was gone. She asked
if I could get up and walk. I nodded.

As she slowly helped me up my feet felt wobbly. I felt as though
my soul had traveled so far that my physical body didn't know
how to act anymore. In baby steps we left the ceremonial place.
When I began to really 'see' my surroundings I noticed the trees
had different, more vibrant colors. I could only stand there in
awe, speechless. Annie looked at me wonderingly. I turned my
head to the other side and a shrub of beautiful yellow green
leaves was smiling at me. As I walked further down the path I
began to notice that all of the plants and trees had different hues.
There was even an ethereal hue surrounding them. I suddenly
understood I was looking at their auras or energy fields. All I
could say to Annie was, "This is amazing. I now realize I had
never really 'seen' our beautiful Earth before." She smiled and
continued guiding me back to our small cottage. This was the
first time I had ever seen auras.

So the *Inka Auditory Clay Kettles Ceremony* was celebrated
successfully once more! And in the process I finally understood
what 'psychonavigation' meant. My dance with nature would be
completely altered as a result.

Healing Experiences at the Gathering of Shamans

Each of the 11 shamans was unique in their approach to healing
even if the intention of wellbeing for the patient was the same.
The workshop had designated two of the five days for healings,

and as workshop participants we were offered the opportunity to take advantage of the presence of these amazing shamans. We could sign up for a maximum of two healings, but with so many attendees that would be a challenge. I was lucky to get my first one scheduled with Ecuadorian shamans Doña Maria and her husband Antonio, and the second one with Maya shaman Eduardo. Interestingly both healings got scheduled for the same day, which coincidentally happened to be the 'day of healing' in the Maya Tzolkin Calendar.

After the lunch break I headed to the healing cabin of Doña Maria and her husband Don Antonio. It was widely known that she commanded the healing and he was her assistant. Late the night before Annie and I had found out that many Ecuadorian shamans required their clients to be naked during the healings, stripping us of our 'western cover.' They maintained that we hid behind our clothes and if we wanted healing we had to come in our birthday suit. Doña Maria was one of them and I found myself facing an internal conflict imposed by my own culture. "What do you mean I have to be naked?" I had asked when I found out.

"That is not all," the person responded, "there will be people witnessing your ceremony and holding the energy." So not only did I have to stand stark naked in a hut in front of healers, but I had to allow everyone that chose to attend to see my original suit. Forget about prudishness and self-esteem, I thought to myself. After a few hours of facing extreme inner resistance I decided to just surrender to the experience.

When I first saw Doña Maria at the opening ceremony, all four feet of her, I felt a pull in my heart, an overwhelming gentleness and a deep recognition of her soul. She locked eyes with me and with the most beautiful smile said in broken Spanish, "Hola, comadre." This is a term used in Spanish to denote a certain recognition or endearment to someone ... and acceptance into the inner circle. Her first language was Quechua, Spanish being a second language ... a language learned in order to survive in the post Conquistadors world.

I held her gaze and from my heart said, "Hola. Un placer." (Hello. A pleasure). I felt as though we had reconnected ... an agreement made lifetimes ago to meet again. She was known to be an expert with female bodies and female issues, and aside from our mutual recognition it was her gentle yet firm demeanor that had attracted me to sign up with her. I was determined to heal that part of me that was ready. We were instructed to bring two eggs, two red carnations and one white candle to the healing.

As I entered the small, wooden cottage I was ushered to a chair on the right. There were chairs all around the room. The individuals receiving healing moved along the right wall. Those holding energies and 'watching' silently shuffled along the far wall. Doña Maria and Don Antonio had set up their healing artifacts alongside the brown, wooden wall on the left, directly under the only window in the cottage. The entrance was to be left free of chairs, people and objects. People were especially discouraged from standing in or near the door for they could absorb the dark energies released by patients that were being blown out.

As I waited for my turn I watched Don Antonio open the entrance door and blow out dense energies from the eggs. Then I turned to my right and noticed everyone along that wall was naked. The moment for my healing had arrived and after a deep breath I began to take my clothes off. I sat again, feeling ever so vulnerable waiting for my healing. Don Antonio instructed me to rub the white candle all over my naked body; after doing so I handed it to Doña Maria and she placed it on the side. She would close the healing by 'reading the candle.'

Within minutes I was called by Don Antonio to stand on a blue nylon mat; this was his healing station. He began by 'camaying' *(cleansing) me, which involved spitting Florida Water all around my head, shoulders, back, arms, legs, and then the front of my body until I was covered with it. Then he grabbed the eggs and furiously rubbed them around my body, using one egg for my front and the other for my back. Eggs are used in many shamanic traditions to remove dense energies from a person. After rubbing for a while he held the eggs in his hand, leaned towards the entrance door and blew the 'bad energies' collected in the eggs outside. The eggs were then thrown in a trashcan.*

He grabbed two more eggs from his bin and continued camaying. He verbally encouraged bad spirits to leave in his native Quechua, so I was unable to understand. Every once in a while however, Spanish words would come out. On one occasion I heard, "Sanación, sanación, sanación … curación, curación, curación. Hay carajo vete ya." (Healing, healing, healing … curing, curing, curing. Damn spirit leave now.) I was now ready to move into Doña Maria's post. Before leaving Don Antonio I asked him to open one of the eggs in the trashcan. Although the eggs had been purchased that morning from a grocery store it was completely black inside. I had never seen anything like it!

Doña Maria worked hard, invoking the assistance of the Holy Spirit, the Virgin Mary and Jesus for my healing. She wrapped the two red carnations together with a string. Then she joined them with one of her sacred stones (known as huacas) and blessed my third eye and head. She hung the red carnations around my neck with another string. I was instructed to get up and go to her workstation where a white sheet on the floor waited for me. I lay on my back on top of the sheet. She manipulated my lower organs with her small yet powerful hands, moving them around as though she was exploring the internal landscape of my body. Then she turned to me and said, "You have worms."

Having experienced the Maya throughout my upbringing I realized that she was speaking metaphorically and it was up to me to figure it out. I said to her, "Where are the worms?" She turned me and moved her knowing hands to my lower back, stopping at my left kidney. "Here is one!" she said. Then she moved to the other side and cried out, "And here too. There are several on this side." I then realized the 'worms' were kidney stones!

She called upon a man from the circle to step forth and grab my feet, while she and another woman grabbed both sides of the sheet and shook me vigorously above the floor several times. They pulled the sheet up and down, rhythmically moving my body from side to side. As I came back down to the floor I felt as though I had been agitated inside a washing machine. Doña Maria then told me to get dressed and come sit by her.

She blessed two wafer cookies and handed them to me. Then she grabbed an orange drink and blessed it by putting carnation petals and some of her huaca stones in it. As I was eating the wafers and drinking the orange drink she lit the candle I had rubbed all over my body. I noticed her attentively speaking to her guides as she proceeded to 'read' my candle. She told me that I had been crying and that I would still have a few more days of crying (while the kidney stones came out), but after that there would be no more crying. Because the flame was rising straight up she said it meant I was ascending rapidly and would not cry anymore with pain ... only of joy.

As the healing finished she gave me instructions for the completion of my healing process. She told me not to shower for three days, no eating pork/meat/seafood for three days, and no intimacy for three days. Carnations were to hang from my neck until they dried, and then I was to put them under my pillow until they disintegrated in time. Every night I was to rub the candle around my body and then light it.

The entire healing was absolutely transformational! It felt as though Doña Maria and Don Antonio had lovingly transformed the pain that had been held in my kidneys, and which no doubt had a lot to do with my latest relationship! Annie was waiting for me outside the healing hut, her healing having finished. I came out in a daze. She glanced at me and then looked intently into my eyes. "Your eyes have changed", she said. "Not just their color, but also their intensity." I headed down to the lake to sit, ponder and integrate the powerful healing I had just had.

That night I dreamt that I went into a deep, spiraling cave trying to retrieve a 'small light' at the end of a hole. Then a monster appeared and it got bigger as I fed it with my fears. When it became gigantic I surrendered and released my fears, sending love to the monster from the depths of my heart. The monster immediately disappeared. As I began my ascension from the hole I pierced through prisms of light. It got brighter and brighter after each prism I passed. When I finally came out of the hole and into the full light Doña Maria was waiting for me. She gave me the warmest and most loving embrace, as though I was her child being welcomed into the light!

A couple of weeks after the healing with Doña Maria one of the 'worms' (kidney stone) she had seen came out with no pain. About one month later I began to feel a strong discomfort in my lower back and bladder, and within a few hours another 'worm' came out. This last one was about ½ inch in length and very thin. When I took it to my urologist he was amazed that the stone came out without causing major complications. In his words, "It was so long it could have perforated your ureter. You have no idea how lucky you are." But of course I knew! I have had no kidney stones since and like Doña Maria had said, "No more tears of pain."

The second healing was scheduled for early in the afternoon with Eduardo. Aside from having an air of impeccability and a martyr-like disposition he reminded me of my Mayan heritage. This is why I had selected him for one of my healings.

We gathered in a group around a fire built by Eduardo, the Maya shaman from Guatemala. There were eight of us in the group. He began by approaching each one and giving us our corresponding Mayan birth sign. Then he arranged us in a circle around the fire according to the order of our birth symbol. Eduardo told me the general meaning of mine was 'water, paranormal visions and prophetic dreams, changes ...' We prayed thirteen times to each Mayan symbol according to the thirteen doorways that each sign has in the Tzolkin Calendar. Each Mayan symbol was called out loud as we prayed. If someone in the circle had this sign as their birth sign they would come forth to the center for their individual healing; the rest of us held sacred space.

Before the individual healings began we each approached the fire and blew into it four times, setting our intent. The sacredness of the space was palpable. Eduardo had given each one of us a lemon to rub around our bodies with the intention of cleansing, purifying and removing 'negative' energies. When Eduardo called out my Mayan sign I came forth to the center. He took the lemon from my hand gently and then offered it to the fire. The lemon fizzled and whistled as the fire took the denseness from it and transmuted it into light.

He then placed a candle in my right hand and another one in my left, which I held for what seemed like an eternity. I began to lose track of time and as the smoke permeated my eyes I sank into a space where everything seemed to move in slow motion. I became aware of Eduardo again, this time perceiving him as a priest from ancient Mayan times. He proceeded to 'camay' (cleanse, bless) me, spitting a vodka concoction all around me. I stood barefoot on his quilt, a colorful and beautifully knit Maya cloth. Getting lost in the weavings I went back in time to my native country and the rituals I had witnessed as a child. I stood there transfixed. He grabbed his mesa (a square pouch containing a shaman's healing instruments) and after circling it around the fire several times he rubbed each of my thirteen chakras, cleansing me further. In Mayan practice these chakras—also known as energy vortexes—correspond to the main joints of the physical body.

I began feeling ever more light and ethereal as I knelt in front of the fire offering my two candles. I stepped back to my space in the circle feeling reborn. Any remaining heaviness had disappeared. It felt as though an essential piece of my being had been restored. I looked around and did not recognize anyone. Obviously I had shifted enough that I was looking at their original faces, not their human faces. I stood in silence as each person had their own individual healing. Upon leaving I realized the entire ceremony had lasted over two hours.

In the late afternoon, after my two healings, I felt the need to be alone with nature. I spent several hours by the river lying lazily on a hammock. The feeling was magical. I felt myself communicating with the trees, the river, and the birds. I began to feel the Earth merge with me as I melted in reverence. The trees were swaying and bowing to my imminent initiation. The birds and animals gathered to witness another awakened soul walking the path of light … and for the first time I could 'see' the world with my heart and all my senses! It was bright and alive, a golden ribbon of light joining everything. I felt an indescribable feeling of belonging and peace, a oneness. It was a reverence I had never felt before.

Sacred Ceremonies at the Gathering of Shamans

We had the privilege of experiencing several amazing ceremonies. Each one was very unique and special and moved us further into a space of stillness and peace. The first one was the Coca Ceremony.

This one was followed by the clay kettles ceremony described above. Then we had a Maya ceremony, followed by a Shamanic Initiation ceremony, and lastly the ceremony symbolizing the merging of the eagle and condor. My experience in each one follows.

An Inka shaman led the Coca Ceremony. She told us this was a dying ceremony because of how the 'white man' was using the Coca; their venerated ceremonial and spiritual leaf was now being used for entertainment purposes, threatening all their rituals that used Coca leaves as a sacred passage to the plant kingdom. We were each given Coca leaves and instructed to assemble Quintus. These consisted of three leaves stacked together and once the prayer was blown into it with full intent, the Quintu was ready to be offered to the fire.

During this ceremony I prayed for my birth family members. I felt myself merging with the heart and soul of each one, the intensity of which I had never felt before. It was as though the merging was happening at different levels and in different dimensions simultaneously. The only physical sensation I had was of tears rolling down my face, falling onto my forearms, ever so slowly ...

On the fourth day we had the privilege of witnessing a Maya ceremony. It began with us facing the four directions. A candle symbolizing each major human race was placed in each of the four cardinal points: the white on the East direction (symbolizing Europe), the yellow on the West (symbolizing Asia), the red on the North (symbolizing Native Indians from the American Continent), and the black on the South (symbolizing Africa). We called the 13 doorways and the 20 energies of the Mayan Tzolkin calendar as we offered candles and ocote (splinters of wood wet with pine resin, which ignite easily).

The ceremony lasted about two and a half hours and we were told this was the condensed version! The regular ceremony would have taken about eight hours, as each energy and doorway would have been honored and prayed to in greater length. I had a tingling in my heart which usually signified a deep familiarity I felt when my soul had witnessed this before. It left me highly energized.

We were almost at the end of our journey with the group. On the fourth evening we gathered around the fire for the Ceremony of Initiation on the Path of the Shaman. Everyone was given an instrument to participate: a drum, a rattle, or a tin can. People seemed lighter, more joyful. Prior to our initiation we were to set our intent on what we dreamt our mission with Pachamama (Mother Earth and the Universe) to be.

The ceremony began. I started drumming and felt my body begin to move slowly to the rhythm of the drum. I stood in one of the three lines that people were forming, walking slowly toward an arch made of vines and flowers. The arch symbolized our entry onto the Path of the Shaman. Right before I entered a mix of aromas and sensations lulled me further into the rhythm of the drum. Once under the entryway the shamans began to camay me with the four elements—water, fire (sage), air, and earth. They cleansed me so that I could embark on my path. As I passed the archway I felt layers of my own baggage being stripped away, preparing me for a deeper spiritual awakening. I knelt by the fire to make my offering and whispered my intent for Pachamama. Then I rose and returned to my space in the larger circle feeling exhilarated!

That night in our cabin, as we lay down to sleep, Annie began describing a vision she was having of me. "He's an older, heavier man with a white beard, dressed in purple. His hat had stars that revolved around his head." As she continued I realized she was describing Merlin the Magician. I understood then that the magic had just returned to my life!

On the last day we participated in an incredible ceremony to celebrate an ancient prophecy shared by both the Inka and the Hopi. It is said that the land of the 'heart'—symbolized by the Condor—would merge with the land of the 'mind'—represented by the Eagle, creating the necessary balance to go forth into the new millennium and into a world of light. This ceremony is symbolic of the union of the Americas, from Canada to Chile. It began with a guided shamanic journey and ended with a spiritual dance.

We laid down to the beat of the drums, then transformed into an Eagle soaring the skies and drifting with the air currents. Our departure point was somewhere in the Northern Rockies and we began to fly south. Destination: the Andes. The mountains were clear and the sun was rising. I saw myself flying past Mexico and Guatemala, seeing the mountains, volcanoes, rivers, lakes ... all below. Once I reached the Andes I was met by a Condor and we began to engage in a beautiful ritual dance high above the mountains. This was a mating dance representing the union between the North and the South. Slowly breaking out of my shell I shapeshifted into a hatchling. After getting up gradually I began to fly. (At this point we were to find a person we had not met before and conduct a silent dance.) My partner was a woman with long, dark hair and sky blue eyes. We stared into each other's soul through our eyes and then flawlessly began moving in a rhythmic and complex dance of two birds. I felt her spirit inside of me! We were engaging in a universal dance we had learned long ago ....

The night after returning home I had my culminating dream. I shapeshifted into a snake and slowly began to shed my skin. Feeling lighter I glanced at my new skin ... it glistened and shone with the light of the sun. My rebirth was imminent! And the gathering was complete.

Shapeshifting

Shapeshifting is also known as 'transmutation.' It involves a tremendous transformation at the energetic level, which then affects the emotional, mental and physical bodies. It is accomplished through continuous shamanic journeying in a short period of time, traveling to different dimensions or realms in order to access the maps of our soul. It is at this level that deep healing takes place. The drum leads the way, beating to the pulse of Mother Earth. It is very important to always set your intent before journeying, whether that is healing, retrieving information, establishing balance on the Earth, harmony, or any other reason.

This second shamanism workshop took place in an old monastery by the water in North Palm Beach, Florida. The topic was 'shapeshifting,' and it would set a strong foundation for my shamanic practice. We would be having more than 16 shamanic journeys in a five-day period! Following are some of my most incredible journeys.

Sometimes we journey for ourselves, while other times we journey to help others. This journey was for another person and the intent was to retrieve a sacred object (plant, animal, or object) that would allow that person to 'open their heart' safely. This object is known as a 'huaca' and since this journey was specifically to open the heart we were to retrieve a 'heart huaca.'

Everyone shuffled around the room to find a partner and a space to lie down; I felt a tap on my shoulder. It was a lovely woman with an Australian accent who said, "Would you care to be my partner?" I nodded and we prepared our floor space. I was to retrieve her heart huaca first, so I set my intent. I lay down carefully next to her, on her right side, insuring we had a common side touching from shoulders to feet. As the drumming began I felt myself being pulled to another world. My breathing started to mirror my partner's. Just then I saw a big, white bird; it seemed to be in a hurry and after I jumped on its back it took me to an absolutely magnificent rainbow. I asked the rainbow, "Are you my partner's heart huaca?"

It responded, "Follow me." I went along and within a few steps a beautiful waterfall shaped like a horseshoe appeared. I asked the waterfall if it was my partner's heart huaca and excitedly it said, "Yes!" I reached out to grab the waterfall and brought it into my own heart, holding it so that it would be safe during my journey back to ordinary reality. Once I returned I got up and kneeled in front of my partner. I blew the heart huaca first into her heart chakra and then into her crown chakra to balance her energy body.

I then helped my partner up to sitting position and as she opened her eyes I could see a spark emanating from them. I told her about my journey and her heart huaca, and her jaw just dropped in astonishment. We had just finished a journey to find our sacred place before this one and she had gone to a place with a beautiful waterfall, shaped like a horseshoe! She told me that waterfalls were one of her favorite places.

The following journey was to help us overcome obstacles that have prevented us from reaching our dreams. It was an intense journey and unlike any other I had ever had.

The drumming began as I finished setting my intent. The rhythm took me deeper into my sacred place. I walked down a familiar path and as a fork on the road appeared I took the road to the right. The road to the left looked like an easier, brighter, cleaner path. However, something had compelled me to go in the opposite direction. This path was filled with rocks and branches, seemingly more dangerous and less traveled than the other one. My friends, relatives and loved ones appeared suddenly, cheering me on.

As I continued the path I saw a cave. I approached the cave, peeked inside, and saw a huge dragon sleeping. I realized that the only way to get to my goals and dreams was to get past the dragon. "Abundance is on the other side," a voice said inside my head. Soon my loved ones realized where I was headed and stayed behind. I was on my own now. All I had with me was a sword, but the dragon was so huge that the sword looked tiny in comparison. I decided to go ahead and give it my best.

As I moved into the cave the dragon awakened, opening his eyes wide. He looked angry, for he was the guardian of all dreams. He exhaled fire while whipping his enormous tail towards me. I stabbed the dragon with my sword, hoping to distract him so that I could to get past it. As it chased me I stabbed it again and again until the dragon fell to its side and collapsed. I ran to the other side of the cave as fast as I could without looking back and discovered I had succeeded. Yet I felt a strange sadness for the dragon. I knew it had been a part of me and had always been there; now it was gone. After a deep breath I reached for my treasures and took them outside the cave. There were no obstacles to abundance in my life now!

This next journey was a very special Tibetan guided meditation where we would meet five new spirit guides that would help us throughout our mission and life. We would be led to a place where we would find a 'Tree of Refuge.' The leaves of this tree contained magic and as we energized them with our breath they would come alive right before our eyes. There were a lot of different transmutations within this journey.

We lay down once again stating our intent before beginning. I felt myself transported smoothly to my sacred place, feeling very relaxed. I glanced at the horizon and saw a pond with a small island in the middle. There was a giant lotus plant in the island. As I approached the lotus began to open up in all its beauty, growing until it became a tree. At the top of the tree was a leaf that invited me to lie on it, where I could observe all that was happening. I became part of the tree. I then glanced over at a branch and saw someone sitting on one of its leaves.

I energized the leaf with my breath and it turned into my 'compassion guide' ... a beautiful white dove. I talked to it and asked it to help me have compassion for all people and for all my relations. Once I felt the work was complete I thanked it for being there. My attention moved to another leaf on another branch and I energized it again with my breath. I saw it shapeshift into my 'counselor guide' ... a Lama Monk with round glasses and a brown tunic. I got closer and asked him to help me with my mission and my dealings in life. After he nodded I thanked him, continuing to look around the tree until I saw another leaf and energized it. My 'healer guide' came to life. An old Native American Indian woman appeared, several teeth missing as she smiled. I asked her to help me with my own healing and she said, "I will do so and also prepare you, for you will be healing others very soon." I thanked her, took a deep breath and looked around the tree once more. I saw another leaf and as I breathed on it the leaf changed into my 'warrior guide' ... a Viking warrior. "My name is Gregor and you need not fear anything." I thanked him for his fearless demeanor and moved on.

Looking to a far branch for the last spirit guide I saw something pirouetting over a leaf. I breathed into the leaf. A ten-year-old girl appeared, running around me saying, "I am your 'wild one guide.' Don't forget to play!" I hugged the little girl and thanked her for her blessings and innocence. In one leap I descended from the lotus tree. Looking up at my guides I thanked them, promising to return throughout my life for their help and guidance. I then left the island and returned to my sacred place. Slowly I became aware of the ordinary world.

After the second day's journeys I went down to the water and pondered. It was minutes before dinner. The journeys of the past two days had been profound; in one of them I was shown my future as a speaker to large audiences. My friend Bonnie came to sit next to me, silently. I shared a couple of my journeys and told her I must have been delirious, especially the one about becoming a speaker. It was not close to my current job so unless it hit me in the face I was not going to pay attention to that one. So much for trusting my spiritual messages and guides! We got up to go to lunch and entered the cafeteria. A woman I had not met before came over and said, "My name is Susan. I have been wanting to meet you." Surprised I said, "How come?" She said, "I represent speakers and lecturers, and I think you would be a sensational speaker." My jaw dropped. Bonnie choked on her drink. It had certainly hit me in the face!

On the last day of this five-day intensive workshop we were to work with a partner to retrieve a logo that symbolized our mission and dream. I worked with a new partner. The logo she retrieved for me had a 'spiral', symbolizing the road we travel in life; it also had a 'goddess,' which symbolized the feminine. Outside of it was a 'sun,' giving light and energy to the spiral. Several years later as I wrote about my mystical experiences, I realized that the logo of my then new company—**Awakening the Soul**—had a part that was identical to the image given to me three years before! Was it time to stop being so amazed at the continuous synchronicities in my life?

My drive back from the workshop was challenging. They had told us to be careful on our return home for our physical body may feel a little off. I didn't know what that meant, but I was soon to find out. My house was about one and a half hours from the workshop location. Driving had always felt natural for my mother had taught me when I was ten. She had raced cars when she was young and wanted us to feel confident on the road.

About 30 minutes into the drive I had a brain freeze and forgot how to drive. My body no longer responded and my driving skills were non-existent. It was obvious I was vibrating in another dimension, but I had no fear. I asked one of my power animals, the bald eagle, to take over and get me home. I surrendered and about an hour later found myself opening the door to my house. I thanked my guides, angels, and especially my eagle.

I lit a candle and put a drumming CD on, intent on journeying to my sacred place. My intent was 'gratitude,' for getting me home safe and sound and for the workshop. As I sat in front of a beautiful stone altar I realized a figure was walking towards me. I began to squint and rub my eyes not believing what I was seeing. It was Jesus! He was dressed in a long white and light blue robe. I said to him, "What are you doing here? I have not called upon you since I was 11, when I left my religion." He looked at me with beautiful, loving eyes, and said, "I am your teacher on the other side and have always been with you while you're on Earth." He told me that he knew I had moved away from him because I had a hard time looking at the crucifixion image that our culture and religion portrayed. He also said I should let go of the pain I felt when seeing him with the crown of thorns. He explained we had missed the point by focusing on the crucifixion and that we needed to remember him resurrected and happy rather than suffering. This episode changed my life! I have felt Jesus close to me since then, and at times during my meditations I see him. His presence has given me a peaceful and humbling feeling.

Although I knew the transformation from the shapeshifting workshop had been intense it would take me several weeks to realize just how powerful it was. One thing was very clear though. The time had come for me to fully commit to my spiritual path and discipline. So I set forth to find a program that combined my two passions: shamanism and energy medicine ... as well as my two cultures: Latin America and North America. I asked the

Universe for help and began my search. Within a few days I found a mystery school that seemed perfect.

Mystery schools date back to Egyptian times, and later Roman and Greek civilizations. They were schools where you studied the 'sacred.' I promptly enrolled, committing to seven weeklong seminars over the course of two years; the curriculum included many homework assignments. Another interesting element of this mystery school was that the teacher liked to weave mental anthropology with shamanism, which meant the mind would be invited along on this path of magic. Anthropology was his traditional educational background and his shamanic training followed the Inka Q'ero teachings. The Q'ero are known as the keepers of the Inka medicine path, maintaining the knowledge and teachings of their ancestors through an oral tradition. They even moved to heights of over 15,000 feet in order to keep their wisdom intact and escape the Spanish Conquistadors.

The Mystery School followed the shamanic Medicine Wheel, a healing and learning roadmap that has been used for over 100,000 years. The intent of the Medicine Wheel is that as you 'cleanse and heal' yourself you also learn how to heal others. The responsibility to heal your story is yours, and this is a priority before embarking on the path of teaching, healing or being.

Some of the greatest frustrations I found during my spiritual quest were healers or teachers who felt they have no responsibility to confront their own ghosts and heal themselves, or those who compromised their ethics and did not walk the path they taught. I know there are people born with amazing 'gifts' and they are meant to share these gifts with humanity and with the Earth. But as souls we all came to learn and this means we must do our own work before embarking on any spiritual mission. And as we enter the path of service our responsibility to continuously improve ourselves and walk the world with humility becomes greater.

The Medicine Wheel is a shamanic process that is still alive in many indigenous cultures around the world today. It engages the student in a path of self-healing as well as spiritual enlightenment. In the lineage I follow we begin with the work of the South, which involves shedding your past and bringing forth only the lessons taught by the challenges of the past; it is symbolized by the serpent for the shedding of the skin is a metaphor for us shedding our stories. We do this both as an act of love and of power. As the Medicine Wheel moves clockwise we arrive at the work of the West. Here we face our fears, including the greatest fear of all: death. We also die to who we have been up to this point: our identity, thereby obtaining the gift of freedom. Next we embark on the work of the North where direction is no longer taken from the past or from our fears. Here we have access to our ancestors and to our guides, to our angels. We also become intimate with our Higher Self, that eternal and wise part of us that is a part of God. In the North we learn a different concept of time: shamanic time. The shamanic lineage resides outside of time but expresses itself in time. It is only when we go outside of time, into infinity, that we meet Great Spirit or the Creator face-to-face. The Wheel ends with the work of the East where we begin to create based on what we can become, envisioning a world filled with light and with infinite possibilities. In other words we remember to dream the world into being from a pure blueprint!

After stripping many layers and completing the Medicine Wheel we finally allow our soul to shine through, our primal essence. We emerge more joyful, no longer prisoners of a world that subscribes to the thought of human limitations. We understand our divinity and our connection to the Divine, taking responsibly for creating our future at every moment. The world of magic and synchronicities becomes mainstream and we begin to live each day and each moment with absolute ecstasy. This is not to say that challenges and difficult situations have left our lives. We are in this school called Earth for our soul's learning, always realizing that with these tools we are better able to deal with such challenges and learn from them instead of falling victim to them. In the stillness we observe ….

The Shamanic Medicine Wheel

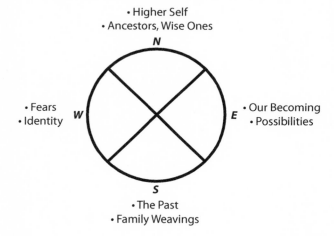

Healing the Past

"It is not the mountain we conquer, but ourselves."
—Sir Edmund Hillary

AT THE TENDER AGE OF 39 IT SEEMED I HAD LIVED AN entire lifetime between family, career and relationships. It had been an intense life up to now and even though there had been hardships, the joy and beauty far outweighed any of the 'stories' I carried with me about the issues and situations I had faced. This didn't mean I could stand still and just continue replaying the same broken records, not in my mind nor in my heart. With my last relationship I realized that I needed to take the time to heal old patterns or I would continue attracting experiences that became ever more painful. In addition, although my career was heading in the right direction in terms of allowing me more freedom for my spiritual deepening, it was not motivating me as it did before. My family continued to pose challenges in terms of the time and commitment they demanded and expected from me, and this was affecting both my personal and professional lives significantly. Spiritually I was beginning to fill the void that I had felt over a decade ago, but my purpose in this life was still eluding me. It was perfectly clear that a lot needed to be healed and changed for me to live life to the fullest, and the responsibility rested entirely within me!

In just a few years of delving into spiritual topics I knew that we do not heal just by understanding situations we have encountered. If energy is the source of everything, then healing needed to start in the spiritual realm—with the energy body. Of course the emotional body would provide the roadmap for me to enter into the lessons of my soul, and eventually the mind would come on board with massive realizations and enlightening shifts. I had seen my mom spend decades attempting to put her life back together through psychotherapy and the results had been negligible and definitely not lasting. So I knew there had to be a deeper way to move through the memories and their corresponding wounds, and that analysis would never be able to mend my soul. I also wanted to learn about unconditional love, particularly self-love. *It was time to break paradigms about healing and write a new story!*

In shamanic traditions what we **experience** is what is true, not what we are taught or think. In fact most spiritual disciplines focus on that internal 'knowing' as truth rather than on 'beliefs.' Beliefs are created based on someone else's experience, which may not necessarily be our own. I was ready to have my own shamanic experiences. The first venture of The Medicine Wheel was the 'Work of the South,' and in early August of 2001 I was on my way to Joshua Tree, California. For the next seven intense days and nights we would be introduced to Inka Shamanism with a Western anthropological flair. There was an intimidating aspect to the notion of joining over 100 other potential shamanic practitioners, especially because I was embarking alone. Yet my soul was ready for the challenge! It was only a matter of physically moving the human part of me forward and the whole Universe conspired to make this happen.

A couple of concepts must be clarified before going forward as they will be referred to throughout my shamanic experiences. First is the shaman's *'mesa,'* which is a living energetic being that helps us engage with the energy world in an intimate way. It consists of a sacred cloth that holds power objects charged with light, many of which become healing tools. A lot of these power objects are added to the mesa as we go through the entire Medicine Wheel, but they can also be adopted as we walk our spiritual path. They can be stones, crystals, feathers and anything else that we feel is special and want to include in our sacred pouch. As we move through the shamanic initiations the mesa eventually becomes a mythic and energetic map of our soul.

The **sacred fire ceremony** is at the center of shamanism. It connects us to a mythic domain outside of time and space. It is very important to always set our intent when doing ritual or ceremony. In the South direction the intent is to release everything from our past that needs healing … anything that we carry in our personal 'heavy backpack.' Once it is released at the mythic level we surrender and watch lightness gradually manifest in our physical world. Fire ceremonies are done to celebrate a stage of life, to cleanse or heal from a challenging situation, to surrender issues to the Divine, to grow the archetypal seeds of our chakras, to honor someone or something, to celebrate Mother Earth, and to thank for a healing done to us. They also merge us with Mother Earth and all her children, as well as help us thank our spirit guides and angels for their help. Fire ceremonies enable us to commune with and express gratitude to Great Spirit, and our whole relationship with everything around us is realigned. After each ceremony I usually emerge peaceful and introspective, having connected with the realm of my soul.

Sand paintings or **mandalas** have been used for many centuries by Tibetan Buddhists and by Native American Indians. They are created at the mythic level as a powerful healing tool or as a source of wisdom and form of meditation. They chart a person's life symbolically yet will manifest in time at the physical level. There are many reasons why sand paintings are done: health, creativity, to simplify our lives, to appreciate who we are, or to understand a situation in our lives. They also help us let go of that which no longer serves us, track what we are becoming, change behaviors, or ask for guidance. Again as with sacred ceremonies we must **always** set our intent before starting one, allowing the Universe to be informed so that it can align behind us. Native Americans also use it for healing, for divining and for creating powerful shifts.

Sand paintings start with a circle either on sand or the earth, utilizing burnable materials to symbolically represent aspects of our lives. These materials are best if found on the ground. It is an exercise of expression not of perfection. We put our intent into the sand painting and then start by making an outer circle with our finger; subsequently we use the natural elements to design, for example, what our lives are like now. After patient observation we begin to move the natural elements we placed inside the circle in order to create shifts in our lives at the physical level. It is important to keep our mythic story as a compass—always. Sand paintings are extremely powerful and help us modify aspects of our life in a domain that is friendly and engaging (mythic), rather than one that could be challenging and reactive (literal).

When relating to the world we learn to utilize and move between *perceptual states*. These are common practice in psychotherapy, but can also be used in shamanism. Although there are many perceptual states the most commonly used are the following four.

- The first one is the *Literal* domain, which is the one we are taught and 'learn' to live in; it is the level of the body, of the five senses, of details and facts.

- The second one is the *Symbolic,* which is the level of the mind and of the emotions, of the personality, the imagination, and of creativity.

- The third level is the *Mythic,* which is the domain of the soul … of stories and mythologies. It is our 'story,' from the perspective at 50,000 feet.

- The fourth one is the ***Energetic*** or ***Essential***, which is the domain of the Spirit, of energy, of all that is.

Once we learn to work consciously with all four levels we understand that the Essential informs the Mythic, which in turn informs the Symbolic, finally informing the Literal. It is akin to our Spirit informing our Soul, which then informs the heart and mind, and lastly our physical body. Although we may not be aware of it before our spiritual awakening we already operate on all four levels; still many begin and remain in the Literal. Jean Houston calls these 'the four most common levels of the psyche.' The closer you work with the source or Essential level the less energy you spend. Ideally you allow the Essential level to inform the other three levels. Since it is the Source of all things it is the most effective perceptual state to work with, but the hardest one to grasp.

The language of the Literal and Symbolic levels is the 'Word,' the language of the Mythic level is 'Images,' and the language of the Essential level is 'Energy.' For example visualizations are much more effective than words for they involve the five senses plus our intuition. So the shaman or medicine person develops the ability to consciously shift levels of engagement with the world, selecting that domain which is the most empowering for a given situation and which utilizes the least amount of energy.

In the majority of cases we try to reach consensus with others at the Literal level, whether this be with a partner, friend, spouse, co-worker, boss, employee, or group. This is what we have been taught to do. However, it is very hard to reach an agreement with just words and details for people have different interpretations of a given situation. This is why we have established rules and definitions, in an attempt to bridge perceptions and reach consensus. Poets for example begin their engagement with the world at the Symbolic level, where metaphors and symbolism provide a loving language to attempt to reach the soul; consensus *may be* possible at this level.

Even further along is the medicine person who knows she can reach consensus at the Essential level. It is in this and the Mythic levels where we can dream our future into reality. Once we learn to operate in these two levels we begin to walk the path of the Peaceful Warrior, where we no longer engage from an ego standpoint, but rather from our soul's perspective. So if we have something hard or stressful come up at the Literal level we elevate our perception to the Mythic or Essential levels in order to gain perspective and shift it, rather than reacting at the Literal. We can elevate to the Mythic or Essential levels through meditation, prayer or by doing Sand Paintings.

Releasing Imprints

The chakras tell the story of how the person 'absorbs' a particular event, pattern or trauma in life. An imprint may form if the negative emotions associated with it are not dealt with and healed. To allow the chakras and energy body to return to health we must find and remove the imprint. This means we must elevate perceptual states and work at the Essential level of a person, evaluating their energy body and assessing how the chakras have been affected by a given issue or situation. Once the imprint is removed it will reinforce or alter the physical, emotional and psychological levels. We utilize a shamanic process to remove them for it allows us to heal outside time and space, thereby allowing us to access the *origin* of a wound. Sometimes a person can recall instances related to what they are healing as far back as the womb and tremendous healing occurs in just a few minutes. Clearing the chakras helps us break free of time plus it brings understanding of how we hold our stories, our wounds.

In traditional psychotherapy, one works inside the client's story. Shamans, on the other hand, work outside the story and motivate their clients to break free from the story. The philosophy is that once healed wounds from our past leave behind only lessons, thereby freeing us from our stories. Revisiting and continuously reevaluating our stories can increase their energy and therefore attract similar situations into our life.

We want our history to stop informing us in the present moment. The intention is to let go of the attachment to a story or to how things happened, thereby freeing us from our past. Who we are today begins to define the possibilities of what we can become in the future. We create our future in the present and healing helps us drop past wounds so that we can re-inform our soul and free it to create the future it wants. This is one of the basic shamanic premises:

**We heal first, whether we understand why
things happened the way they did or not,
then we dream our world into being.**

In order to start healing our past we must begin by identifying our current map. A map shows how we process and hold situations in our lives, and we utilize the chakras to illustrate this. The key is to get a very clear emotion related to the issue being healed so that our energy body engages. Once the energy body engages our map emerges. This is the part of the healing process where we drop our current story and redo how we process issues. It results in a new map that lessens the damage and is more empowering, allowing us to change behaviors that no longer serve us.

Healing is a journey and most of the time we are 'in-process.' Once the healing seed is planted it grows and begins to inform the body and the mind of our intention. The closer we get to the Essential the greater the wisdom and consciousness, and less details and matter. The closer we are to the Literal level the more matter and specifics, and the less wisdom and consciousness. So we want to keep our perception where we can get more wisdom for this will assist us in releasing old stories. The shamanic process we use heals the Energetic level immediately, yet its expression into the physical may be gradual.

My own experiences with releasing imprints were life altering. I started by selecting the three most challenging issues throughout my life: family, the caretaker, and setting limits. Then I selected three stones and blew one issue into each stone. The stones would help transmute all three issues. The healing process began, one issue at a time.

The first issue involved **my family** and the excessive expectations they placed on me. I had been trained to respond to those expectations since I was very young and therefore allowed it, but I didn't know I had a choice in how I responded to them. I eventually understood that I had to come from a position of power when I responded to their calls for help.

I began by blowing several memories about those situations involving my family into one of my South mesa stones. Four out of my seven chakras were adversely affected. The process began ... One family member emerged first. I saw a dark tunnel with an opening of light at the end. Intuitively I pushed all the darkness up towards the opening and it siphoned out.

Then a second family member emerged and I saw a long dorm-like hallway with many doors opening and closing simultaneously. When I asked the doors what they were they told me they each held an issue or an illness for this family member. I filled the entire hallway with light and compressed it from both sides. Using my intent I sent it all to the stone that was on my root chakra. The stone absorbed it, taking it away from me.

Then a third family member emerged and I saw a lit disc. On one side was all my love for this person and on the other side all of their issues that I had been pulled into. For an instant I hesitated in giving the disc to the stone because I was concerned that my love for them would be combusted too. Then a moving, revolving sphere of light came and asked me to send the disc to it. I did, releasing it.

The fourth family member had been healed through the first three. I felt so much lighter and noticed the love for my family members had grown tremendously as well.

The main message I got from this healing was that the greatest love is to say, "YES," to yourself first before giving to anyone else. Only then are you complete enough and able to fully give to others from a position of abundance and of power.

The second issue of being a **caretaker in relationships** was something I learned very early on while in the womb. When we are young we don't know how to heal these situations so we form an imprint. This affected me in such a way that I began to repeat that story in my love relationships as an adult. My first serious relationship lasted more than a decade and I quickly began to see patterns similar to my parents' relationship. I was the caretaker/rescuer, be that love, financial, mental strength, curiosity in life, and the one that took care of issues and anything that arose. My partner was the victim, perceiving that life was unfair and everyone was rotten to him. Although I was aware of the caretaker and how it was affecting my life I did not yet know about imprints. I was able to identify the pattern and understand it, but not heal it.

So I repeated the same pattern in my deepest and most intense relationship that followed. In this case my partner was absent from his life and therefore from our life together. Being deeply in love with an absent person is one of the hardest things I had ever dealt with. It was like finding the deepest soulmate yet one of the two is suddenly not ready to show up for the most beautiful dance in life! It was the deep ache from him not being present that motivated me to heal the rescuer, that perpetual cycle of caretaker and victim that continued to manifest in my life. It was also one of the main factors influencing me to commit to the Shamanic Medicine Wheel and put my spirituality first, and for that I will always be eternally grateful to him.

I proceeded to blow two of my most intense personal relationships into the second stone of my mesa, one at a time. The chakras were checked and three of them were affected. When I blew issues related to the first relationship I saw a picture of a dark castle with many black chimneys and black smoke; all the surroundings were black too. I didn't know what to do so I asked my 'Elder Healer Woman Spirit Guide' to assist me. She said that I had to begin to 'paint' the image with white, for light can only enter once the darkness leaves. I began with the chimneys and smoke stacks, then the castle, last the surroundings. Once all was filled with light I lit a fire under my solar plexus chakra and combusted everything. Instantly I felt tremendous relief!

Next I blew the issues related to the second relationship into the stone and the 'Elder Healer Woman Spirit Guide' asked me if I liked being a caretaker. I said I liked caring for people I loved but wanted mutual caretaking in a relationship. She asked if I was ready and willing for someone else to also take care of me ... was I willing to receive? I said a resounding, "YES," and promised to learn to receive. She asked me if I was ready to let go of 'people needing me' and, after thinking about it for a few seconds, I nodded. She combusted the issues that had been blown to the stone and I sighed with relief.

We can still take care of those we love, yet there is a light side to bring caretaker and also a dark side. The light side is when the victim is ready to heal and asks for help, understanding that they have to put their own energy into healing themselves. They understand that they have access to the same Universal energies we have if they choose to tap into them. We merely act as a spark to help them initiate healing. The dark side of the rescuer is when we jump in to take care of someone but they haven't asked and therefore are not ready to help themselves. In this latter one the person we rescued usually repeats the issue that we jumped in to help them with but at greater intensity. Why would we wish that someone repeat a wounding situation with greater intensity? This has been one of my greatest lessons! I have eventually learned to embrace both the light and dark side of the caretaker, understanding that I always have the opportunity to choose how I want to participate.

The third healing dealt with **setting limits**. Many times we are afraid to set boundaries because we don't want to hurt someone or maybe we are culturally trained to always say, "Yes." Regardless we usually end up in a place of resentment because we betray what we really feel and therefore ourselves.

I picked up the third stone and blew into it several situations in my life where I had not set limits and thus had been taken advantage of. I did it one story at a time, slowly. During the healing I saw the faces of all the people I had not set limits with. One face melted into the next and the next to the next. They all appeared in a round orb, even ones I did not remember and incidents that had happened long ago. I filled the orb with light and sent it to the stone on my heart chakra. As I combusted the toxic energy tremendous liberation took over me. I felt free and powerful. I felt no attachments. A big weight had been taken off my shoulders.

When we learn to set limits we learn to stand up for ourselves. Self-respect is at the core of a life of stillness and a strong Divine connection, for in respecting yourself you have the platform to respect everything and everyone else. In fact, out of self-respect I also made a commitment to my soul that until I had healed significantly I would not enter into a relationship other than with myself. I did not want to repeat any of these patterns again. This brought forth the gift of becoming present in my relationship with myself. I learned that only I can complete myself, and only when I am complete I am ready to enter into relationship with others. It was a great step forward!

All of these experiences have taught me that when faced with a tough emotional situation I have a choice: I either face my pain and move forward reinventing myself in the process, or regress to what I was before I faced the painful situation in an attempt to recapture a time when I did not feel that ache. One allows you to heal and love deeper; the other takes you into complacency and denial, and eventually opens a much bigger hole. Moving forward is the undeniable choice!

Soul Parts and Original Faces

After healing imprints I engaged in other journeys and processes which would help me continue healing my past. First was a 'soul retrieval journey,' that involves bringing back a fragment of our soul that left due to a traumatic event. Generally a shaman does this process for a client, but, because I was engaged in the Medicine Wheel, I did it for myself. This would also help me begin to know the landscape of the Lower World. The Lower World is usually where we find lost soul parts and answers to issues related to our current incarnation. It is not good or bad, it just is. In every soul retrieval journey, the intent is to 'seek that which will make us whole,' that part of our soul that we left behind as a result of trauma.

The first soul part I saw was my fourteen-year-old self. She left during a horrible earthquake in Guatemala in the mid 1970s. I began by seeing flashes of this teenage girl's experience. It started with her being yanked out of dreamtime by the loudest roaring of the Earth and then the continuous shaking back and forth. Windows exploded everywhere ... pictures fell all around her ... devastation. No light. As she came outside of the house she saw Death all around her. She was very scared. The Lord of the Lower World, in a kind and gentle manner, helped me bring back the lost and scared soul part. It wanted to feel safe and it took some convincing for her to trust that the 'adult me' would protect her, but she agreed to return. Now I understood why any sudden noise or movement scared me after the earthquake. I also needed a light nearby to be able to sleep. It had all come about as a result of that little soul part leaving!

Once she returned I began a dialogue with her, not only to fully understand why she left, but also to know what she needed in order to integrate with me. "Who are you?" I asked her. "I am a playful, carefree girl," she responded. "Why did you leave?" I said. She responded, "I was scared, confused, and felt all alone." I asked, "Why were you scared?" She said, "Loud thundering noises from the Earth; hard shaking that dropped me to the floor ... the bed canopy going wild; running downstairs with windows cracking and everything falling in front of me ... going outside the house ... looking for my puppy; the smell of death ... the continuing trembling ... the loss of shelter."

"What are your gifts?" I continued. "Comfort in aloneness, being carefree, and I bring excitement to any situation," she responded. I probed further, "What is your medicine?" She smiled and said, "Mother Earth will always take care of me ... as well as those meant to die." Finally I said to her, "How can I make you safe?" She sweetly said, "Just love me and hold me in your heart regardless of what's going on around you in the outside." I promised to hold her lovingly as a tear escaped from my eyes.

Once she was safe with me I glanced to my other side and saw another soul part of mine. It was a five year-old girl sitting on the beach. My family was swimming. All of a sudden my mother screamed for help, my younger brother clinging to her neck. My father realized they were being dragged out into the ocean by an undertow. He managed to grab my older brother who was right next to my mother. He threw him towards the shore where the five year-old took hold of him and dragged him out.

Then my dad swam to my mom and younger brother only to be caught in the undertow. My mom began to panic and threw her arms around my dad. He screamed at me to go get help. It was a desolate beach, but the little girl began to run into the forest beyond the sand. She was barefoot and the sand was extremely hot. Her soles were burning with pain. Finally she found a disheveled, toothless man; she was sure angels had put him there. The old man retrieved a rope and ran toward the ocean, slowly pulling each family member safely to shore. The little girl breathed deep, relieved, yet a part of her soul essence left her. Witnessing the story helped me remember. I did not bring that soul part back at that time though.

The next soul part I saw was a little girl about twelve years old. My family had been involved in a strange accident right before New Year's. We were shopping for groceries on our way to the beach. A pickup truck ran through a red light, tipped, and rolled toward the trunk of our car. My father and two brothers were packing the groceries into the trunk. My father saw the events developing out of the corner of his eye and managed to push my older brother out of the way. He then got out of the way himself, but was unable to reach my younger brother. My younger brother's head got trapped between the trunk of our car and the pickup truck that rolled over. I witnessed it all from the entrance of the supermarket. My brother's head cracked open and I saw the blood spurting out. I wondered if he was going to make it alive. Just then the pickup truck rolled back miraculously and exploded into flames. My younger brother's head was released. I watched as my soul part left, literally scared out of her wits.

The fourth part I saw was from when I was forty-one. My mother had had a devastating heart attack and had miraculously returned to life. Heart doctors in Guatemala could not help her because her condition was so rare. We had to take her via air ambulance to the Cleveland Clinic in Ohio so she could see a specialist. Once there we discovered they could not perform the necessary operation for she had stomach ulcers and they needed to heal first.

She was told to go back to Guatemala for a couple of weeks, but instead decided she would stop over in Florida to spend New Year's with me. My father and older brother came as well. Doctors were testing a variety of medicines on her and we were told to monitor her closely. One of these medicines was giving her severe convulsions and I was usually the one to hold and calm her during these episodes. They were very scary as her eyes rolled back and my heart could feel her terrified soul. On this one occasion she was going to bed upstairs for the night. As she reached the turn in the steps she looked back down and I saw the blank look in her eyes. My father, who had sat down on the step next to her, did not notice she was about to have another convulsion. I ran upstairs with a stack of pillows in my arms barely in time to catch her from falling face first down the stairs. I sat next to her, calming her down and holding her lovingly. As soon as she relaxed, I fainted. At the time I thought it was because of a hypoglycemic attack, but later I realized it was that a soul part of mine had left because it was so terrified to be holding the 'potential death of her mother' in her arms.

Soul retrieval journeys are part of the healing process. The fourteen year old who came back to me was the part I needed to feel 'whole' at that point in my life, and the other three parts were revealed to me so that I would know to go back and get them at a later date.

After the soul retrieval journey I participated in an exercise to 'track the self.' The objective was to glance at the many faces of my previous lives. I was to use the four perceptual states, where the **Literal** meant 'seeing things as they are;' the **Symbolic** was 'seeing things as they begin to change for nothing is as it appears to be;' the **Mythic** followed, where 'things get still;' and the **Essential** was about 'seeing the original face.' I worked with a partner and sat directly across from her.

I worked with Katie, a wonderful and powerful woman from Canada. We looked into each other's left eye and moved through the perceptual states until all became blurry. Many faces appeared, one morphing into the next and then into the next. The first face I saw was a woman with a veil circa 1820s, either Egypt or India. The next face was a tall man in Asia, almost Mongolian looking. The next one was an eight year-old boy in the America's, maybe Native American, and as I held the image I realized the boy was killed at that young age. We finished the exercise yet that last face had shaken me. I felt compassion for the young boy and for Katie, assuming I was seeing the faces of her past lives. Suddenly I realized all those faces were mine. This exercise was not about her; it was about me! Katie was actually a reflection of my past lives. So this was all about awareness.

After numerous other exercises and rites of passage my sensing was elevated to a new level. I began to perceive the invisible world in a manner I never thought possible, while realizing I was only beginning to glimpse pieces of the totality of my being. Within days and later weeks I started having major realizations about my soul's path and some of the experiences I had originally signed up for.

- The first realization was that death had been close to me on several occasions. I seemed to be the witness of my family's potential deaths yet to my relief they hadn't actually manifested.

- The second realization was that I needed 'to love and respect myself first and foremost.'

- The third one had to do with my teachers and my wish to have a female spiritual teacher. I thought a woman spiritual mentor would involve learning with love and be more nurturing. Men, from what I had read, used trickery and sought power for power's sake. After this workshop however I realized Andres's work and teachings did not follow my preconceived notions. We were like-minded with similar experiences. Then I came to the realization that throughout my life's path there had been many male teachers: all the men in Corporate America, my father, my brothers, friends and previous partners. I understood gender was actually irrelevant as long as I was willing to hear the messages. We all have feminine and masculine energies, and it is essential to develop both. Men taught me many valuable lessons such as 'how to set limits,' 'how to be assertive yet flexible,' and 'how to give recognition to myself.' They have been great teachers indeed!

- The fourth major realization had to do with the fact that 'sadness is a signal from the soul.' It alerts us to the fact that there is a piece inside of us that we must shed in order to move forward in our paths. If we go deep within to find the wounds that made us feel sad we can heal them and see the gift sadness brought us. If we hide from it or keep repeating to ourselves that we feel sad we may end up in a depression or our life can become paralyzed. Sadness can be used as a bridge to the depths of our soul, and in the healing voyage we resolve to shed it.

Facing My Fears

*"Security is mostly a superstition. It does not exist in nature,
nor do the children of humans as a whole experience it.
Avoiding danger is no safer in the long run than outright
exposure. Life is either a daring adventure or nothing."*
—Helen Keller

HAVING FULLY EMBARKED IN MYSTERY SCHOOL AND AFTER reframing my past it was time to face my fears. I needed to become free of them so that my creations would only include possibilities of wonderment rather than what I didn't want to happen. The overall intention was to move from a place of *disempowerment* to one of *empowerment.* But facing my fears would involve many aspects of my life, such as my identity, my ancestral lineage, the many lifetimes I have lived and how they affect who I am today, and also confronting the greatest fear of all: Death. There was anticipation as well as uneasiness at the thought of 'Death.' I had heard the 'Work of the West' was one of the toughest directions in the Medicine Wheel so I just took a deep breath before taking a step forward.

A large part of the identity that was holding me captive was an expectation of behavior based on 'what I did.' Isn't that the first question we ask someone so that we can place him or her in a category? It doesn't matter if we are really good at it yet it sets the framework for how others see us. Soon we become attached to describing ourselves in that way, using it as our introduction card; in our society our identity is meant to place us in a certain position vis-à-vis others we meet. The time had come to shed it and begin to redefine who I was. My professional identity as the Corporate Executive or the Strategy Expert or the Global Business Leader was about to dissolve.

In addition this work was also about shedding judgment and ego, which is done through awareness and impeccability of thought. We become fully aware of our mind, its ego, its judgment and its chatter, so that we can begin to release it and be free from its grip. Just by learning to observe it we have ceased to participate and be part of it. This change in perception demands respect and humility and leaves no place for the ego.

Shamanism is a sacred practice, but by no means a technical one. Shamans take their work seriously, like a Divine calling. Yet many are playful and don't take themselves very seriously. This discipline involves an engagement with everything and everyone around you whether in this ordinary reality or in alternate realities. As humans we are taught to describe things and to source ourselves from the physical reality, but as shamans we want to experience the extraordinary side of reality. Moving into altered states helps us access this non-ordinary reality but in order to do so we must enter absolute stillness.

I recently heard an amazing world-renowned environmentalist and shaman explain this concept in a very simple way. He says that there is a physical side to our existence and there is a spiritual or sacred one. The former is ordinary reality, while the latter is non-ordinary. Both worlds are part of the reality of the ONE so we must pay attention to both. It is the shaman who bridges these worlds and creates harmony between them by connecting the spiritual to the physical.

So what is ordinary versus non-ordinary reality? Ordinary reality is the one of our five senses ... the human perception that we have been taught. It is what we can see, touch, taste, hear and smell; that which we can 'explain' and 'manipulate.' It comprises the material world—the world of limitation—and defines what we can and cannot do, what is and not possible. It is the realm of linear space and time where either one or both limits us. Ordinary reality is where most of us grew up and where the majority of the population still lives today. It contains and maintains a system based on beliefs that life is a duality of love and fear, of good and bad. It does not and cannot explain the spiritual aspects so it has to define them as 'miracles.'

Non-ordinary reality on the other hand, is a reality where time and space cease to exist. The most subtle movement or action in one area creates an effect somewhere else, and the effect happens *simultaneously* in two different physical places (where it originated and where it ended). It is a reality where we have additional senses to the usual five, intuitive senses that defy explanation or logic. A place where our experience rules, what we perceive is 'real' to us. Non-ordinary reality is the reality of our soul, where it is free to be, do and sense whatever it wants. It strips us of limitation and everything is possible; *if you can dream it you can do it.* It is seeing what you failed to notice: a heightened sense of awareness to the spiritual nature of all living things and a sense of connection and oneness with everything and everyone. Non-ordinary reality contains ordinary reality within it, but not the other way around.

A feeling of absolute peace overtakes us when we dwell and meditate in non-ordinary reality. It is as though we are swimming in the ocean of outer space. Shamans can enter non-ordinary reality through drumming, through breathing patterns, or by doing ecstatic dancing. Non-ordinary reality is also very powerful when doing healing work for it opens a doorway that helps clients move into a place of 'no time and no space.' In this way they can remember situations or incidents from their past which are relevant to what they are healing. In many instances they can return to the original wound of what is affecting them today and heal it. It is a magical space where incredible things happen.

The Emerence of the Peaceful Warrior

The Peaceful Warrior is the individual that has no enemies and doesn't need violence or revenge in their lives. He or she always practices Peace regardless of the circumstances. In order to get there however, fear and anger must no longer live within us. We must release the Dark Warrior inside so that we can step beyond fear. The first step for the Warrior of Light to emerge involves breaking free of the triangle of disempowerment. This triangle is imposed upon us by the Western mentality, where power is taken from others. It is a shadow we grow up with and follows the old paradigm of the Victim, the Rescuer and the Perpetrator. It is an ancient model where the violent warrior is fed by a loss of power, which is part of the World of Fear. The three archetypes exchange positions continuously and create a never-ending cycle of fright, dependency and suffering. But we are never a victim when we walk the Medicine Way. Even if we get harmed, once we decide to walk the medicine path we cannot fall into the victim archetype. This means no more rescuing, no more victim and no more perpetrating!

Shamans release this triangle by learning to embrace their own power, which means stepping beyond fear. We begin by facing the greatest fear of all: *Death.* There are two centers in the brain that are next to each other but opposite in their function. The center for 'ecstatic communion' is next to the center of 'anger.' Medicine people recognize that fear is the absence of love. So by disengaging our Energy Body from our Physical Body through the 'Death Rites' we separate these two centers. It results in an experience of deep communion with life. Most of us know that we will die yet we don't know when. *But after we intentionally step beyond Death while incarnated we touch infinity in the most miraculous way!*

Death Rites of Passage mark great transitions. They allow us to stay out of violence. We cannot do anything out of anger or fear because ours is a practice of non-violence. Anger no longer sits with us; we can get angry, but we let it go and do not react. In the West direction we learn the practice of non-engagement. If you **must** engage it needs to be fast and decisive; do not drag it out. The shaman picks his battles *rather* than the battles picking him.

My first experience with 'Death' was more of a 'near death' experience rather than full death. I would learn later that full death would happen in the last direction of the Medicine Wheel as a culmination of our ability to journey between worlds. Regardless, disengaging the Energy Body from the Physical Body is a very delicate undertaking. It demands only to be done if engaged in the Medicine Wheel and the individual is in the presence of an experienced shaman.

Someone was sitting at my head while another person read the Eulogy I had written, and yet another one began the dis-engagement of my Energy Body. One by one my chakras were opened starting with the first one, spinning each one counter-clockwise. Initially all I saw was light. I felt calm and safe. As the Energy Body was raised from my Physical Body I began to see black. This was not an uncomfortable black, but rather a calming infinity. When my Energy Body was above me I saw my Physical Body from above. The only thing I was fully conscious of was my breath. There was a luminous cord coming out of my belly that connected my Energy and Physical bodies. When you touched this cord it felt warm, yet the rest of the body felt cold. The cord was wide, soft, and palpable.

The feeling of my Energy Body above my Physical Body was beautiful ... so beautiful and calming that I was ready to leave with my Energy Body. There were no regrets about leaving my Physical Body. This feeling is likened to having an 'out of body experience.' As the Energy Body was brought back to merge with my Physical Body I saw light again. There was a certain sadness when both bodies were rejoined, sadness for tying down my free soul once more and for realizing that I was human again!

The night after my 'near death experience' I had wild dreams; all of them were about resuscitation, both in this lifetime and in others. It must have been part of what my psyche needed to release. There were at least four dreams of dying and coming back to life. Following is what I could vaguely remember.

*In the first dream I was in a moving vehicle talking to my friends. I was sitting on the passenger side and there was a mirror in front of me. I glanced in the mirror and saw the face of a woman. Instinctively I knew **She** was Death. I took a second look and she was still there, smiling. Somehow I understood it was my time to die. I said, "Goodbye," to my friends and left with her. As I joined her thinking she would just escort me away, I was surprised that she took my hand in hers, turned and walked towards Heaven ... in an angelical yet distant way. Just as I resigned to the thought of dying I saw people I loved grieving. In an instant I came back to life.*

In the second dream one of my miniature schnauzers from childhood had died in my arms yet kept coming back to life over and over. I did not understand how she revived, but was so thrilled I gave up the need to know and just accepted the gift.

In the third dream I was clearly in another lifetime, driving in the countryside with my beloved; he was driving an old, 1920s car. It was a beautiful day and we were very much in love. Then something happened. I couldn't recall exactly, but I did know there had been an accident. I saw myself lifting from my body. My beloved was holding my physical body while crying uncontrollably. Suddenly I was pulled back to my body; as I opened my eyes I embraced him deeply. He couldn't speak! After an eternity of holding each other we realized we had been given another chance.

The other dreams I couldn't quite remember. I woke up the next morning very calm yet incredibly energized, knowing that something inside of me had definitely shifted. It seemed the 'death experience' had opened pathways to my soul although I was still unaware of the full impact of it.

Working to Release My Ancestors

Before incarnating and from a blessed place, our souls select the lessons we are to learn and the services we will offer while on Earth. These lessons provide more than enough challenges, yet if we learn from and heal them immeasurable gifts abound! However, there are other major influences to our experience in this lifetime, such as our *genetic lineage*. Previous generations affect how we live and how we react to certain events, people and situations. Whether it is a consequence of their attitudes and beliefs, the stories they pass on to us, or because of the genetic matrix that is part of our energetic makeup, in a strange way they continue to live through us. The Western culture is the only one that does not honor ancestors as the rest of the world does. So our intention in healing ancestral lines is to honor our ancestors yet at the same time extract them from our energy body.

My ancestral work began by identifying and then releasing ancestral lines which had hindered my freedom. I selected three ancestors insuring that they came from both parental lineages. Then I tracked where they lived within me energetically, identifying the specific chakra(s) and area of my body associated with each one. I concluded by removing them from my energy body, setting them and myself free. The three ancestors we select act as 'hooks' for *all* our ancestral lines. We don't need to clear any other ancestor after that as those three released them all.

The shaman always chooses to remember her past as a positive legacy. It is an act of power and of love. Regardless of the wounds and lessons learned that relate to her ancestors, she forgives and releases them. They no longer live in her physical, emotional, mental or spiritual bodies. This way she changes how she chooses to remember them, acknowledging the positive heritage they left her.

In one ancestor releasing exercise I worked with five other people; the intention was to 'clear ancestral lines.' The person clearing her ancestral lines would stand in the middle while each of the remaining people would hold one of the four directions (south, west, north and east). We had previously assessed which chakra(s) and which part(s) of the Energy Body where affected by each ancestor. To unravel the ancestral lines we used three small wooden sticks and one of our own mesa stones. The unraveling was done with counterclockwise movements, weaving the energy strands of the ancestral lines onto the stick and out of our Energy Body.

Later that evening we had a fire ceremony and we put the three sticks to the fire. This would free our energy from the ancestors and ancestral lines we had just unraveled while elevating our ancestors in the process.

I stood in the middle of the blanket doing the Seven-Breath exercise designed to move me into natural altered states of consciousness. Closing my eyes I began to see a web matrix of light in front of my third eye. I grabbed my first stick and the stone, and wound the cords of energy threads into the stick using counterclockwise motions. As I was winding the web revealed the threads I was picking up. I continued to wind the threads into the sticks and the web began to clear out. I kept going all over my Luminous Body until the web was gone and only light was left. The Seven-Breath exercise took me into a trance state, helping me enter non-ordinary reality quickly. Since non-ordinary reality moves you outside of time and space it helps you clear ancestral lines regardless of whether you knew your ancestor or not. One of my ancestors from the paternal side had a hard time releasing and as I wound the energy strands I sensed as though I was disengaging shackles that had been put on me. Once they were gone I felt a mixture of grief and ecstasy, although the grief lasted only a few seconds. Two of the three ancestors were from my paternal side. Interestingly both of them affected my crown chakra; this had created a blur in understanding my mission for this lifetime and also affected my communication with the Divine. Once I put the three sticks into the fire that evening I felt the final release from those ancestors.

Ancestral lines provide us with great understanding. Once removed we feel liberated. Ancestral energies don't belong to us and we must strive to be released from them. However, we should not try to do this alone for we can get entangled in our own threads. We need four other shamans to hold sacred space for us.

In the storytelling of medicine people it is said that we carry our mother on our hips and our father on our shoulders. I have come to fully understand this after doing many healings on people whose parents are deceased and who exhibit pain in either their hips or shoulders, depending on which parent died. At other times, when we are young—even as early as the womb—we make deep energetic agreements to take on issues for our parents and loved ones thinking we can help them heal their wounds.

A fellow medicine woman performed an extraction in the Underworld for me. Feeling she was going to find something major in this healing she asked the Lord of the Lower World to accompany her as she began her descent. He responded that both her and my power animals would be there with her and that she should not be afraid. A few seconds passed. Then I heard a scream! She discovered a room that looked like a library, blood-stains covering the walls. (Remember that this image is usually metaphorical.) The blood she found was from the people I had helped throughout my life. I had empathized with them, 'owned' their pain and tried desperately to resolve whatever situation they were facing. I was the typical caretaker. It was a contract I had made while in the womb: 'to own the pain of the people I loved so that I could make it go away.' The medicine woman proceeded to destroy the old energetic contract I had made, which in turn revealed my original contract. My Divine mission was to be a 'spiritual teacher' in this lifetime. She said it had something to do with 'helping people find their own star.' The medicine woman felt I had originally been so excited about incarnating because of my Divine mission; yet after making the new contract of 'owning the pain of others' while in the womb I became terrified. Before ending the healing she blew a 'star' into my heart chakra.

Liberating Myself From Reincarnatory Lines

Another major influence to our experience in this lifetime has to do with our *past lives*. Our past incarnations bring forth 'karmic' lines that affect how we act, how we perceive, and how we relate to others and to ourselves. Our ancestral (biological) lines inform us at the genetic level while the karmic (reincarnatory) lines inform us at the cellular level. These two lines converge in us and we must work to heal them so that we can clear the influence they have on us. Both of these lines exist outside of time; we usually do ancestral (biological) work first and then clear reincarnatory lines (past lives). In clearing them we may remember our past lives and memories as well as the ancient stories that belong to the collective and which we have heard before. In these instances we connect to and are informed by the lineage of Medicine men and women who have existed since the beginning of time.

Shamans walk consciously between the ordinary and non-ordinary worlds; the latter is also known as the world of Spirit. In order to liberate myself from ***past incarnations*** I moved to non-ordinary reality and began by journeying to three former lives. In each I was instructed to see 'who I was', 'how I lived,' 'how I loved,' and 'how I was loved.' I worked in non-ordinary reality so that I could observe without being involved, and so that the person I was in those lives would understand that all was forgiven and released. After observing I would help myself die, and then follow my Spirit. A Light Being would then invite me to come Home.

*I used three stones—one for each lifetime—and imprinted them with what I had been so that I could be released from those karmic lines. The intention for the first lifetime was to travel to that **life in which I suffered the most.** I placed a stone in the affected chakra and allowed myself to be guided on this journey. I was a black man in Africa, the second son of a very poor family. Our family was quite large and we lived in the outskirts of a village. As I went into the forest one day to hunt and gather I ran into a beautiful woman; both of us were awestruck and fell madly in love. At the time neither one of us knew where the other came from. All we knew was that we loved each other deeply and that we could rest eternally looking into each other's eyes.*

Later I would find out that she was the daughter of the village chief and realized our union would not be acceptable to her family. But the love we felt for each other was immense and neither could conceive life without the other. We continued to meet and love each other in the forest for several months. Then one time as we were making love in the wilderness the guards of the village came upon us. They took her away and killed her for dishonoring her family, and then proceeded to exile our family from the village and into the forest.

We were so poor that my younger siblings began to die from hunger. Then my mother died of sadness from seeing her children pass and being unable to do anything about it. My father was tremendously upset and decided to oust me from the family. I went deeper into the forest, living in a cave alone with animals as my only company. Several years passed while living in nature without any brush with humanity.

Then we were instructed to move to within five minutes of our death and to notice our surroundings and the eyes of those around us. I was in the cave, about 32 years old, and the only ones there at the time of my death were two wolves. As I lay dying and looked into the eyes of the two wolves accompanying me I recognized the eternal love of two of my present life companions: my two puppies!

*The second lifetime I traveled to was the **life in which I had the greatest knowledge and power and misused it.** I placed a stone in another chakra and began the shamanic journey. I was a white woman in Massachusetts born into a family of witches. Our expertise involved developing potions, using a variety of herbs and sacred incantations. My mother and grandmother started teaching me at age 12 and I quickly learned to develop potions. Since I was so young when it all started I didn't understand the application of ethics and morals as they*

related to people's requests. I believed that I was playing more than helping. I began to misuse my power by giving potions to people who wanted to manipulate situations, such as having someone fall in love with them against their will or others who were looking for revenge for a perceived wrong.

As I moved forward in that lifetime I discovered I was married and had two children: a son and a daughter. When my husband found out that I developed potions that could be used to manipulate situations he left me. I moved in with my grandmother, my main teacher, and brought my children with me. As I was urged to move to the last five minutes of that life I found myself lying on my deathbed with both children at my side. Their eyes spoke the anger they felt towards me for ruining their lives. I died poisoned by someone who had been wronged by one of my own potions!

The third lifetime I journeyed to was the **life in which I had the greatest wisdom and served well.** *I placed my third stone in the corresponding chakra and allowed the journey to take me there. I was a man in a very powerful Mayan village, born into a noble family of a lineage of kings (caciques). I was the second son in my family. My brothers and I were thoroughly trained: hunting, leadership, compassion, medicine, history, family, and death. The village council of elders was responsible for selecting the cacique that was to lead the tribe and also for de-selecting them when they didn't serve their people well. (This structure is similar to that of the Lakota in North America.)*

They picked me over my oldest brother as their next king because of my open heart, my compassion. My oldest brother was furious and left the tribe. The village loved me so much that when I addressed them from atop a temple they lifted the face of a 'sun' towards me, symbolizing their approval. One of my greatest powers in this lifetime was 'divination' and I knew how to govern and lead based on seeing the future. I married the love of my life and we had two children: a boy and a girl.

After 25 years of leading the tribe peacefully the Aztecs began to encroach upon our territory. They wanted our riches and were preparing for war. I saw this in my divinations some years before, but hadn't addressed it because I didn't want to go to war and watch my people get killed. The elders told me I must face what I had seen and fight for our people. In the last five minutes of this life, as I was leading my tribe to war, a spear penetrated my abdomen. I died looking into my son's loving eyes; he was in the battle with me. I also saw my older brother's face; he had joined the Aztecs and was fighting against us.

Removing Intrusive Energies

After ridding myself of ancestral and reincarnatory lines it was time to cleanse my energy body of unwanted energies. There are two types of intrusive energies that can penetrate our energy and physical bodies: crystallized and fluid. **Crystallized energies** are those that have hardened in the physical body of a person. Many of these energies have emotions associated with them and can sometimes have psychological manifestations as well. They may or may not be from this lifetime; most are very ancient. The middle part of our brain is called the limbic brain, and it remembers emotional issues we have had across thousands of years and therefore across lifetimes. It is the second brain we developed and is responsible for emotions and for our ability to have empathy. When we touch a crystallized energy in a person, memories stored in the limbic brain get activated. The story recalled by the person may be a metaphor for a condition in their current life or for one in a past life. The shaman may also see the story. There is always a chakra associated with a crystallized energy and this can provide more information about the story.

In order to remove a crystallized energy the shaman begins by tracking it, sensing its shape, temperature, and material, before trying to name it. Then the energies around it must be removed so that it can be extracted. This is similar to digging out the earth around a root or a rock that we are trying to remove from the ground. Once removed crystallized energies lose their memory. We return them to nature so that Mother Earth can transmute them.

When I first heard about this concept I was reluctant to accept it. How could something that happened in a previous life physically manifest itself again when we are in a different body? Even more incredible is that it usually appeared in the same physical spot where it had been in that previous life! I could not fathom the whole concept. But the Universe has a way of aligning us with what is. My personal experience would change my mind.

My partner for this exercise began to track my body for crystallized energies, starting with her hands and continuing with a tracking stone. She was not touching my physical body, but rather scanning it several inches above. There was a definite 'hot spot' right under my right breast, piercing my liver and ribs and all the way back to under my right shoulder blade. The chakra associated with this 'hot spot' was my second chakra although the physical area was within the perimeter of the third chakra. My partner proceeded to do an Illumination on the navel chakra. Then she began to clear the area around the crystallized energy so that the extraction would be easier. When she began sensing the energy she described it as a hollow-like crystal that had entered through my back and went all the way to the front of my body. There was a sharp tip on one end of it pointing towards the front of my body. It was important to track the shape for its removal would depend on where the sharp edges or points were.

She held the object and moved it around to dislodge it. I could distinctly feel something moving inside my flesh. She asked me to breathe deeply and then exhale rapidly several times. As I did she began to pull from the back; I visualized pushing it to the back from the front of my body. She continued to pull. I felt as though a large part of my back was being taken out! She stopped for a while to allow me to rest and then continued to pull with both hands until it was all out. The entire time she was pulling the object was vibrating significantly, so much so that she had to hold it tightly with both hands.

Once out she cleansed the area around it and told me to imagine blue-green water cleansing the infected area; then she asked the wind to come into the hole left by the crystallized energy and fill it. I felt a rush of air slowly seal the emptied space. She continued to cleanse the area of any final residue and then harmonized my second chakra so that I would not have any more affinity to this energy. The crystallized energy was huge! It was a multi-faceted, transparent crystal about two and a half inches in diameter and about eight inches in length. After the extraction I felt a massive cylindrical hole under my right shoulder blade with tender spots all around it. The area hurt as I moved or sat and continued to hurt the rest of the evening and through the night. I felt as though physical surgery had been performed!

One week later, as I was having a massage by the therapist I had had for many years, she said, "What happened in your right middle back? The spasm you have had since I have known you is gone!"

It is important to point out that the story behind the huge crystal is irrelevant. Healing precedes understanding, so if I were meant to know more about it time would tell. However, I *am still incredulous as to how this physical object could reen-ergize itself in a physical body from a different incarnation!*

A *fluid energy* is very different to a crystallized energy. It runs through the nervous system and is not localized or stagnant like crystallized energies are. It attaches itself to the nervous system—to the fluid of the spinal cord—in order to survive for it needs energy to live. It is important to mention that many of these energies are unaware that they have attached themselves and are generally relieved once they have been released.

Intrusive *energies* and intrusive *entities* behave similarly yet are different in character. An 'intrusive energy' is fluid and moves through the acupuncture meridians. An 'intrusive entity' is also fluid, but attaches itself to a person's chakras so that it can feed from the fluid of the nervous system. Both energies may have an emotion attached to them—such as sadness, grief, or anger—and are always associated with a chakra. After extracting it we must change the energetic affinities within that chakra in order to protect it. Intrusive entities are not common, but intrusive energies are extremely prevalent. There are many possibilities as to where they come from yet that need not be our concern. Instead our focus needs be on getting rid of them so that our own energy can fully permeate our Energy Body and bring about healing. Entities can come from many sources: someone who passed and was afraid to die, a previous incarnation of ourselves competing for energy, or loved ones who either died traumatically or were severely medicated and generally felt trapped between the worlds.

An intrusive energy, on the other hand, is more common and most of us have dealt with it. Anyone who has a pathway to our soul can send an intrusive energy even if they are still living. They penetrate our resistance because our Energy Body recognizes them and doesn't identify them as intrusive. Someone who feels anger, jealousy, or rage towards us, or someone that is sad from a breakup can send an intrusive energy. The term 'stabbed in the back' is a clear metaphor for someone sending you dense energy, which may or may not become attached to your energy body. The more open we are psychically the more available we are to these intrusive energies. We always strive to become increasingly open spiritually yet want to remain protected from these intrusive energies or entities.

Fluid energies and entities can both be easily extracted. Some shamanic practitioners extract them with a red cloth, others use their breath and some utilize a crystal. I prefer the crystal not only because I feel safer, but also because it is more comfortable for the entity or energy to go into as it is Light. The crystal acts like a vacuum extracting the energy comfortably and effortlessly. Crystals must then be cleansed and this is when you can sometimes tell if what was extracted was an energy or an entity. However, keep in mind that the most important issue is to heal and be free of them, not to know where they came from or what it was.

Sometimes energies or entities are very reluctant to leave and sometimes the person is reluctant to let them go. That is why we must startle the energy or entity to persuade it to leave. Someone who is continually sick more than likely has an intrusive energy or entity. They may get momentarily better and then they mysteriously get very sick again. They can only return to health once the energy or entity is extracted and the chakra's affinities harmonized. Extractions can be done either in a group or alone. If done in a group people are assigned to a specific task, with one person doing the extracting and the others supporting.

There were five of us in the group. We were going to take turns doing each aspect of the extractions. Two people tracked the energy or entity from a distance; a third person ran 'hot' energy along the spine of the client (to dislodge the entity or energy from the chakra it is feeding from) and a fourth one, me, did the extraction. While I was extracting the energy in the person looked like a jellyfish with a very long tentacle. The tentacle was holding on to the person's medulla and moving up and down her spine into her brain and around her neck. Once extracted the person's sight was significantly restored. She also professed gaining a sensation of lightness and peace almost immediately.

Then it was my turn to be the patient. Initially I had tested negative for an energy or entity yet one of our group members said that they sensed something in me. Sure enough the energy was hiding behind my heart chakra and didn't want to come out. It was black in the middle and then gray with a red rim as it moved outward. Once it was extracted I felt a very deep sense of relief in my lower back. Shortly thereafter I had an image of an ex-partner who sent it to me, obviously hurt over the breakup.

The next person had a similar situation in that she initially tested negative. We somehow knew her mind was in the way and suggest she count backwards while retesting her in order to distract her from her thoughts. The intrusive energy was like a swirling disk, hiding behind her neck.

The next member to be tested had told us that he had suddenly gotten sick the night before and felt someone had purposely sent him something energetically. I was the one running 'hot' energy along the spine and could distinctly see a dark and very long energy that looked like a worm. It tried to hold on to his spine for quite a while until it was too hot to stay. It finally came out. We were all exhausted after the five extractions—yet each one of us felt so much lighter and relieved!

Doing extractions alone is much more challenging because the shaman must do all the steps in quick sequence. It is best not to inform a client that they may have an entity or energy until the time of the extraction, for their mind informs the energy or entity and it may hide in its refusal to come out. During the extraction the shaman holds the crystal in one hand; the fact that she is in non-ordinary reality creates a mirror effect that duplicates the crystal to the shaman's other hand.

After obtaining a base strength test from my client I began to run energy down the spine. Just as it was heating up I saw a round, light circle on her left shoulder blade. I began to entice it to come towards the crystal I was holding in my right hand; it started moving to her right shoulder and then stayed there. After a little while it began to come down the right arm very slowly. I waited and then startled it so it would come out. When I tested her chakras her throat one was affected; it had attached itself there. Interestingly enough she had had throat problems for the past several years and doctors had not been able to help her. After this her throat felt great!

Spiritual Pilgrimage to Peru

After shedding the past and facing my fears it was time to travel to one of the pillars of all these teachings: the Inka Q'ero Indians. My shamanism teacher had prompted me on several occasions to accompany him and his group to the sacred mountains of Peru. This time, without hesitation I cleared my calendar and then immediately called my spiritual friend Dana to see if she would like to share this mystical journey with me. I told her my teacher would be our main guide and master shaman. She was so excited she could barely respond. It was to be a rugged and tough shamanic pilgrimage, starting in P'isaq and the Sacred Valley of the Inka and then to Ausangate—a sacred medicine mountain located above 14,000 feet; the trip would end in Machu Picchu with ceremony at night.

In June of 2002 we traveled from Miami to Lima, stayed in Lima overnight and then headed to Cuzco the next morning. We arrived in our hotel in P'isaq the afternoon of the following day, patiently awaiting our instructions and observing others who would be our travel companions on this adventure. I recognized several fellow Medicine Wheel participants some who had become my friends. Within a couple of hours the local medicine people that were to accompany us started to appear. First came the Q'ero: Doña Bernadina, Don Francisco, Don Humberto, and Don Mariano, all very serious and with their full regalia. Then came a medicine woman from Cuzco named Doña Berna whose energy and disposition enchanted me. She was the only one who spoke Spanish and we quickly began to reweave energies that seemed so familiar to one another. The rest of the medicine people spoke only Quechua.

Our trip began in P'isaq where we visited local ruins. We had the place all to ourselves! We wanted to set our intention for this amazing journey and our teacher began with a Despacho Ceremony. A Despacho is a bundle of prayers done at the mythic level, assembled over delicate tissue paper and made of flowers and many colorful nature elements. There are several types of Despacho depending on the intention. This one would be a Harmony Despacho, which is designed to bring harmony into each of our lives and to Mother Earth. It would be held in the center monument of the P'isaq Ruins: the Temple of the Visionary. The local shamans brought out their nature elements, which included 'coca leaves' (sacred to the Q'ero), cotton, flowers, and above all pure intentions and unconditional love. The coca leaves would be used to assemble Quintus, consisting of three leaves stacked on top of each other. We would blow our prayers into the Quintus and then pass them forward so that they could be placed in the group Despacho. At one point Doña Berna from Cuzco approached me and offered me two Quintus saying, "One is for your work transition and the other one for your utmost wish." Then she immediately added, "Your utmost wish is Authentic Love. I see it in your eyes." I hadn't spoken a word to her yet but she knew! I suppose Authentic Love is probably everyone's wish.

We visited a couple of sacred sites and on the second evening returned to P'isaq. We needed to rest and get ready for our incredible journey to the highlands of Peru. That evening Don Mariano held a demonstration of an Inka Divination practice using coca leaves. Each one of us got to ask him a personal question. When it was my turn I said, "Will I be released from my Corporate work soon and jump into my Spiritual work? When will that happen?" Don Mariano threw coca leaves onto a mat and responded, "YES, it will be very soon for a window will begin to open for you by the end of 2002. However, it will also depend on how fast you can let go of your current work." My whole body had chills! As it worked out I made my decision to leave the corporate world in January of 2003, right after the window opened! By August of the same year I was developing the outline and strategy for a mystery school.

In the morning we left P'isaq for Ausangate, the sacred mountain of the highest-level Q'ero shamans. It was a very long trip, first by bus then smaller vehicles, horseback, and finally by foot. We left civilization completely and entered a desolate terrain with only rocks, soil, and breathtaking glaciers and lakes. We hiked to our campsite at 14,000 feet, right next to a magical and beautiful turquoise lagoon called Azulcocha (translates roughly to 'Blue Lagoon'). We were right at the snow line, the impressive Apu Ausangate standing before us as a protective father. The temperature during the day was around 60 degrees Fahrenheit but by 6:00p.m. it had dropped to the 30s and by 9:00p.m. it was close to zero degrees. It was freezing even with five layers of clothing on!

After several ceremonies, rites of passage and stories, it was time to hear the Inka Prophecies. This was one of the main reasons I had been lured to this trip. "The Pachacuti Inka is coming back", the prophecies said. "In fact there will be nine Pachacutis waking up simultaneously, then another nine until the whole planet turns to light! Soon it will be the end of our world, as we know it. It will be the end of Western medicine, of our economy, our governments, our legal system, our corporations, and of our educational system. All will collapse, because they no longer serve the needs of the people or of Mother Earth, and it will happen around 2012!" Interestingly 2012 marked the beginning of the Fifth Sun for the Maya, forecasted as a period of over sixty thousand years of light on Earth! 'So maybe these systems have to collapse and be developed anew for this new beginning,' I thought.

Those are big statements regarding the end of five of our major systems (economy, government, education, medicine, legal). When probed further the Inka elders alluded to people's impatience at the fact that old systems no longer fulfill the current paradigm. They have grown so much yet they have not evolved. For example *Western Medicine* today is more focused on keeping people alive, but not necessarily with great quality of life. Medicines help us improve an area, but side effects affect other areas. There is very little responsibility given to the patient, although it is the patient that commands its own healing.

World renowned doctor, Andrew Weil, says that the patient needs to be at the center of the wheel, with all types of allopathic and energy medicine possibilities around the wheel. This will allow the patient to select a combination of modalities that can help them heal. They can choose to involve experts or check in with their own inner wisdom. Allopathic medicine on the other hand has placed itself at the center of the wheel, the patient being around the wheel with other possible healing modalities. In 2012 the total amount of dollars spent on 'alternative sources of medicine' exceeded the amount spent on traditional medicine by more than 20%. This percentage has only grown as more people realize current offerings are not healing them.

The world's *Economy* has become a gamble as major countries hold tremendous amounts of debt, which in turn is funded by unstable economies of other major countries. Smaller countries are severely affected by this gamble and placed in positions of enormous uncertainty as to how they can stabilize and sustain the wellbeing of their population.

Legal Systems have become so cumbersome and filled with processes and laws that they don't provide justice as it was originally intended. The majority of time and resources are spent in navigating the processes rather than in obtaining fairness and results. The *Government* entities have lost sight of their objective to represent the needs of their population. And finally the *Educational System* no longer supports the learning needs of today's children, but rather tries to force them into a mold that is obsolete. It was interesting that the prophecies of the Hopi, Maya and Inka were in agreement about these systems yet were developed at different times ... in different places. This was a lot to digest, but nevertheless an interesting proposition!

Before leaving the amazing site of Ausangate and heading to Machu Picchu we took a trip to 18,000 feet, the 'top of the world' as it was known there. The intention was to see the 'Bridge between the Worlds' (the ordinary and non-ordinary worlds) as well as meet its gatekeeper, a very high level Q'ero shaman known as Don Mariano. The site was completely surreal: a turquoise lagoon below, several gigantic sacred mountains, and a pristine glacier between the mountains close enough to almost touch. We had reached natural altered states of consciousness just by being there!

Traveling to Machu Picchu took all day, but in our current states of consciousness time and space had disappeared. Once there we were given time to tour the citadel during the day and told to stay around for reentry at night. Our adventure was just beginning, as we were about to have this amazing sacred site all to ourselves; void of tourists, tour guides, and vendors ... just the ancestors, the full moon, the stars, and us.

All was dark as we began to reenter. The citadel felt as though it was fully populated though. The energies were intensely palpable, our ancestors gathered to welcome us home and to support us for the upcoming challenges. The aroma of smoke from ancient times began to permeate our surroundings. The wind was still. It was as though you could touch the veil, but not describe it. Under the starriest of nights we climbed tenaciously to the top of Machu Picchu. We arrived at the original entrance, a small hut to the side and the mythical Death Stone resting in the middle. This special place is usually off limits to tourists, but we had been cleared to have the run of this powerful site.

Our teacher began by explaining the concept of the Death Stone and as soon as I heard the word 'death' and remembered the beautiful experience I had had with 'death rites' in the Work of the West my body pushed itself to the front of the line. Shamans entering Machu Picchu were to take a 'death flight' on this stone before entering the citadel, so that they would 'die' to who they were in their ordinary reality before their energies were allowed to permeate such a sacred place. It was done to honor the holy site as well as to cleanse before entering. He began organizing the group. First he positioned one person on the entry side of the Death Stone to help usher people onto it. Another person was assigned to the front of the stone to assist in releasing the Energy bodies of those taking the 'death flight' into the sky. Two other people were placed on the backside of the Death Stone and were responsible for receiving the Energy bodies of those returning from flight. Three people would wait on the exit side of the stone and assist those who had come back from their flight and were ready to step back into their physical bodies.

I went onto the Death Stone first and stood facing the West with open arms, welcoming Spirit and stating my intent for the imminent flight I was about to take. Then I lay down with my mesa under my head. My teacher was right next to me and proceeded to open several of my chakras with his rattle; then he stood and softly ushered my Energy body forward into cosmic flight. I left my physical body fast, first visiting numerous stars and constellations all at once then saying, "Hello" to long, lost friends and familiar places. This was home ... a memorable place that allowed my soul to be free and whole, one with the Universe. I felt so held and so unencumbered. It lasted a few minutes yet it seemed like an instant. Suddenly I was abruptly pulled back into my physical body. I did not want to come back! My teacher used his rattle to re-spin the three chakras he had opened initially, bringing me back to the present moment. It was hard for me to get up and stand firmly. Karla received me and helped me come down from the stone. She held me until I felt integrated with my physical body. Even if my mind wanted to take a step my body would not respond. There was no fear just acceptance. The simultaneity of the experience was fascinating to me. I could visit stars, constellations and galaxies at the same time!

All this happened within four minutes, which is the maximum amount of time your energy body can be outside your physical body without the possibility of physical damage occurring. At least fifteen minutes passed from the time I came back into my physical body and the when I felt fully integrated with it. It remains one of the best experiences of my life to date!

We moved from the Death Stone to the Main Temple. It all looked magnificent under the light of the full moon. The light beings were definitely present. The citadel had a vibrancy and aliveness that penetrated my soul. I had changed the batteries in my flash light right before re-entering to make sure I had a source of light while climbing and descending those steep steps. However when I tried to turn it on after the first ceremony nothing happened. So I resigned to the fact that I had to 'feel' my way through a place that I had walked so many times before. We moved towards a 'U-shaped' monument and three women from the group began the ritual of offering coca leaves. Everyone sat around this 'U-shaped' building, our backs against the walls. I wondered how many souls had placed their backs on these walls. This was yet another area that was off-limits to tourists.

What ensued was completely unexpected! Dana had told me several days before that she had seen a vision of me in the South Pacific (Australia) with a gift upside down. This meant I had not opened the gift in that lifetime. The gift contained ten bands of protection, but I never had the chance to open it. Five years ago when I was in Machu Picchu I had had a spontaneous regression to a life in Australia where I owned and captained two large commercial vessels. The Indian Ocean was so treacherous that the captain of the vessel had to journey forward in time to chart the course for the vessel's upcoming trip, anticipating storms, winds, and waves. I died in that lifetime after my vessel capsized, overturned by an unforeseen typhoon. If I had returned to Australia I would have undergone a special ritual of protection, but since I never made it back I never received the gift.

When we got to the main temple I glanced to the mountains on the left. They were majestic! Memories of a very dear friend of mine came pouring through. She had died in those mountains some years before and I never had the chance to say good-bye. My heart was completely open especially after the Death Stone experience. I began to hear her voice. Tears poured down my cheeks. As I was sitting in the 'U-shaped' building with my back to the wall my friend said to me, "It's time you open your gift. I'm here to help you install the additional bands." She somehow knew I already had five bands of power that had been woven around me so she proceeded to carefully put the other five bands around my Energy body.

I could feel the power of the ten bands as they began overlapping. I asked her what the additional bands were for and she answered, *"It's for you to have direct access to the Heavens any time you wish, and for absolute protection in this lifetime!"* *She told me that I could feel and talk to her and my departed loved ones much easier now and, that any time I wanted, I could access the power and wisdom of the Universe. "You are getting fully prepared for your mission," she said. I was unable to speak for a long time.*

Dana knew that I was having an intense altered state experience and she compassionately observed me. The group had descended to the next ceremony location yet I was completely unaware. She moved towards me slowly and whispered in my ear, "Come back ... we must go now ... you don't need to say anything ... I'll take you." With that I got up and held her hand, walking slowly to our next destination.

We had another ceremony after that, but I felt as though I was floating somewhere else. I remained silent during our short bus ride to our hotel and through dinner, unable to put words to such unbelievably magical and mystical experiences! We returned to Miami a few days later. I had definitely come back a different person than the one that had departed.

A New Lens Emerges

"The real voyage of discovery consists not in seeking new landscapes, but in having new eyes."
—Marcel Proust

ALMOST A YEAR HAD PASSED FROM THE TIME I HAD embarked on the Medicine Wheel. Everything around me felt different now that I had shed a significant part of my past and faced some major fears. I was learning to trust that I lived in a benevolent Universe, one that was always conspiring to 'assist' me. For example, after moving beyond fears related to abundance and past perceptions I may have grown up with regarding women providing for themselves, I deeply understood with every fiber of my being that each of us has access to boundless resources. We just need to get out of the way, feed thoughts of abundance in order to manifest it, and be grateful for what we receive irrespective of what that is. This is what Native American shamans call the domain of Buffalo, where unlimited abundance is within our reach. These reserves are symbolized by the hump on the back of the Buffalo. It is in the North direction of the Medicine Wheel that we learn to tap into them, as they are available at all times.

The liberation from ancestral and reincarnatory lines allowed me to see the world with new eyes, almost as though the lens had completely changed. Add to this the transformational trip to Peru and I felt as though I had just been reborn. Continuing my journey to wholeness I now had to focus on regaining any energy I had lost throughout this incarnation. This would help me connect to a much wiser part of me as well as begin a conscious interaction with the Higher Realms. My whole existence was moving away from the linear reality I had grown accustomed to and into a more mystical and unexplainable world. Yet I felt good, even if my mind couldn't fully understand nor control my 'reality.' The lure of magic made my heart race! It was time to surrender and move forward, feeling and sensing rather than thinking.

In many shamanic traditions you have three stones for each of the four directions of the Medicine Wheel plus a lineage stone. The lineage stone is special as it bridges the solar and lunar calendars, which in turn gives us access to the sacred calendar. The lunar and solar calendars coincide every fifty-two years and then reset themselves. This connection of both calendars symbolizes the synchronicity of the masculine (solar) and the feminine (lunar) in relationship to time, which is also indicative of the integration of both energies within. It is also the 13th stone in the mesa. This is a sacred number for the Maya as it signifies transmutation, magic and stepping outside of time. The lineage stone is given to you when you take your seat as part of the lineage of shamans that exist across time, which happens in the Work of the North. Once we are part of the lineage we get help from wise people that live in multiple dimensions. This in turn increases our ability to travel across dimensions, which significantly impacts the depth of our healing work. Now we are not just 'connected' to a lineage, *we are the lineage!*

For South American shamans the North direction of the Medicine Wheel is the domain of Royal Hummingbird. She is revered as the bringer of joy for she knows how to drink the nectar of life. In addition this little being embarks on a great journey each year, flying over 2,000 miles in spite of its limitations: not having enough wing energy, fuel, or food. This had great implications for me at this stage of my life for in spite of the uncertainty facing me in my world I was only limited by my own imagination. Hummingbirds are masters of **stillness in motion.** Metaphorically we understand that regardless of whatever happens in our life there is always a core part of us that must remain in **stillness.** When we are in 'stillness' we do not disturb the ripples of life. We become like the palm trees, swaying with the wind but never falling. Domestication, on the other hand, teaches us to project what happens to us in an outward fashion mostly through our thoughts. However, we must learn to be still inside, even from our own thoughts and perceptions. So hummingbird is here to teach us balance between 'unlimited energy' and 'absolute stillness.' I was about to become one of hummingbird's most avid students, seeking stillness inside … amidst a sea of change.

In order to move further into this mystical world of non-ordinary reality and enter the realm of Divine magic I had to learn to **step outside of time.** In the Western world we are prisoners of the law of cause and effect as we follow linear time. This is the 'human' concept of time where Western society belongs to time. Even our mythology of creation is based upon specific time parameters. We divide time into seconds, minutes, hours, and this is precisely what we must step out of. We cannot divide time to 'stop it' so we must learn to move vertically in between time to reach 'stillness.' The ultimate intention is to achieve 'Mastery of Time,' where we are no longer held in its grip.

One of the keys to stepping outside of time is **invisibility.** It has to do with becoming transparent and allowing our true self to be 'seen.' It is about dropping our identity and therefore having nothing left to hide … no image to maintain. We are no longer defined by what we 'do' or 'have done.' We have ceased the ME projects where the ego is fed. We do not leave tracks and must become adept at getting out of our way. Sometimes we may even stand or walk by others yet they will not 'see' us.

Stepping beyond linear time means going to a time before the Universe was created and after the end. Even though the shaman may be able to glance at events to come in her future or view future possibilities for others, she must *keep the present inno- cent, authentic and filled with beauty.* She must maintain it a secret even from herself and return to the present without being affected by it. This allows her to participate in the Moment with total authenticity, keeping it fresh and pristine. If we lived our life based on the glimpses of the future that we can see we would not be able to live in the present moment.

Everything is happening much faster on Earth today. We may face events on a given day which used to take weeks, maybe even months, to happen in the old energy. Our planet has been catapulted into the realm of Divine Manifestation, and there- fore, so are we. Our creations manifest rapidly whether they are beautiful things or fears. So awareness of our thoughts and intentions is key. Therefore it is now more important than ever to view occurrences outside of time so that we are not trapped in it and become overwhelmed. How do we 'step outside of time' and practice 'stillness?' *By observing the events in our lives with detachment, and by stopping our roles!* We stop all that we DO: have to do, must do, think we need to do, can do. This involves stopping expectations from others and from ourselves on us. When we see people as being in a horizontal continuum rather than hierarchical we release them from those roles which confine them, and we release ourselves from the roles imposed upon us by others and by ourselves.

My experience with transcending my roles was profound. The intent was 'to no longer be confined to a given role even if I still do that role' (i.e., caretaker role). First I put into a sand painting all the 'roles' I have played in my life, with one of my North stones in the middle representing me. The roles in my sand painting

*were numerous: mother (people around me and my puppies),
daughter, consultant, leader (business, community, friends),
rescuer, friend, rebel/non-conformist, caretaker, seeker/explorer,
teacher, student, sister, sister in law, aunt, and godmother.*

*Then I started tracking energies within my sand painting,
intent on following each role to its natural unraveling. I asked
myself, "When do I stop that role?" I grabbed the object representing each role, closed my eyes as I held it in front of my third
eye and called upon my spirit guides and the lineage to help me
'see' its unraveling. Once I saw my destiny for each of the roles
it became clear that the 'rescuer' and 'caretaker' roles no longer
had meaning; I removed them both from the sand painting. Then
I took the remaining objects that symbolized roles and placed
them outside the mandala. I grabbed another North stone from
my mesa, blew into it, and tracked my possibilities for each role
... each life destiny. What possibilities weren't included in my
existing roles? I followed them beyond my death and tracked my
becoming. This resulted in me adding the 'healer' role, symbolizing the light side of the 'caretaker' and the 'rescuer.' I couldn't
wait to see how this would all play out in my life!*

Stepping outside of time also helps us track several possible
destinies instead of being locked into one. We no longer talk about
probabilities, but instead concentrate on possibilities, which are
again only limited by our imagination! So tracking our timelines
and the possibilities within them allows us to jump into our destiny consciously. We can therefore **choose** the best path to follow
with full awareness and align with our ultimate destiny. When we
step beyond time we can also heal things before they are born,
before they manifest physically. We can do this for ourselves and
for others, and it can also be applied to events in our past.

Our destiny lines follow a 'cone of probabilities.' We have many
destiny lines available and when we choose one it solidifies and

later becomes our history. The majority of our probable destinies are within the cone of probabilities, and maybe 1-2% of possibilities are outside of it. We track the cone so that we can increase the probability of the 1-2% alternate destinies. The cone of probabilities is conditioned by our current life: our culture, our perceptions, our thoughts, our past events and our attitudes. It is defined by our roles and by our identity ... the 'coat' we put on and take off. But we are not our 'coat or identity,' and the moment we step out of it we can track the possibilities outside the cone.

Once we find the alternate destinies we shift the cone energetically, which eventually informs the physical reality. And how do we find these alternate destinies and shift the cone? We begin by setting our intent and then we journey to the Upper World and track those possibilities. If someone has a terminal illness for example, the healer can track the 1-2% of destiny lines not in their current cone of probabilities. As this future 'healed state' destiny line is brought forth it informs the present so that the cone of probabilities can shift. The only caution when doing this shifting of the cone is that the patient **must want to heal,** for they will have to consciously work to change behaviors and beliefs as these come up.

Our intent is always to break free from that destiny that is not our highest possibility so that we can find the one that is and step fully into it. For example, although my career in Corporate America taught me immeasurable lessons and brought amazing gifts it would have eventually led me to a destiny that didn't hold the highest possibility for me. So by tracking alternate destiny lines and shifting the cone I embraced a higher possibility for my soul. Eventually this resulted in me leaving my Corporate career and moving fully into my spiritual path and mission. This is where we learn to 'be *in* this world but not *of* this world' ... of 'participating *in* this world yet not being *possessed* by it.'

We must all reach for the highest destiny—for ourselves, our family, our community, our planet, our Universe. We track consciously for those two or three destiny lines that Spirit is showing us and then fully embody one. Spirit will then align behind us and help us move fully into that higher destiny. Each one of us must **choose** to embody that alternate destiny and then change accordingly. We cannot impose it upon anybody else. *But remember that we live in a benevolent Universe and once we commit it conspires to assist us!*

By now you have gathered that shamanic time is a different kind of time. Shamans and Quantum physicists deal with circular time, where we can influence both our past and our future because events are not sequential. So the beginning of time is now and to reach the beginning you must go through the past. This is why the Solar Disc of the Inka is circular, since time is circular. So medicine teachings did not develop incrementally in time. Rather they were complete from the beginning because they existed outside of time.

In non-ordinary reality time and space don't exist so it is easier to experience infinity. Shamans can step beyond time **after** the Work of the West, after we are no longer stalked by our ultimate fear: Death. Now we can listen to and honor our ancestors. We cease the search for Truth because we understand that *we* are responsible for **bringing** 'truth' to our lives, to our environment; we no longer search for meaning in events, people and things, for we know it is up to **us** to **bring** 'meaning' into the now!

Working With Perceptual States in a More Conscious Way

All of us perceive life in different ways, choosing how we see and hold the events and the people in our lives. Our 'stories' are based on these perceptions and they can either strengthen or weaken us. My shamanism teachers would always say to me, "Change your story and your life changes accordingly." At the beginning it was a hard concept to grasp. Later I came to realize we all have the power to shift how we 'see' an event, and as we consciously change the way we hold it within us our entire life changes.

In the North direction we learn how to select the perception that strengthens us. As I mentioned before the four most common perceptual states are: literal, symbolic, mythic, and energetic. To reiterate:

- The *Literal* level is the body, the physical, the details; its archetype is the serpent.

- The *Symbolic* is the mind and the emotions ... the spoken word; we use jaguar as the archetype for this perceptual state.

- The *Mythic* is the level of the soul, where our grand journey resides ... it is the perspective at 50,000 feet; the eagle is the archetype.

- The *Energetic* level is that of Spirit, it involves sensations and dissolves into the oneness.

We must learn about each one intimately so that we can naturally shift between them in any given situation and move to the one that is the most empowering. And remember when Spirit heals it heals the soul, which then heals the mind and the heart, and finally the physical.

Perceptual states can be used in many different ways; they are extremely powerful in reading people and situations. In most cases we begin by tracking at the symbolic level to give context to a situation. Then we move up to the mythic level so that we can see the grand picture, and then surrender to the energetic level. On the other hand when we want to step outside the box and dream the world we want into reality we always start at the big picture level.

Once we map at the mythic, in time it will manifest at the literal. We cannot map at the literal level because with so many details we cannot step outside of the box or the cone of probabilities.

When healing others however, we track at the perceptual state the client is in so that we can relate and feel the heaviness of their dilemma. Then we can move back and forth to the other perceptual states so that we can track deeper and get more information. For example we go to the mythic level when the client needs a global perspective before delving into details, or we go to the symbolic level when there's fear or anger in the client.

The Upper World

The Upper World is the place where our Higher Self resides. It is the realm of destiny and of unlimited possibilities, where we taste the passion for the possible. It is where that which has not manifested exists in pure potential. It is also the kingdom of the Masters, the Star People, the Light Beings, and the Angels ... where we touch Divinity. Our Akashic records are here as well as what Carl Jung called the collective unconscious. In order to have access to the Upper World we must have cleansed from the past and from fears so that we can enter with absolute purity. Duality does not exist in this realm.

In the medicine tradition the Lower World is associated with *time past* ... with recovering soul parts we have lost in the past or with altering how we hold events from our past. The Upper World, on the other hand, is associated with *time to come* ... with our future possibilities. This is where we track destiny. The first time we go to the Upper World our intention is to become familiar with the landscape, to 'map' it. Since it is a realm of such purity however, we must be stripped of everything that is not our essential Self. So in order to gain access we begin the journey by going to a cavern where we are energetically dismembered.

There are a multitude of levels in the Upper World. Some shamanic lineages I studied have seven, others use three, and yet others have more than ten. Some mythologies include dangerous or dark levels while others choose to work with friendly realms. The number of levels is not as important as the mythology you choose to work with. I feel comfortable with a friendly mythology and for now will describe what five levels might look like:

- The first one is the *Stone domain*, a mineral domain. It can have large rock formations, boulders and/or small river rocks. It is not a great world if you are a human, for it is void of light.

- The second level is the *Plant domain*, a green domain that appeared after the coming of the light. It has flowers, trees and plants. Humans may come here to cleanse and purge before going to 'heaven.' It is also the domain where our 'plant medicine' is and upon visiting it we start becoming familiar with our plant allies. It is important to mention that if we find relatives when journeying to the Stone or Plant realms we must not engage or interfere because they are usually purging; we must respect them.

- The third level of the Upper World is the *Animal domain*, animals reside here. Our power animals guide and protect us when we journey to this level.

- The fourth one is the *Human domain*, also known as Heaven. This is where we came from and where we go to after we die. It is also where our ancestors live. We share this realm with dolphins and whales, which are the keepers of life in the oceans and the holders of the crystalline grid blueprint.

- The fifth and last domain is the *Lineage domain*, which is the world of our becoming … our destiny. This is where medicine men and women are, and where cities of light are being dreamt into being.

We currently source ourselves from the Human domain. But according to the Inka, Maya and Hopi prophecies, we will soon begin to source ourselves from the fifth or Lineage domain. This will happen to each of us as we awaken spiritually and begin to dream a world of light into being. Shamans must develop allies in each of these five realms, although as medicine people we are protected in each domain. Our mesa stones help us in the Stone domain; plants we are drawn to become our allies in the Plant domain; power animals and archetypes help us in the Animal domain. If an individual is not a shaman, then only people who have died can travel to the Upper World levels.

*My first experience journeying to the Upper World was vivid and intense. I entered the **Stone Domain** and saw big boulders and mountains interacting with each other. Then I saw canyons with huge overhangs that created amazing designs. As I looked beyond I saw someone I knew. She saw me as well and tried to reach me, but I was not allowed to engage. This was a reconnaissance journey. Then I went up to the **Plant Domain** and saw extensive land with gigantic forests, colossal trees reaching up to the skies, and beautiful flowers. One of my spirit guides appeared and told me I was now ready for her to teach me. She was a plant medicine wise one and made me aware that Eucalyptus and Sage were part of my plant medicine. Then I entered the **Animal Domain** and saw my power animals were waiting for me. There was a lush forest with animals everywhere: boas ... tigers ... lions ... insects ... birds.*

*I went up one more level into the **Human Domain**, and saw lots of people and spirits. One of my ancestors came forth. It was my paternal grandfather Don Beto. He just looked at me with deep love and said, "It's about time you came to visit." Then I saw the dolphins and the gray and blue whales. The Orcas also came and told me to 'trust.' That once I tracked my destiny I would need to surrender and have the conviction that it would all develop to reach that destiny ... as different as it may seem to my current life! At this point I went much deeper in my journey receiving profound information from them.*

*Lastly I entered the **Lineage Domain** and saw groups of Inka and Maya priests gathered, holding the lower four domains and many other levels above them. Then I saw domes of light formed by students who were vibrating at the same level and making the light glow brighter. As soon as class disassembled the dome disappeared, magically. It was as though the gathering of light beings created 'temporary' buildings of light! I also saw trees tossing sparks of light everywhere, sharing their luminescence. Amazing to realize that this is the domain that we will begin to source our lives from!*

During our journey we were guided to engage in dialogue with the Orcas and request a message. The information I received from them was unbelievable:

Our world needs to be re-imagined so that we can emerge as luminous beings.

Right now you are training to be one of those agents of re-imagination.

Can you hear your ancestors calling you to action ... are you really listening?

Are you ready to trust and surrender, to envision your destiny and let it morph your life without interfering?

I wrote this right after returning from my first Upper World journey and to this day I cannot believe their message. Each time I read it I get chills for it is exactly what happened in my life **several** years later!

Soul Retrieval

Soul loss is one of the main causes of illness according to shamans around the world. Psychology calls it 'dissociation.' It happens when part of our soul essence is lost due to trauma or an impacting situation. In shamanism we can bring the soul piece back to the person and this is called soul retrieval. It is one of the most beautiful healing practices I have ever encountered, both for the client and for the shaman. A client needs to seek an experienced shaman to have a soul retrieval done. *Only trained shamans can do soul retrievals on themselves, and that is not always the best course of action. As with many situations in life we must be humble enough as a shaman to recognize when we need help.*

In old civilizations returning a soul piece was done within three days of the incident. It was considered critical for a person to get their life force back, in order to help them heal and rebuild their lives with greater strength. In today's world many people from Western societies walk around with significantly less life force than what they need to be creative, unable to take advantage of the amazing opportunities they encounter.

How do you know to seek soul retrieval? There are many signs but the most common are: a reduced life force, a disinterest in life, and a lack of creative force or passion. In order to recognize 'soul loss' however, we must identify patterns that force a person to return to a particular situation or to certain behaviors. If the part of our soul that is missing took with it the attributes that help us deal with a certain pattern it is very difficult to break it.

A soul part leaves in order to survive; it is a wonderful process that allows us to preserve our Divine spark. When bringing that soul piece back we must be willing to change many aspects of our lives in order for it to integrate. In a few cases the part that is recovered has been rejected rather than wounded. For example you can return a soul part to bring back 'expression,' such as the ability to draw or write.

There are three essential parts to soul retrieval. First the soul part we loose has been disowned and therefore has been exiled into the shadow. To find it we must go to unknown terrain, which is generally the Lower World. Second the soul part retrieved is going to force us to get our life in order. Soul loss is always around the core Self and is usually much bigger than the issue we bring forth. A significant amount of energy is lost at the time of trauma and it usually comes back with the soul part. The third part of soul retrieval involves 'mapping' a healing strategy, which means designing a mythic map so that the soul part can be integrated. This usually involves dialoguing with the soul part and as mentioned above, the person receiving it will more than likely have to change behaviors for the soul part to feel comfortable.

The Soul is the vital part of the Self. Regardless of what happens during a soul retrieval journey the soul part is more important than the information received. In fact the information is useless without the soul part. But apart from the procedure of bringing the soul part back, integrating it into our lives is the most significant aspect of soul retrieval. So the 'mapping strategy' is critical for us to be able to integrate the returning soul part. If not the soul part may leave again and be less willing to return afterwards.

Creating a Framework for Soul Retrieval

Soul parts are usually found in the Lower World and when journeying we must engage more than our five senses to find them. If a soul part happens to be in the Upper World it has not been embodied yet … it has not incarnated and we have not become that. In the mechanics of soul retrieval we first ask the keeper of the Lower World for permission to go in. Remember we have allies in all journeys and places of non-ordinary reality. This is one of the most beautiful aspects of shamanism. Once the keeper greets us it is very important to state our intent: 'I have come to get that which will make my client whole.' Sometimes we may be denied entry, if for example we have an affinity to the person we are doing the soul retrieval for and therefore cannot be impeccable.

Each shaman has different ways of journeying to retrieve soul pieces and again, different shamanic groups have their own mythology. On many occasions while studying with some of the best shamanic teachers I journeyed to chambers or 'lands' that were intimidating or just plain scary. As I mentioned earlier in the book, when journeying to the Upper World we can decide how we engage with non-ordinary reality. I choose to be as creative as possible, selecting a shamanic mythology that has friendly terrains, void of fear. We also have our spirit allies, be that our power animals or spirit guides, and they accompany and assist us in our non-ordinary endeavors. For soul retrieval I generally work with four chambers of the soul. This is a framework one of my favorite teachers shared with me while I underwent a Medicine Wheel:

- The first chamber is the *Chamber of Wounding,* where one goes to discover the original wound that caused the soul loss. Often the wound happens early in childhood when the world was no longer a 'safe place.' It could have also happened before the client was born. A story begins to develop here and it is mostly a metaphorical one. During the journey the shaman is usually able to experience the way the wound lives within the client.

- Next is the *Chamber of Agreements,* where you find out what your client's sacred contract is. This refers to the promises or agreements that the soul part made as a result of the wound. We will more than likely destroy or renegotiate those contracts on behalf of our client. They have been poorly written, for they were made at the time of wounding or fear. These are energetic contracts, but will manifest in our ordinary physical life and sometimes force us to repeat behaviors that may be harmful to us. In rare occasions the wound stems from a previous life.

- The third one is the *Chamber of Enchantment,* where we discover the client's passion or life force that has been missing because of soul loss. This passion must be witnessed and acknowledged because if it weren't for the wound it would still be here. It is an area where we observe what the soul longs for, watching how the client may have behaved if there had not been soul loss.

• The last one is the ***Chamber of Gifts,*** where we discover the client's deeply hidden treasures. These are usually the biggest assets we have: gifts, possibilities, capabilities. In this chamber we retrieve a gift that is symbolic of those treasures. We may find: a stone, a disc, a feather, a power animal … or we may retrieve the 'artist,' or the 'expression,' or the 'poet.' This gift is key in the integration of the soul part.

After we have journeyed through the four chambers and done our work we ask the keeper of the Lower World to take us back to the entrance. Our power animals also help us return to ordinary reality. Generally we bring back three pieces: the soul part (provided it wants to come back), a power animal (which is symbolic of the instinctual aspect of that soul part), and a gift or treasure that serves as a bridge for the soul part's integration. If the soul part doesn't want to come back we must still bring back the power animal and the treasure to our client. The soul part may ask that the client change aspects of their lives before returning, and bringing back these two pieces may create enough sense of urgency for that to happen. Once we return to ordinary reality we hold the soul part tightly to our heart chakra, and then proceed to blow it into the chakra of the client that we have been instructed to engage.

The next step is to develop a mythic map that will help the client redo an existing map that no longer works. We map at the mythic level for this is the level of the soul. The map is not practical unless the client can relate to it. You may have to use a metaphor they understand in order to make it relevant to them. Gifts or treasures brought back also help with the integration as they create a bridge between the 'old map' and the 'new mythic map.' This is extremely important or the client returns to the 'old maps,' the old behaviors. Then it's time to share with the client that part of the journey that is important for their healing.

We must be careful not to bring back a 'story' that will shock the client or that can bring forth another trauma. For example I once had a student that had just completed soul retrieval for a client. It is not uncommon for the shaman to see several soul parts of that client when journeying, but only one or two need to be returned at the time. After the soul retrieval and when she was sharing the healing journey with her client, she mentioned another part that was missing because of sexual abuse. The client did not remember and the 'story' relayed to her was so shocking that she was unable to integrate the soul part that had been brought back.

Another way to integrate the returned soul part is to do what in psychology is called a 'sacred drama.' This is a reenactment of the drama at the time the soul part left, including the participants that were part of that situation. It can be done with other people or we can do it alone. If alone we may utilize mesa stones or symbolic elements to enact the different chambers or characters, therefore assisting the soul part in dialoguing with the adult it is integrating with. It is best to limit the sacred drama objects/stones to two or three. If a soul part is left behind in the Lower World because it doesn't want or isn't ready to come back, we want to leave a sense of curiosity with the person but not so much that it becomes an obsession for them and then they don't do their other integration work. We must keep in mind, however, that when a soul part is lost we are affecting our future parts.

Soul contracts are usually found close to the corresponding soul part. All soul contracts have some benefit for the lost soul part as they are enacted in order to protect it. A soul contract is an agreement we make with our soul at the time of trauma in the hope of receiving something that we usually don't receive.

Many times we do soul contracts for a sense of validation or protection from someone, and this is usually related to why the soul part left. For example a person that lived with an alcoholic parent that had violent reactions when drinking may loose a soul part. If that parent was the father the soul contract developed may be along the lines of 'never trusting men.' This is not a healthy contract for that soul and if activated can create havoc in all relationships that person has with men.

Keep in mind that a soul part may be found in any of the four chambers. There may be *no energy* in a particular chamber so don't keep looking for it there. The soul part may be in the Chamber of Gifts rather than in the Chamber of Wounding; or the client may need to have one of their passions for life returned so we may find the part in the Chamber of Enchantment.

After the soul retrieval is completed we may provide additional tools for that person to use during the integration phase. I always insist my clients set time aside to engage with the returned soul part, asking a series of important questions. It is critical to find a quiet space in order to listen to the soul part's answers. Some of the questions are:

1. Why did you leave?
2. What are your gifts to me ... what are you *teaching* me?
3. Bring the soul part up to date on the positive aspects of your life, from the moment the soul part left to the present.
4. What do I need to *stop* doing for you to feel comfortable with me?
5. What do I need to *start* doing for you to feel comfortable with me?

Once this dialogue is carried out for several weeks integration begins to take place. Receiving a lost soul part is like having a baby and it must be nurtured, welcomed, spoken to, acknowledged, and loved. When the work is done diligently the rewards are enormous and amazing.

As part of my shamanic training I had to do both 'solo' soul retrieval journeys as well as work with colleagues that were also engaged in the Medicine Wheel. Below is a soul retrieval I had done during a Medicine Wheel that was profound and very healing. The issue I was trying to heal was the 'caretaker' pattern that I have lived with for so long, many times sacrificing myself in the process. It was a pattern developed before being born and which has carried on into all type of relationships. The caretaker is a basic role for females all over the world and especially in the Latin American culture I grew up in.

*My shaman in this exercise was Ariel, a colleague I've grown to respect tremendously. In the **Chamber of Wounding** she found a six year-old girl in a pink dress. She was in a corner, protected by a 'gardener-like man.' He was certainly not a nurturing man. As Ariel went on to the **Chamber of Agreements** she found that the little girl compromised and 'adopted the powerless image of femininity' that her culture expected, and which was directly in conflict with the independent expression included in her original contract. She renegotiated the contract, returning it to the girl's Original Contract: 'to live the full power of the Universal feminine ... nurturing, loving and tremendously creative.' In the **Chamber of Enchantment** the little girl was climbing a tree and the higher she climbed the more the tree grew. The theme was one of adventure with a tinge of adrenaline, which the little girl loved but wasn't a part of her culture's image of femininity. On she went to the **Chamber of Gifts,** where Ariel brought back a 'magic wand.' This was to help me change perceptual states and shift perspectives when needed, and to always have the MAGIC around and within me. A Cheetah came as a new **power animal.** It was able to climb to the very top of trees and run the fastest. At the top it could watch everything and make sure all was safe for me; it would also help me to run faster than anyone to either reach a place or escape fast.*

171

Solo soul retrieval journeys also helped me tremendously. Not only did they assist me in mapping the Lower World landscape for future endeavors, they also allowed me to be aware of traumas where I had lost a portion of my life force. We may choose to just observe the parts we find or we may decide to retrieve them. I must mention that in my experience across the years however, it is always best for another shaman to help us with soul retrieval. This is because our own journey may be filtered by how we perceive our lives.

As I went down to the Lower World I found a soul piece I had lost in one of my most intense love relationships. I was in my late 30s and had given my heart and soul to this love partner. This relationship had been the deepest I had had so far, but also the most heart wrenching. The piece I brought back had my innocence and passion for authentic love, and had left because it felt betrayed by my soul companion's absence. The greatest lesson from the soul piece that came back was: 'I must shed the fear of being hurt and betrayed in relationships so that I can be whole again and thus be ready to love unconditionally.' During the period of integration I realized there had been many more blissful lessons and learnings in this relationship, and for that I am now grateful.

It is important that shaman or energy healing practitioners place great emphasis on healing themselves before engaging with clients. Although offering healing gifts to help others is of paramount importance, if we don't heal ourselves first we may influence the healing with our own filters and unhealed wounds. Ego may also affect the healing session if the practitioner hasn't traveled the road of self-healing. To this day I continue to have soul retrievals done as I encounter situations in my life that need healing. In fact before resolving any issues that arise I usually begin with healing myself. Taking responsibility for having participated in creating situations in order to heal them is very important. It keeps us humble and open to integrating with a wiser part of us. Once the life force returns and the healing is in process we are stronger to face and resolve any given situation from a higher perspective.

Removing Energy Wrapped Around a Person's Soul

Some people have energy so entwined around their soul that it just doesn't flow. In other words the energy is entangled in 'who' they are and the person usually feels stuck in a particular situation, issue, or pattern. The shaman must go into the Lower World with the intention of 'looking for that which is wrapped around the client's soul.' As with soul retrieval one must journey to the four chambers of the soul and track the energy that is enveloping the person's soul while at the same time rattling to call forth the Spirit or Essence of the person. The shaman has a crystal in hand and when prompted must be ready to extract the restrictive energy by winding it counterclockwise. This energy may be found in one specific chamber, in between chambers, or moving around them. It may also be necessary to do soul retrieval after the extraction is completed.

When is this type of extraction done? There are many possibilities. If a client has trouble breathing (may be hyperventilating) yet they do not have a crystallized energy. Also when one cannot find anything else on a client, but they have clear symptoms of being paralyzed in some way. It is also appropriate when we have done different types of healings and the situation hasn't improved. In addition if we cannot 'see' anything as we journey—just blackness or blurriness, that's a clear signal that an extraction in the Lower World is needed. It is also done if we hit a wall when trying to heal and remove imprints. And finally it should also be done if the person is not conscious of what is holding them back or what could be the cause of a pattern.

Being raised as a 'caretaker' meant that others expected I rise to the occasion when necessary regardless of what was going on in my life. There was a silent understanding that I could take care of myself. This did help me become resilient and driven, yet all caretakers hope someone will help them as they helped others. As I moved through my own healing journey I noticed that the 'caretaker' pattern was continually being addressed. It would still raise its little head in some situations and with some people, but each time to a lesser degree. Nevertheless it kept appearing when I least expected it. I always felt this pattern had emerged in my early years. Little did I know it was an energy I had carried since before birth!

My experience with the removal of an energy wrapped around my soul was intense plus it created a shock to my energetic system. Lara was my shaman in this healing. She set her intention, opened my solar plexus chakra and then began her journey to the Lower World. As soon as she descended she found a slimy, green energy that was stuck all around my body. Getting her crystal out she started winding, working it until it was all gone. Then the soul agreement I had made emerged and it dealt with my loved ones. It had to do with them 'giving me everything and anything I needed to survive and to thrive in this lifetime **except being present when I needed help!'**

From the beginning of this lifetime until now I would be expected to help when they needed it, yet they would disperse when I needed emotional help. That contract was made in the womb, before birth, and there were several major soul lessons that stemmed from it. One of the greatest lessons was to recognize that those who came forth when I asked for help of the heart were my 'soul family' ... an eternal family who loved and accepted me *unconditionally, no questions, no expectations and no judgments. From a very young age I learned that dogs were part of that 'soul family.' They would not disperse or abandon me when I needed help plus they allowed me to express myself fully. Another of the soul lessons was to learn to fully love and accept my 'loved ones' for who they were. They were playing the perfect roles for my learning and with my soul's blessing. Lara proceeded to replace the old contract with a new one, which read: **I have a soul family that hears my voice ... I can talk to them and to myself about anything. I must learn to TRUST my soul family and myself. Only then would I learn to trust humans.***

A huge third soul lesson related to my loved ones surfaced: I was to learn to 'watch their dramas at the edge of the river ... just observing, without judgment.' In other words observe the drama without getting involved. They had a right to learn their own soul lessons. The implication was that I also had to learn to shed any concerns of being alienated or judged by my loved ones for not stepping into the river. So Lara blew the new contract into my third chakra and then blew Eagle as a power animal; Eagle would help me observe and listen keenly without flying into the drama. In addition my throat chakra was given a voice so that it could express itself ... to my loved ones, to my soul family and to myself.

The healing was done in the morning. An hour or so after it was completed I began to feel strange inside. At lunch I had started to withdraw from ordinary reality, hearing people's conversations from very far away. By the afternoon, as we were doing 'Destiny retrieval' exercises, I felt very off. I asked my healing partner Sophie to test my chakras AND THEY WERE ALL GOING BACKWARDS! My energy body was shutting down due to the severity of the new contract that was blown into me during the previous healing. She did a mini healing to realign my chakras and try to temporarily jump-start my energy body.

I went back to class and approached my teacher. Just moments before, during break, he had come by to chat and ask about my childhood. I thought that was very strange. When I approached he told me that he had been tracking me and that my energy body was coagulating (crystallizing). He said I needed shock therapy NOW! Shock therapy meant I would have to alternate between very hot and very cold showers for about twenty minutes. This would jump start my energy body and I would slowly begin to stabilize. If I did not do it immediately my energy body would crystallize and eventually my physical body would collapse. So I asked Sophie to drive me back to the hotel where I was staying. Shock therapy began and I woke up right away. Then Sophie did a healing to balance my chakras and this brought me back to life.

At the fire ceremony that evening I thanked my teacher. He smiled and began rattling all around me, tracking me once again; after a few minutes he said, "You are flying now, Beatriz. Has entrado en tu nuevo contrato de lleno y veo gente que quiere seguirte pero no puede ... estas ya muy lejos." (You have entered into your new contract fully and I see people that want to follow you but can't ... you're already too far away.) I hugged him, thanking him profusely; I felt euphoric! There was a sense of timelessness and infinity. As I sat by the fire I could feel the lineage of elders next to me, welcoming me to take the place they had been holding, feeling honored to become one of them.

The lessons we came to learn open pathways to our soul and to our Divinity once we heal them. ***There is nobody to blame or hold responsible for the patterns and issues that surface in our lives.*** Once we identify them it is our task to heal them, then move on. Just our intention to heal them provokes the Universe to conspire on our behalf, bringing forth an army of light beings to assist us. The people that have helped me have been placed in my path the moment I send out that intention. I am grateful to have learned these lessons in a loving environment and to have had the freedom to search for what resonated with me.

Destiny Retrieval

On the last day we journeyed on our own to the Upper World in order to track our Destiny. The drums began and I went to the cave to be energetically dismembered. I set my intention to track my becoming and then followed the cord above my crown to each domain. I did not enter any of the four lower levels. When I got to the Lineage Domain I crossed the threshold and sat patiently, witnessing the World Becoming. Then images began to appear.

First I saw a dome of light that expanded and pulsated, encompassing people and opening them to unlimited possibilities. Each person that came through the dome created their own dome and as more people joined the greater dome kept expanding. A colony of interdependent yet independent domes formed. **Lecturing, teaching, nurturing, being a beacon of love and light, protecting Mother Earth ... this was 'my becoming!'** *No rescuer or caretaker in sight. "Wait for the message and request help before moving," I heard them say to me. "Don't offer to solve 'their' world or heal them, but rather wait for Spirit's message ... just listen!" Spirit's message was clear:* **wait, listen and love ... don't rescue ... wait for Spirit!**

Then we worked with a partner and the intention was 'to see the contract of our true essence.' My partner was incredibly clairvoyant. We began by tracking left eye to left eye until the person's face disappeared and she began to see my destiny unfold.

My partner asked me to pick a stone from her mesa and blow my intent of 'seeing my destiny' into it. Then she began to see and said, "You will be redefining spiritual teachings and taking them across the American continent including Latin America." She turned to me and added, "It's big, Bea, real big ... and it is about to begin in less than one year." It actually began eleven months later ....

The Work of the North had been magnificent, a strange ethereal quality to it. As we stepped beyond time to reach 'infinity' we were no longer stalked by death or fear ... we had shed our story. We now had the tools to speak and negotiate directly with God, to talk to and merge with the rivers, the mountains, nature ... all of our relations, and to participate in the creation of the World Becoming. Taking my seat next to the council of Wise Elders I felt solace and deep peace.

One month later my Medicine Wheel teacher asked me to participate with him in a TV interview for a program called 'Primer Impacto.' This is an entertainment/news program of the Spanish channel Univision and the segment would be aired throughout Latin America and the United States. The interviewer was one of the main spokeswomen for that program. My teacher explained that we would collaborate on doing a healing for a person during the interview.

My teacher and I got ready for the healing, each on either side of a mat. The lady we were to work on came towards him and although I could not hear what was being said I watched her leave the room. I did not understand what was happening. He then turned to me and impromptu said, "I will be doing a healing on you Beatriz. We will be filming it live." I was stunned, but the program was starting and I had no choice but to acquiesce. I had sensed him tracking me from the moment I arrived and did not know why. I proceeded to lie down. He used his feather to cleanse all around my energy body, especially in the region of my head and heart. "Your heart is springing open to take you to new levels of absolute unconditional love," he said. "You have been carrying a lot of pain for your father. His visit is an opportunity for you to do healing work on him, which in turn will be greatly healing to you. It will explode your heart open."

Interestingly enough my father was arriving the next day from Guatemala. He had called a month before asking if I would help him work on his fears! However, I had not told my teacher that my father was coming.

Entering
Stillness

Practicing Energy
Medicine

"Life is not measured by the number of breaths we take,
but by the moments that take our breath away."
—Vicki Corona

SO WHEN DID THIS ALL BEGIN … THIS DEEP CALLING TO
become an 'energy medicine practitioner,' a 'healer?' Did I even
have a 'deep calling?' As a soul I would say it was many lifetimes
ago, for I spontaneously began to remember healing practices and
techniques that I had not learned in this lifetime. The spontaneous memory began when I decided to focus on Shamanism and
Energy Medicine in the mid-1990s. With time I have understood
that it is an innate ability we all possess, for each one of us is the
'expert' in healing ourselves.

Our cultural beliefs, however, have educated us in a different
manner. We wait for a dis-ease to manifest before we pay attention
to our wellbeing. For most of us this means turning the responsibility to 'cure' us over to a Traditional Medicine Doctor who has been
taught that people fit into categories of existing illnesses; in other
words, we will be diagnosed based on symptoms that are compared
to previous cases and then prescribed medication accordingly. This
is a noble attempt at helping someone yet it is reactive; people

aren't educated on how to prevent diseases altogether or on how to jumpstart their own healing by commanding their cellular structure. We have been taught to handover our health to someone else instead of taking responsibility for our own healing and wellbeing!

The desire to see people feel better has been with me from the moment I was born, especially those I love. My mother battled serious illnesses and health conditions from the time I was barely one year old. She withstood tremendous pain and discomfort with courage and patience, yet had become more and more limited in her ability to live her life fully. Being one of the closest souls to me in this lifetime it pained me to see her suffer. I had been by her side in most of her serious situations and as I mentioned before, attempting to be the best 'Florence Nightingale' I could be.

However, all I could do before embarking on my spiritual path was offer words of comfort, loving massages, taking care of doctors/nurses/specialists on her behalf, researching alternative scenarios, and above all, unconditionally loving and supporting her. Even so I noticed that each experience seemed to take a piece of her essence away, and with time she looked more tired and resigned. Although she would deal with whatever would come her way, I cannot say Western medicine helped her feel much better nor did it give her the ability to confront life with all her might. Eventually depression set in, and rather than taking responsibility for healing herself, she was disappointed that doctors couldn't do more to help her.

Yet, as I moved into Energy Medicine she was a willing participant. And although I noticed she had the courage to try new and sometimes out of the ordinary practices, the mindset that someone else had to heal her remained. To this day I wonder if it was just a product of her upbringing or if she didn't have enough energy to invest in her own healing.

My father also had serious health situations that developed later in his life and felt as though he dealt with one illness only to be confronted by another one. The leukemia came out of nowhere and caught him completely by surprise. In fact it caught all of us by surprise. He had always been extremely healthy, barely ever having a cold. And even after he managed to go into remission from his leukemia through alternative medicine, continuous complications in the heart area were never ending (pleurisy, water and blood in the lungs, blocked arteries in the heart).

Both my parents were prescribed numerous medications to address a given situation, which in turn caused 'side effects' that later created something else. This was a never-ending vicious cycle that went on for many decades. When confronted doctors would just raise their hands and say, "We tried to address the imminent problem, but there are always possible complications." 'It shouldn't be that way,' I thought. Needless to say my experience with Western medicine left me so frustrated that I embarked on a quest to find something 'different' to help my loved ones. This was the beginning of Energy Medicine for me.

All of us have had questions such as:

• Where did this illness come from?

• What is the source of this disease?

• Are there emotions or attitudes associated with it?

• Can these be addressed **before** an illness manifests physically?

• What do you mean, "It can come back?"

• How does each person heal?

• How can I help someone I love feel better?

There are many variations of these questions that we may pose to ourselves when confronted with any of these situations. However, we are not as powerless as we have been led to believe. In fact, we already have within us most of the ingredients to help ourselves as well as others.

A healer is someone who comes from a place of deep love and compassion, and attempts to 'jump start' an individual in order for them to want to reach a healing state. When most people ask me about healing I reply, "The healer might do 10% of the work but the other 90% is up to the patient."

It is not the healer who does the healing, but rather someone who agrees to be a vehicle for healing energy to move through them and into those who need it. It is as though the healer becomes the observer of an amazing process unveiled right before their eyes. From my experience the main ingredients of a healing practitioner are: impeccability, purity of intent, humility and unconditional love. We all have this! As one of my teachers said, **'healing'** is unplugging our energy from certain places, people or events in order to make it available to invest in something creative today; **'curing'** on the other hand, is returning someone to the place they were at before the onset of the illness.

In my path as a healer I have always wondered why some people heal while others don't. Two patients may have similar situations and undergo comparable healings, yet one heals while the other one doesn't. Although there usually aren't general answers that address each situation I have come to understand that those who heal have taken responsibility for their own wellbeing, and generally have an internal drive to feel better, to change behaviors, and a determination to return their four bodies (mental, physical, emotional and spiritual) to health. So the responsibility for healing comes back to each one of us. We have the power!

I also noticed that when I was going through a rough period in my life there was an increase in patients that wanted healing. Each healing seemed to not only reveal an issue that I as the healer needed to address in myself, it also brought me to a state of wholeness where I could do deeper healing work. The specific situations being addressed didn't necessarily mirror mine; yet engaging in the issues of healing others sometimes took me to a place that facilitated the 'Aha' moments for me.

One of my favorite teachers always said, "We engage in healing others not necessarily because we want to, but because we can."

After a couple of decades of being involved in Energy Medicine I came to see the truth of this statement. The journey has been amazing, and with each instance, my wonder and reverence for the Divine has increased. We truly do live in an extraordinary Universe!

Following are a few patient studies that greatly impacted my view of life and the power we have as souls in this human experience. The fragility of it all and the miraculous resolve of many have been deeply humbling. I have felt like a 'special witness' who has been allowed to peek at these life changing experiences. The following ten studies I share with you crossed my path in the first few years as an Energy Medicine practitioner and significantly altered me in amazing ways. It has been a magical experience! (As is the case in this book, names and locations have been changed in order to protect the privacy of those that have allowed me to be their witness.)

Make Room for the New

Several years ago I met a wonderful woman from Latin America. Ana was married, early forties, and a kindness in her eyes that emanated from deep within her soul. I met her through her mother, who I had recently done a healing on as she traveled through Miami. At the time of her first phone call Ana shared her deep desire to have children. She and her husband had tried for more than seven years. They had had all the relevant tests done yet there didn't seem to be a physical reason for her not to conceive. She wanted to know if I could help her with this issue to which I replied, "I cannot help you to conceive for that is a decision between you and the Creator. However, I can try to help you move past the persistent desire so that you can carry on with your life." There was silence on the phone.

I had already learned that you couldn't offer certainty nor predict what would happen; whatever was to be would unfold in the moment of healing and in the days after. Although as a shamanic practitioner we are taught to engage in direct negotiations with Great Spirit (God) we cannot offer the client any certainty about the outcome. What is meant to happen will, and both the healer and the patient must learn to surrender. Everything is in Divine and Perfect Order!

Once Ana got her breath back she was able to ask what I suggest she do to prepare for her healing. I offered to send her guided meditations that would help calm her mind and told her to call me when she felt ready. (Healing occurs when the client is ready not when the healer is. This is one of the hardest parts of being a healer, for even if you sense that people are in pain or discomfort you cannot interfere until they ask and are ready to put their own energy into healing themselves.)

Three months later I received a phone call from Ana saying, "I am ready to come see you. Can I come at the beginning of July?" I looked at my calendar and noticed I would be in a shamanic pilgrimage to the highlands of Peru for the second half of the month of June. Those intense spiritual pilgrimages brought about deep energetic changes that usually took me several weeks to process. However, something inside told me to agree so I did. Many times, when the client comes from abroad, I agree to see them for several days in a row. Ideally your client needs to process each healing for several weeks before moving on to the next phase. However, this is not possible with international patients that want me to be physically present; they cannot remain in the United States for several weeks, maybe even months. I knew the work with Ana would be intense and very deep.

She arrived at my healing office on July 1st. The apprehension in her was palpable yet there was also a quiet resolve. I was still trying to 'land' from my magnificent trip to Peru; it had only been one day since I had returned. Being in a natural semi-altered state would prove to be extremely helpful in this case. At the same time a traumatic situation had emerged in my life immediately upon my return; my precious puppies and home had been seriously violated by someone I trusted to take care of them. Ana's healings would prove to be very timely for my own healing as well.

She began to relay most of the major events in her life with intensity and emotion, both triumphs and traumas. Usually I do not encourage someone to go into detailed incidents of their life, for reliving trauma can reinforce it in their energy body even more. However, I sensed she was still trying to feel comfortable with her healing practitioner, so I allowed her to continue for a few minutes. While she was relating the story of her life I began to 'see' a little girl about six years old standing next to her. I decided to only observe, for it was my first time with Ana. In addition my spirit guides were insisting that today was a day to work on balancing her energy body and getting her to a relaxing place ... that was all. So as I concentrated on her chakras and saw them start to light up I knew it was my cue to start. The first session consisted of releasing the frustration and anxiety she had accumulated from not being able to get pregnant. There were deep emotional and cultural issues at play. It was a day to begin detangling the web!

On the second day Ana was calmer and the speed at which she was relating her stories had greatly decelerated. After a few minutes I stopped her and asked, "What happened to you at six years of age?"

"I had a traumatic incident," she responded. "Why are you asking?" I told her that a six year-old girl was standing next to her since yesterday, and my sense was that it was a part of her soul that she had lost earlier in life and was ready to return. She was pensive for a moment and then said, "Is this why in the guided meditations you sent to me, when I tried to visualize creating abundance by having a baby, all I saw was a girl about five or six years old?"

"Could be," I said. In psychology this is called 'dissociation' and it happens when we experience trauma in our lives. Many times hypnosis is used to try to recall the memories associated with the incident, yet these may be unavailable. As I mentioned before 'soul loss' is one of the main causes of disease and discomfort according to shamanism. Once soul retrieval is done to return the lost piece to the client, the memory of the event returns as does the energy associated with that soul piece. Soul retrievals are one of the most amazing healing events for the client, and an extremely powerful one for the healer.

Before bringing back the soul piece, however, we had to make sure her energy body was completely clean and ready to nurture it. So we proceeded to do energetic tracking and then removing any interferences found. She needed several fluid energy extractions. Ana was very cooperative and fully engaged in the process, trusting it was all for her highest good. I could feel many light beings accompanying us, ready to assist and give her the necessary strength. For a couple of days we continued with energetic balancing and clearing. Ana said she felt calmer, lighter and more peaceful. She smiled as she said this and added that it had been a while since she had felt so well.

On the fourth visit the six year-old girl was more than ready to return to Ana and she was ready to have her back. There was excitement and anticipation in both of them. I put on shamanic drumming music and set the clear intent of 'bringing back that which would make Ana whole.'

Off to the Lower World I went in search of the child. Once in the Lower World I spotted a cave. I went towards it and noticed a huge, furry man at its entrance. I asked for little Ana and he said, "I don't know them by name, but you can look inside and see if you find her." There were many other children in this cave, no doubt soul pieces many of us have lost in the course of our lives. I saw a small child in the corner of the cave and what gave her away was a ring she was wearing. I have noticed that many times the soul pieces are wearing something that the adult wears today, making them readily identifiable. I headed towards her and asked if she was Ana, to which she nodded. I asked her if she would come back with me … that her adult was ready to receive and protect her.

She responded, "My adult needs to learn to play more and be less serious for me to return." I assured her adult Ana was ready to accommodate her and play. Then she surprised me by saying, "I will come, but there is another part of Ana that you must also get." I asked her if she could take me there and she agreed, telling me, "We will have to go to the Middle World, for she is still there." I held little Ana close to my heart and we exited the cave.

She seemed relieved to be out of that dark place, smiling timidly. Then she held my hand and began to run. We left the Lower World and entered the Middle World, which is the one we live in day to day. She took me to a large house with a long veranda encircling it, the ocean in sight through one of the sides. Little Ana began to look around and after a little while said to me, "There she is. Let's go talk to her."

We headed towards the corner of a large living room, where I found another girl. This one was around eleven years old and had left because she had just entered puberty and was afraid to 'become a woman.' "Why were you so afraid?" I asked her.

She responded, "Because since I was hurt as a child I don't even want to imagine what will happen to me when I become a woman." I explained that adult Ana had faired out well and was a happy person, and that she would take care of her and make her feel protected. The eleven year-old girl was not convinced. I had my 'leopard' power animal with me in the journey and asked it to talk to her. It worked wonders and eleven year-old Ana was ready to return as well. I held both of them tightly to my heart and returned to ordinary reality, where adult Ana was waiting. I blew both soul pieces into her, one into her fourth chakra and the other one into her seventh chakra. When Ana opened her eyes there was a new glow. She smiled widely for the first time since I met her! I related the stories from both soul parts and she confirmed them. Ana was now ready to return home with a new resolve and with lots of homework.

Even though I was still in altered states, a consulting project in Mexico demanded I get ready to depart within a couple of days. I was there for a week of intense strategy work. Upon returning from Mexico a long e-mail from Ana awaited me. She reported continuing with the feeling of tranquility and peace in her life, in spite of the many things happening all around her. The 'girls' (six and eleven year olds) were happy and integrating well. Her and her husband continued their dream of becoming parents, yet their demeanor was more relaxed and she was more open to receive any news from the doctor—positive or not.

About one year later I saw Ana again. She had been diligently working on herself and looked great. This time she shared that she had noticed a specific area in her life where patterns kept emerging and she was unable to stop them. Although she had identified them and attempted to change her behavior and attitude, they continued to surprise her 'out of nowhere.' I sensed something was preventing her soul's contract from unfolding, so I decided to journey and see if this was the case. Ana had said that if I did find a soul contract that was preventing her from moving forward, I had her permission to either alter it or destroy it. I embarked on the journey and promptly found an energy wrapped around her soul. After extracting the energy and destroying the old contract, I wrote a new one that would help her strengthen in her life. She immediately felt lighter. About one month later she reported that the pattern had re-emerged, yet this time she was able to deal with it swiftly and for good.

A few months later she became one of my students when I launched **Awakening the Soul**, a mystery school you will learn more about later. The class had started with discussions about managing energies, followed by a few guided meditations. She then learned to work with the mandala, a mythical instrument of healing and understanding used widely by shamans around the world. In her first exercise she had completely filled the sand painting with nature elements. There was barely a space left in it, which was symbolic of her life.

She sat in front of her mandala and observed it carefully, soon her patience paid off. The sand painting began to 'speak' to her, revealing how much stuff she was carrying that wasn't her own and that was weighing her down. She removed most of it and later offered it to the fire during that evening's ceremony. Her intent: getting rid of that which no longer served her in her life. The wheels of change had been set in motion!

A couple of months later she spoke about how several situations that disappeared in her life mirrored what she had removed from the mandala; as more months passed she felt lighter and freer. After six months she underwent the third of five modules which dealt with 'shedding the past.' Throughout the previous modules and the time in between she had been arduously working on changing behaviors, attitudes, and thoughts; she was also engaging in a daily meditation practice. Ana was anxious to integrate further with her Higher Self!

One month after the third module Ana called and could barely contain her enthusiasm. She and her husband had decided to try once more to become parents, and she was pregnant! I was just as elated and at the same time amazed. This was one of the most beautiful cases I had been privileged to witness. Eight months later I arrived in her country to teach. Her baby boy had been born; he was one of the most beautiful souls I have ever seen!

A Pain in the Back

Celia was a single woman, late forties, who I had known as a friend for eight years. She worked as an artist in South Florida and was raising two children on her own. Celia approached me a couple of weeks after I returned from learning how to release imprints, telling me that she didn't know what to do about a chronic lower back pain she had had for over ten years.

We made an appointment to address her physical pain for the following week. Before coming I asked her to ponder what were the gifts she was getting from this lower back pain, as well as notice when it got worse. When she arrived I explained energy medicine and the chakras, and then how this process worked. Since she had been involved with yoga, acupuncture, and also did psychic readings, she was very open to this energetic process. Her expectations of the process were for her physical pain to greatly diminish, as she was convinced that until she worked at the energetic level it would not heal. She was anxiously waiting for the session.

We began to talk about her lower back pain and about her current map, to try to probe into the root of the pain. She progressed to tell me about her inability to say "No," to friends, finding herself overwhelmed and heavy with responsibilities, plus people always coming over and leaving her little time to herself. This was when the physical pain got worse. I asked her to recall several of these experiences and connect to the feelings associated with each. Once people have decided to heal it is amazing how at the time of their healing they will tell you the root cause of their situation, most times unaware they are doing so. When I proceeded to test her energy body two of her chakras were severely affected.

We went into the process to identify and remove the imprint when her stomach started gargling. Dense gray energies began coming out of her navel chakra, then stacks of white that looked like cotton candy. The chakra was opening to the left of her body and as toxic energy released it slowly moved back to center. An energy dome was forming over the solar plexus chakra so I tapped it. Heat continued to come out of the navel chakra. Once the imprint was removed and the healing concluded Celia expressed deep relaxation; she said she felt much lighter and was fascinated with the overall process. She began to move about and said that the physical pain had subsided considerably. Celia told me she felt the imprint leaving her energy body and also felt when I smoothed her Energy Field at the end. She called me a couple of days later to say that her lower back pain was almost gone and that she felt much better.

The immediate outcome was outstanding for most of the time healing at the energetic level happens immediately, but its manifestation at the physical level is gradual. Celia felt physically lighter and emotionally calmer and more peaceful. One week later she claimed to be rid of ALL back pain and had more energy than ever before. This was the first time she was free of the pain in almost ten years! In addition she was aware of how to change her map so that it would not reoccur. She decided to do a sand painting to help effect her lifestyle change and express gratitude for her healing.

Talking to Heaven

After attending a business meeting one of my clients pulled me aside and asked if I could help her cousin Susie. She lived in the Midwest and had been a music composer and singer. Susie was close to her family and had just returned home after being away for almost seventeen years.

Susie had mental, emotional, and physical issues, all stemming from being stalked by a very scary man for four years. She had undergone extensive psychological therapy and the traumatic experiences she lived through were only now coming into conscious memory. Their impact had caused her soul to leave her body repeated times. She felt sad, afraid and alone. Her mental and physical states were extremely fragile.

When I first met her she wanted to know about my religious beliefs. Her main concern was whether I believed in God, Jesus Christ and the Virgin Mary. Even though I rarely expand upon my personal spiritual beliefs during a healing, I chose to give her my version. She seemed comfortable with it. Susie was a devout Catholic and wanted to make sure that the healing process would not conflict with her religious beliefs. She claimed that if it wasn't for God and her faith she would be dead now. She had an angel-like appearance and light. Although she had never heard of energy medicine before, her sister was a chiropractor and acupuncturist, so she gradually opened to it.

She wanted the stalking experiences to stop haunting her and she was also hoping that her creative musical gifts would reemerge. Susie expressed a desire to feel her soul return to her body, to be able to feel like a whole person again. I explained the process in great detail and said that the outcome was up to God. We began to talk and I asked her to recall the emotions she felt when she began remembering the incidents from the stalking situation. Since her thoughts were very scattered I guided her to three specific instances. Once she felt these I began testing her energy body and chakras.

In order to help her relax I had to hold deepening points in her occipitals for at least fifteen minutes. I also smoothed her Energy Field repeatedly. There was significant twitching in her hands, which denoted toxic energy release. This is pretty common when a major incident hasn't been released. There was lots of heat coming from the heart and third eye chakras. At one point I had to hold my fingers over her third eye to help her regain her balance.

Then the healing process took an unexpected turn. After holding the deepening points for over ten minutes she began to speak out loud to God, from deep within her soul. I heard my guides saying, "Step out of the process." I did not understand what they meant and didn't want to leave Susie halfway through the healing.

They repeated it and said, "Just intend to step out and let things unfold." I stepped aside emotionally and mentally. Then this soft voice began speaking beautiful words to her through me. It was as though God was speaking directly to her. The voice was coming out of my mouth yet it was a different voice than mine, the words were also different than ones I would use. Susie started crying, feeling a slight pain in her heart. I asked her to cross her arms over her heart to slow down the healing process. We resumed a couple of minutes later as she insisted she wanted to continue.

She relaxed to a certain degree during the process, but her anxiety to release the trauma didn't allow her to be fully at ease. After the healing was over she claimed to feel physically lighter and emotionally calmer. Two days later her mother called my business client to say that for the first time in many years she had noticed a significant improvement in her daughter. She proceeded to tell her that this was the first time since the incidents of stalking began that she was able to see a glimpse of who her daughter truly was. Several weeks later I talked to Susie and she seemed like a different person. Although there was still hesitancy in living fully and in feeling safe, she was able to do things she liked and which she had avoided in the past several years. She had also begun writing music again and was able to concentrate on her job for the first time in a long time.

Amazed at the results with her cousin my business client asked me to do a healing on her during my next visit to the Midwest. After I agreed she asked, "Was that your voice that responded to Susie when she was talking to God during the healing?" I replied, "No." She said, "I didn't think so."

I began to notice that spontaneous channeling would occur with some patients during their healing sessions, and most of the times I had no recollection of what was said. Some clients would call me later and ask, "What is it you told me during the healing?" or "Do you remember what you told me? It happened exactly as you said." I usually drew a blank, recognizing that wisdom was sent through me, but knowing it wasn't mine.

Finding the Divine Love Within

Tanya was a powerful businesswoman, owner of a very successful small business. She was married and in her mid-forties. At the time of the healing I had known her for almost 11 years. We were good friends and at times business associates.

Tanya had had lupus for 20 years, which hurt her joints and left her immune system and physical body very weak. I was due to arrive in her city for a massive project within a week. A couple of days before arriving she asked if I would do a healing on her regarding the lupus. I agreed and also asked her to think about the gifts of the lupus before our session. She understood shamanism and energy medicine somewhat due to our personal relationship. She was also aware of and open to alternative medicine. Her expectations of the process were to feel better physically, with more energy, and for her immune system to get a boost. She also hoped for greater understanding of the emotional issues linked to her lupus.

We began the session and she went back to instances where her lupus had started or was activated. A thread related to abandonment and betrayal issues began to emerge. These had started in her early childhood. She shared that when she was first diagnosed with lupus she was pursuing her graduate business degree at one of the top five universities. The diagnosis had forced her to quit school and take care of her health. Others did not understand her decision to leave graduate school; she felt betrayed and abandoned again, this time by her best friend. As we moved into the present she expressed fear that her husband or best friends may betray or abandon her, so she overcompensated and went beyond the call of duty to take care of them so that they wouldn't leave her.

We discussed her map and how to change it; she understood that if she learned not betray nor abandon herself she wouldn't need to fear others doing so. Her understanding of the lessons of betrayal and abandonment was incredible, and an unbelievable shift began to occur in her.

When we began the healing I 'saw' a wall around her heart; it was a wall for herself not for others. Tanya relaxed almost immediately through breathing exercises and pressure on the deepening points. Energy released through her arms and hands. I asked her to visualize a fire under the open chakra and stoke it so that it would burn all the toxic energy sent to it. Building the fire caused many memories to surface and be released, memories related to the issue that she hadn't remembered for a long time. She said those memories provided significant information through which she was able to assemble a puzzle and have big realizations. She emerged very pensive and at the same time relieved of how it all tied together.

Tanya came out of the healing feeling relaxed and with a new understanding of the relationship between herself and the lupus. I felt several light beings around us throughout her healing, as well as a black and white wolf. Her chakras were spinning wonderfully after the healing. She immediately felt physically lighter and calmer. Several days later she began to feel energized and stronger. Emotionally she felt repaired and ready to open her heart fully again. A few weeks later she had to go to a very famous medical clinic in the Midwest for her semi-annual lupus checkup and to her and her doctor's amazement, nineteen of the twenty variables tested for lupus were within 'normal' range. She was taken off her medicine for lupus, which had been causing severe side effects such as blindness. I checked on her a few years after and she was still doing great.

Back to the Light

Maria was a hardworking woman who arrived from Brazil and quickly adapted to the American way of life. She was in her late thirties, diligent, amiable and extremely sensitive energetically. I had met her through mutual friends, at which time she related a story of being unable to sleep at all. When I inquired further she said, "Something takes over me, takes me to dark places and horrible situations and I can't stop it. So I would rather not go to sleep." Sleep is so necessary for our physical body finally rests and our soul is free. In fact it is one of the most important activities we do and which helps return energy to our body. All in all we sleep one third of our lives! I asked her if she wanted to try a healing and she quickly responded that she would love to. We scheduled an appointment for late afternoon the following week.

She arrived promptly yet with some hesitation. I asked her to tell me about the places she gets taken to and the nightmares she had. Several of them seemed right out of a horror movie! I asked her to blow these incidents into one of my mesa stones, and to be clear about her intention for healing. She proceeded to lie down on the massage table. We began by having her relax. Within minutes I began to notice that her eyes rolled back. I asked her to stay present with me during the healing process and although she was trying her best, she couldn't. Guttural sounds began emanating from her throat, her eyes kept rolling back while open and she started writhing on the table. The first time it happened I just commanded for the beings of light to come and help. Maria stopped for a few minutes. Then it began again, the strange sounds from her throat, her eyes rolling back and the writhing. This time I asked the Celestial Court to come forth and help. It stopped again for a few minutes. The third time it began I commanded help from my shamanic lineage and power animals. She stopped and suddenly opened her eyes. With bewilderment she said, "What just happened?" Amazing, I thought, she has no memory of what went on! I realized we had to do some major energetic extractions to help her regain control of her own body. Although she felt calmer and lighter, the healing process had just begun.

The following week Maria showed up early for our next appointment. We were at a park with nature as our guardian. She said she had had a couple of deep sleep nights, but the intrusions to her sleep continued. I had brought several clean and transparent quartz crystals with me ready for the work ahead. I asked her to do her best to stay present for I would not be able to successfully extract intrusive energies unless she was fully there with me.

We began the process and she started to get limp. "Stay with me," I said to her in a firm voice. She did and we extracted the first fluid energy. Seeing the other energies move throughout her body I knew we were far from done. I began to track the second one. Maria became a rubber band and almost collapsed right before my eyes. Again I had to ask her to stay present; you could see the effort it took for her to stay with me. We took out the second intrusive energy. I moved a couple of steps away to continue tracking. Then she arched backwards and said, "Here, on my shoulder. It's painful." I knew there was a third entity so I proceeded to extract again. After this last one Maria stood up firmly and with elation said, "I haven't felt this good since I was ten years old!" She was a different person altogether. Her whole demeanor had changed dramatically.

Within a few days she called and told me that she now slept beautifully through the night, wasn't scared, and had dreams filled with light. I soon realized that Maria was a full medium. When I shared this with her she was not happy so we devised exercises to 'close her gates' until she felt prepared to accommodate her gift. She called a few years after, sharing her dreams with me. She had developed the gift of prophetic dreaming … about world events, local events, her life, and even about situations in my life. What a delight she was to know!

The Magic Stone

Andrew was a boy eight years old. He was beginning to have problems in school, mostly frustration with other children and short of temper. There were also self-esteem issues surfacing. His mother talked to him about a 'friend' of hers that could help him and asked if he wanted to be helped. "Yes!" he told her ... then asked, "Where is your friend?"

"In Miami," his mother answered. He was curious to see how I could be in Miami and he in another city, yet the healing could take place anyway. Remote healing is something most people are not aware of, yet quantum physics has proven over and over how physical distance is no obstacle for energetic healing to take place. There have been many documented cases of prayer groups that affect situations positively from a distance. Most people do not believe it is possible until they experience it. Shamanic traditions work outside of time and space, which allows remote healing to occur. I am still amazed to this day!

We scheduled the remote healing for the next day after Andrew returned from school. His mother was familiar with energy healing, so she would help out with the process. The phone rang and when I answered, Andrew was on the phone. He was anxious to begin. "What is bothering you?" I asked.

He eloquently answered, "I have some children at school that say mean things and they make me mad. Also there are adults who scream at me and make me feel bad. I am tired of feeling this way. And," he quickly added, "I am sometimes scared of things."

I asked him to relate three separate incidents: two that made him feel mad and another one that made him feel bad; he articulated each situation to me with clarity and in some detail. There was clearly anger in this soft and loving child. I talked to his mother for a few minutes, conveying instructions so she could help me. She proceeded to lay Andrew down while holding the occipital points behind his ears … he began to relax. In the meantime I checked his energy body and then opened his solar plexus chakra. Once the chakra was clear of toxic energy and the imprint had been removed, I asked Andrew to talk to his chakra. We did this through his favorite animal, a wild horse. He remained calm throughout the healing, listening to the instructions being relayed by his mother. Once done, I asked his mother if she had a small stone she could give Andrew. The stone would help him if he ever felt frustrated or scared again. He was to carry the stone in his pocket at all times and blow on it if he felt mad or afraid. He thanked me and asked if he could now go play.

Within a couple of days I received an email update from Andrew's mother. After the healing she had taken Andrew to see a few beautiful small stones she had just gotten; they were part of a feng shui set of candles. His eyes opened wide as he grabbed one of the stones and quickly placed it in his pocket. It was his treasure. He asked her where he should put it at night. His mother said he should place it under his pillow, to allow it to collect his fears and frustrations while he slept. Within a few seconds he disappeared, hurriedly. As she followed him she found Andrew had gone back to the place where the remaining small stones were and grabbed two more. He walked into the family room towards his father and handed him one of the stones while saying, "For you dad, for when you get mad." Then he gave the other one to his little sister so that it would keep her safe while she slept.

The e-mail closed with a heartfelt thank you from the mother saying how much the healing had helped her appreciate her children. I later had a chance to send one of my altar stones to Andrew. A few months later I visited his city and met up with his mother. She told me that although he might forget to have breakfast, he never forgets his stone! His situation at school greatly improved and Andrew returned to his sweet and loving demeanor.

I'm Coming to Earth

I was on my way to Latin America again, but this was an especially exciting trip because I was to spend some time with my friend Ana. It had been a year since we had begun all the energetic work. She had called a few months before to share the great news and I couldn't wait to see her pregnant!

Ana asked me to help her communicate with the little soul in her womb. Most of the time I don't do healings on pregnant women because there is another soul involved. But this was a unique request and there would be no energetic healing involved. The intent was to go on a guided meditation and talk to this little soul. Ana had specific questions she wanted to ask him, such as: What do you want to be called? Why did you come to me? What is your mission? How can I best help you?

I had not yet guided anyone on a meditation with the intent of talking to an unborn child, but shamanism has taught me everything is possible. We decided to do the journey in nature, amidst the forest. I still had no idea how I would guide her in this journey; I also knew that it wasn't up to me. Rather, and as I had learned before, I was to step out of the way and just surrender. So we set up sacred space away from people and began concentrating on our breath to calm down and center ourselves.

The meditation began with Ana going to a beautiful garden in the Lower World. There was lush vegetation, a beautiful waterfall, a lake, and the most majestic rainbow across the waterfall. As Ana went into this magnificent area of the garden I instructed her to go to the cave next to the waterfall. Inside the cave she would find a bed of red rose petals, where her baby would be waiting.

She did and there he was, anxious to communicate. I began to ask the questions she had given to me; he answered each one without hesitation. It is almost as though he had been waiting for us to engage with him. He wanted to be named Antonio. Ana had sensed only the last four letters of the name, but they made no sense to her. I had seen the whole name and the last four letters were exactly what Ana had sensed. He had been waiting for Ana to heal and felt this was the perfect time to 'come to Earth.' Antonio asked Ana to make sure he was given the freedom to be creative, for as he put it, 'I am here to revolutionize spatial medicine.' We didn't quite understand what that meant but knew it would all be clear in time. After his answers I brought Ana back through the garden and into ordinary reality. We both sighed, thrilled at the clarity of our connection with her baby. We left the park shortly thereafter and headed home.

I visited Ana and Antonio a little over a year after the guided meditation. He was now 14 months old and a beautiful old soul. When he first heard my voice he became very excited, then hugged me sweetly. Could he have remembered my voice form the journey or was it from the healings on his mother? His wisdom was palpable through the depth in his eyes. It was all too incredible!

Allowing Help

It was late 2002 and I was on my way back to Latin America for business. My consulting job took me to this region quite often. Although I was already deep into my spiritual path and into energy healing, I would not talk about it freely unless someone else brought up the subject. I had learned that some people would dismiss your business prowess if you ventured to speak about 'those subjects.' If they brought it up however, I was more than willing to speak about it. A top executive from my client company had asked me to dinner that evening and I was to meet his wife for the first time. I agreed and was looking forward to it. As our conversation progressed over dinner she brought out a spiritual topic and I quickly engaged. She moved into another spiritual topic, relating an experience she had had. I also shared some of my spiritual experiences. We had a great evening of sharing mystical events and time passed without any of us noticing.

The next day his wife called and asked if I would do a healing on her and also on her friend who had Parkinson's disease. I agreed and we scheduled time for the following day. I headed to their house after a full day's work, somewhat tired, but excited at the opportunity. Her friend's name was Sara. She had developed Parkinson's several years before, and as a hairdresser the trembling in her hands had become a real nuisance.

Sara arrived shortly after I did. We began her session by identifying the gifts that Parkinson's had brought to her. This was a hard exercise initially for she said, "I don't know if I have received any gifts from this disease. My husband and children have had to take care of me and I really don't like that." The energy of the last sentence gave me a key to probe further and try to get to the source of her issue.

I asked, "Tell me about the first time you asked for help and allowed someone else to assist you." She pondered for a while and then began telling me a story of when she was eight years old. While playing with her siblings and cousins she fell on a spot in the grass that was wet. It looked as though she had wet herself and all the other children began making fun of her. She felt awful. Sara continued with stories about her childhood where she was ridiculed and felt humiliated. She vowed never to ask for help and to always take care of others, so that they would never make her feel ashamed. Her energy body lit like a Christmas tree and I could clearly see where the blockages were.

She proceeded to lie down and we began the healing. As forgotten memories kept coming into her consciousness she began to cry. I instructed her to send any memories directly to the stone I had over one of her chakras, without analyzing them. Her energy body was releasing a lot of toxic energy and you could see her relaxing more and more with each release. After what seemed like an eternity she finally smiled. We began to discuss the healing and the mythic map that the chakras had revealed when the gift of her disease began to emerge. Parkinson's was to teach her to surrender and accept help from her loved ones.

This would heal the wound of embarrassment and shame, and begin to balance her masculine and feminine energies. As we were talking about the changes she needed to make in her life she interrupted abruptly, and putting her hands forward said excitedly, "Look, my hands, they are not trembling anymore. Thank you." She began to weep, but these were tears of joy! She had worked hard to heal and the reward had been a glimpse of what would come. She stood up and hugged me.

I last heard from Sara about five years after her healing. She was elated about her ability to allow others to help her, was feeling much better and had even begun to look at Parkinson's as a great teacher … rather than as a cruel disease. Her attitude had changed considerably as had her life.

The Heart is Healed

It is always hard to work on our loved ones yet we must learn to step out of the way and let Spirit take over. My dad used to visit me with some regularity, but physical challenges slowed his visits considerably. Several years ago he came to South Florida for a medical checkup; he was experiencing shortness of breath and a potentially damaged lung. Although the energy in hospitals is quite draining to me I decided to accompany him. The doctors decided to run a stress test to check out his heart. Because of my dad's lung condition the stress test had to be chemically induced. After evaluating the results doctors concluded that an angioplasty would be necessary for there were blockages in several of his arteries. The situation was not an emergency so my dad was allowed to return home. However, the doctors asked to be notified in advance when he planned to return, so that the procedure could be scheduled.

He spent about three months at home in Guatemala. His lung condition had worsened considerably and rapidly. The breathing capacity on his left lung had been reduced to less than 40%, while the other lung had pleurisy and was not at full capacity either. Soon thereafter his situation turned critical and he had to be taken in an air ambulance to the Cleveland Clinic in Ohio, as it offered the best care for respiratory and heart conditions such as his. I flew commercially to meet up with him. Upon seeing each other at the hospital we both began to cry. He looked gray and sad, much different from the optimistic man I had seen a few months earlier.

I spoke to the doctors and they explained the situation. They would have to do an angioplasty for his heart first, and a few days later do thoracic surgery to resolve his respiratory issues. It would be a couple of very intense days for him. "His heart must be ready to help us during the thoracic surgery," the doctor told us.

My dad was scared and felt very weak yet we had to prepare him for the upcoming interventions. He looked at me and asked, "Will you do a healing on my heart before my surgery tomorrow?" I readily agreed and we began the process. Lots of gray energy released from his heart chakra. As his energy body healed his breathing began to calm down. When we were done he felt relief and said, "Do you mind leaving your medicine bag next to my left lung? I think it would help me." I did so for the rest of that day.

The next day I arrived early at the hospital to prepare him for his surgery. He seemed to have surrendered to the Universe and was ready for the challenge. The heart surgeon was one of the best in the world and we both trusted him completely. My dad got sedated and was then rolled away to the operating room. I sat in the family room waiting for the doctor to appear after surgery. 45 minutes later Dr. Cohen appeared, seemingly relieved. "Please sit down," he said in a serious tone. "I have good news for you yet a little baffling. Your dad's heart is perfect. We just ran some tests and there are no blockages. In other words the angioplasty is not necessary. We don't understand how it healed so quickly for we have the tests from several months ago and they clearly show several blocked arteries. This is a miracle and a great outcome! We will be moving the thoracic surgery to tomorrow." Soon thereafter my dad was rolled back into his hospital room. He asked me what had happened and I explained. He then realized that his ability to let go and surrender allowed his energy to flow with that of the Universe and his heart had healed overnight. We both smiled and embraced each other. With renewed optimism he was now ready for his thoracic surgery.

Bringing Pain From Another Life

As my first year of teaching marched on I watched many students evolve and change in beautiful ways ... their demeanor, their words, the clarity of their thoughts, their attitude, their behaviors. The pieces of the puzzle were being revealed as they gained understanding of the spiritual lessons in their lives. The following study happened in Central America.

The group had just done a past life regression with the intent of seeing what lifetime was holding them captive in this one. It was lunchtime so we would have at least one hour before resuming class. Carolina approached me right after the regression and asked if she could talk to me privately. She was a soft-spoken, somewhat timid woman, but her purity and sincerity shined through. "Of course," I said, "Sit down, please."

She was about to begin telling me about her past life regression when her right shoulder started aching so much she winced. "This pain has been with me since I have memory," she told me.

"I just saw in the regression that I was tortured and stabbed in the same area where it hurts." I had her get up and stand in front of a white wall so that I could track her. As I rattled around her I began to see a long spear-like object in her energy body, going straight through the right shoulder blade and towards the right lung. I related to her what I was sensing and asked if it bothered her enough to have it removed.

Bewildered she said, "Can you really take it off? I would love to not feel that pain anymore." Because she had been stabbed from the back, the front of this object was towards the lung. If it had a sharp point, taking it out from the back would 'rip' her insides energetically. So I decided to push it from the back towards the front. When I felt the tip coming out of the right side of her right chest I began to pull ... softly at first, moving it around to dislodge it, then with one fast move just pulled it out. "Ouch," she said. "I felt that."

Once I cleansed the area and filled it with light I asked her to move her shoulder around. "Is the pain still there?" I asked.

"No, it's gone. What happened?" she said.

"It was crystallized energy that was affecting your physical body," I responded. She gave me a puzzled look and then smiled.

A few weeks later I spoke to her over the phone and she said the pain was gone. Many people have pain in certain areas of their body yet X-rays and numerous tests will show nothing. My experience has been that these are physical wounds from a previous life that appear as crystallized energy in this lifetime, causing real physical pain to the person. Once removed the pain immediately disappears! Sometimes the client will have sudden memory of the event that brought it about, but not always.

These studies and my experience as an Energy Medicine practitioner spanned over two decades, starting in the early 1990s.

There were many more clients. I selected just a few to provide you with a sampling of my work in Energy Medicine. Some clients were very fragile; others required more love and kindness, while others showed extreme bravery in the face of great adversity. Yet each one of them taught me that we are remarkable spirits attempting to deal with the issues and situations facing us in the best way we know how. Undoubtedly our own desire to heal is the greatest and most amazing tool we each have. This is what makes the biggest difference!

Letting go of the outcome has been the greatest learning for me. Even though we want to help everyone heal we must understand that every soul must make that decision for themselves. I learned this first with my mother, then my father, and later with many other people I have deeply loved. It is their journey and their soul lessons, and we are merely actors in their play. I also learned that in order to show up to healings impeccably I had to take care of myself. Just because I decided to accept the Universe's invitation to participate in Energy Medicine didn't mean I had the right to do so. I had to be well physically, emotionally, mentally and spiritually. That was always my greatest responsibility to patients, and if I was not in that space I did not move forth with a healing. Lastly, we must also learn to cleanse ourselves after each healing, so we don't take on any of the energies that were moved during a session. This is very important so that we can continue to be present in our own lives.

I am grateful to each client for their trust and might, and for teaching me about the resilience of the human spirit. It has been deeply humbling to witness the many shifts and miraculous healings of so many brave souls. Although I no longer have an active practice, I continue to teach other practitioners as Great Spirit brings them forth.

The Place of Transformation

"I want to know God's thoughts ... the rest are details."
—Albert Einstein

THE MEDICINE WHEEL KEPT TURNING AND WITH IT MY life. A long road had been traveled since I first embarked into the advanced studies of Shamanism in the mid 1990s, and it was time to take my contribution to this world to a much higher level. The work had been arduous and awe-inspiring, and each time glimpses of my true essence kept coming forth. It was amazing to discover who I truly was after many pieces of domestication were unlearned, and after continuing to transmute the wounded emotional and mental bodies. Shedding experiences from my past, changing perceptions of situations and people who participated in them, recognizing and facing fears that appeared when I least expected, and releasing the need to be defined and recognized by my accomplishments was monumental yet extremely liberating. With each step my inner voice became clearer, self-doubt subsided, and I began to live from the wisdom of my open heart.

It was time to begin participating in dreaming the world into being, working with *possibility* rather than *probability*. The 'Way of the Visionary' was about creating in the Present, observing with detachment, and then continuously modifying those creations so that I could always improve upon what could manifest in the future. My imagination was the only thing limiting my creativity. In the last direction of the Medicine Wheel we were to remember how to be supreme manifestors, where everything we dream is possible. I had come full circle to what my mother used to tell me as a child: 'If you can dream it, you can do it.'

Mystics remain in the North, basking in Spirit. Shamans want to bring the mysticism and magic into this reality … into this world. The intent is to experience Divinity by creating and while in creation, participate fully in dreaming a light filled world into being. It is in this direction of the Medicine Wheel that we shed all walls of separation and duality, and the veil starts to come down. Cooperation and sharing become the new paradigm for our world. We truly begin to understand and honor the oneness in the Universe.

The East direction deals greatly with *Transformation:* of the self, of others, of the Earth, and of the Universe. Transformation becomes a practice, and we learn to work with four transformation practices simultaneously: Identification, Differentiation, Integration and Transcendence. Mandalas are used as one of the transformation tools. So I began by making four sand paintings, insuring that all the edges of the circles were touching each other and in a particular order. The first circle illustrated 'what I identify with … who I am now.' The second one, to the right of the first one, was about 'what I have differentiated from … what I no longer am … what I have healed.' Under the first circle was the third mandala, showing 'what I have integrated.' Finally, the fourth mandala sat to the right of the third and below the second one, illustrating 'what I have transcended … the roles I have moved beyond.'

The four sand paintings would help me explore my archetypal journey. These archetypes reside in the energetic state yet manifest in the other perceptual states; in other words they reside outside of time yet manifest in time. Then I put one of my mesa stones from each of the four directions in the center of every circle, so that they could aid in my transformation. I sat in front of my four mandalas in silence so that I could integrate with my life journey. It was amazing to see what I had already transcended!

Two of the most important teachings we would have in this direction of the Medicine Wheel related to reciprocity and boundaries. The Inka called right reciprocity 'perfect Ayni,' which means living in a Universe that mirrors back to us the condition of our love and our intent. Ayni means reciprocity and usually leads to 'balance.' It's not about perfection, but it is about courage. It doesn't mean there will be no storms, but when they do show up they no longer blow us away ... they only sway us. In practicing perfect Ayni we shift our intent and then the Universe shifts to support us! This is how we dream our world into being, by changing our thoughts, our intent and by remaining impeccable. We would also learn that saying *Yes* to life doesn't mean saying *Yes* to everything. Setting limits becomes more challenging, as others can perceive the lightness of our being once we have said *Yes* to life, and they want it for themselves. The key is in helping them be aware that they have access to it themselves rather than through us.

The South and West directions of the Medicine Wheel were about knowing that *we have choices* and thus are not held in the grip of this world. There was awareness at the consequences of our choices, so being conscious when we made them was the key. The North and the East are about freedom—about not needing to make choices—thus about 'choicelessness,' because we are in the flow of the Universe. The minute we think we have to develop a 'what if' scenario we are in trouble! There is no Plan B for we no longer do the deciding. In the North direction we took vows and said *Yes* to life. In the East we bring *home* back to us, to our communities, to our village, and to our possibilities. It is here where we finally enter the stillness of Divine wisdom!

Perceptual States

As we move deeper into living the way of the shaman we learn to shift perspectives in any given situation we face. We select the one that makes us stronger, that helps us feel more peaceful or that provides the greatest understanding. It is this continuous shifting of perceptions that liberates us. I learned that the moment I felt trapped in any given situation, I was to ask my higher guidance to shift perceptions so that I could move forward with possibilities. In the East we lock each perceptual state into our mesa, which allows us to easily move between them at any time.

All perceptual states are of the same quality and value, and one has to learn when to use each one. For example, if a snake bites you on your arm you want to go to the *literal* state to heal it. If you go to the *symbolic* you will probably freak out and engage the flight or fight response; in the *mythical* you would want to find the meaning of the bite while the poison travels up your arm and gets you into further danger; in the *energetic* or *Inka* state you would leave this world and not heal your arm. So it is very important to learn when to use each perceptual state.

The *energetic* state is where we participate in dialogue with creation … with Great Spirit, but we cannot bring our *Self* or ego with us. It is a natural state for our souls where we are able to just *be*. Nevertheless it is a hard perceptual state to reach. Now that it is connected to our mesa we can access it much easier. We also receive assistance from the lineage in reaching this intangible state.

Patterns of Behavior

Archetypes are organizing principles of behavior. From a collective standpoint the tribe teaches us how to respond to the situations we may face in life. However, from an individual standpoint, we must identify the patterns of behavior that affect how we respond to given situations in our lives. Our own experiences allow us to develop these unique patterns or archetypes. The key is to identify what archetype participates in the different situations, acknowledge it, and manage it in its light. If we allow the dark side of the archetype to rule our lives we will remain stuck in certain situations and repeat soul lessons.

For example, if we are grieving the loss of a loved one we don't want to keep analyzing why they died or if we could have done something to prevent it (literal), or getting stuck in describing over and over how we feel about their loss (symbolic). Rather we want to elevate to the mythic level and see their overall passage through our lives, realize the soul contracts we had with them, understand that we agreed to their death or 'physical departure,' and remain grateful for the lessons learned. At the energetic level we realize that their energy has shifted and we must shift enough so that we learn that there is no real separation.

Another example would be when building a house. We want to begin at the mythic level, where we have a greater perspective as to what this house will mean for our soul. We want to become a mythical character in the story of our own life and see the big picture. Creating a mythic story about our home is a great place to start, dreaming about all the possibilities. We engage the energetic level to sense the house and dialogue with Creation about it. Then we can shift to the symbolic where we begin to feel the actual space and allow our mind to engage in giving a context to the mythic story. Finally we end up at the literal, where we select the designer, builder, architect, and on into the specific details of the house. If we engage the dark side of our archetypes, our 'ego' probably leads in the creation. Self-importance, status or stubbornness might begin the process at the symbolic level, and we end up with a place that doesn't fit into our lifestyle or that blows our budget from the onset. Or we may bring in details at the beginning phase, which when put together will show a lack of cohesiveness and will not allow us to see the overall picture of this massive creation.

The main question we should ask ourselves in order to move from our human-self to our spiritual-self is: *Who does my Higher Self serve?* The norm is to default into the 'collective' archetype—the peer group, thereby doing and being according to what the tribe does and has delineated is acceptable. The key in this direction is to transcend this tribal identification process and develop our own individual map. In order to evolve we must differentiate ourselves and identify with the larger picture of the Universe. We all came to do something much bigger than what human minds can conjure, and we are all links in an amazing chain. But we won't reach our highest potential until we heal ourselves from tribal patterns and honor our own path.

To identify our own archetypes we need to know which patterns of behavior we use to respond to a given situation; in other words which are our default behaviors and reactions. One way to track those archetypes is to write a mythic story. One of my favorite methods utilizes the Tarot cards, not to read the Tarot but rather to use the cards as archetypes that inform us. We form small groups of three or four people, and each person picks a card from the deck. We begin by individually writing a story with whatever comes to mind, regardless of whether we know about the Tarot or not. Then we read our story out loud to the small group. The listeners track what perceptual state the reader is most comfortable in; this is usually where we go in a given situation.

Once we identify the archetype where our energy gets trapped, we unravel it so that we can develop a *new map.* The new map is always the key, just like in soul retrieval! If we don't remap we fall into the same archetypal patterns over and over, and more than likely get stuck again. We must also identify which archetype the reader barely uses for this is the one they have to work hardest at mastering. This is the key piece in developing the new map.

My experience with tracking my own patterns of behavior allowed me to understand why I viewed the world and life the way I did. The cards my group picked were: Death, the High Priestess, and the Angel of Temperance. The following is my story:

Once upon a time a knight with shining armor came into a town that had decayed from the obsessions of its inhabitants. Upon arriving the knight began to notice the stench of decomposition; people were dying of hunger and disease, and chaos seemed to reign. He gazed upon an elder in a yellow cape and was amazed that this elder was the only one who seemed to be well. He trotted around town in his horse, trying to understand what had caused such death and doom in this beautiful mountain town. He had just passed a town that seemed to be the exact opposite of this one. It was filled with love and light, children's laughter, and the whole community was fully alive. He had met the high priestess of that shining town and her aura was one of abundance, sharing and love.

He returned to that lively town and asked the high priestess to accompany him into the next town. He explained to her that death and decay were everywhere in that town, and asked for her help. The high priestess gladly agreed and shared with the knight that her town had once been dead too, but had managed to find the source of love inside each one of the inhabitants and this had transformed the community. She asked if she could bring four of her most trusted and open hearted priestesses with her to the next town. He agreed and on they went.

Once they arrived in the dead town they began a ceremony of light to call in the angels. The whole community approached, surprised to see light and struggling to remember the last time they had participated in a ceremony. The priestesses' helpers took sparks of light from their hearts and multiplying the energy of these, began distributing such light and love to each

219

inhabitant. The momentum gathered more and more followers, and soon even the trees and flowers started to sparkle. The colors changed and the people realized their true essence. Death had been a necessary step for this beautiful rebirth to occur. The knight thanked the priestess and her helpers, and continued on his path to the mountains ahead. THE END.

The interpretation of my mythic story by the group was that it went through symbolic, mythic and energetic perceptual states. However, mythic was all over the story and definitely my default perceptual state. The one missing was the literal, the details. This meant that the archetype I got stuck in was the mythical. So my remapping involved learning to use the literal state more often, even if I was not comfortable with details and the slowness of them. This awareness would also help me when one of my students or clients delved in minutiae, which happens to be one of the most common perceptual states used by people. Remember that developing new maps is key, for it helps us heal old patterns and become empowered. As shamans we always map at the mythic level (outside of time).

Now that I knew my default archetype it was time to identify the archetypal map I followed in this lifetime. What was the script I abided by in life and how did my patterns of behavior support this script? We would utilize the Tarot cards again. This time my group picked: the Universe, the Fool, and the Fool again.

Once upon a time, in the Universe of Light and Possibilities, a stork was told it should find a singular place for a very special soul that was to bring the Divine into Earth. The stork was given four Divine helpers to assist in selecting the perfect place for this little soul to incarnate. The four Divine helpers had never had an assignment like this before so they were puzzled as to where they should begin. One of them concentrated on trying to find the exact location and family for this baby, the second one focused on the traits the baby should exhibit and how its gifts should be revealed, the third analyzed how this baby would remember its connection with the Divine and hear their messages, while the fourth one concentrated on how they would clear the obstacles for the baby to follow its true heart and mission.

The stork was baffled at all this discussion and decided to take flight with the baby before a decision was made. It searched and looked, in valleys, mountains, lakes and villages. Finally it saw a family that wanted a child, but had been unable to conceive one. It decided this was the right place. As the family woke up the next morning they found a beautiful shining baby in their living room. Elated they began to spread the news to everyone in the village.

The stork returned to Heaven and the four Divine helpers were up in arms. This was a special baby that needed special nourishment, and it had been dropped in a remote village that prized itself on its isolation. They talked and planned, discussed and kept thinking, yet nothing could be done fast enough. The baby grew up. As a teenager it was already exhibiting its Divine traits and personality. The mother nurtured this beautiful baby like no other mother.

The four Divine helpers continued pondering what to do. The baby's family decided to move to a place where their daughter could flourish to her highest possibility. As the stork observed from a distance it realized everything was unfolding as it was intended. The four Divine helpers were in awe. After all, the stork simply allowed itself to be guided by Great Spirit and had delivered the baby to the best place it ever could have. THE END.

Life is most certainly a mythic journey! Interestingly, when I wrote this story I had not yet started the mystery school or fully embraced my mission of connecting with and bringing the Divine to Earth. However, I am convinced that many old souls agree to participate in the Corporate America setting to bring light and an open heart into the environment, as well as to transmute the dense energies that permeate that atmosphere. According to two of my preferred teachers and writers—Jean Houston and Joseph Campbell, being able to see our life as a mythic journey is one of the greatest gifts from the Universe. And soon my life would unfold to mirror that mythic story!

Embracing the Storyteller

The Work of the East is the path of the storyteller, the one who impregnates the world with her breath. Shamans the world over are known for their storytelling because we have heard and can connect to the ancient stories through the lineage. We can also journey to the beginning of time where the teachings are held pristine. In addition many of the shamanic teachings were kept intact through an oral tradition, so storytelling was the chosen way to share wisdom. The path of the storyteller is an invisible path, as it is the path of the Creator of all creation.

It was time to begin to work with the *energy of creation* in order to bring about a massive transformation in ourselves. Our four sand paintings illustrate a mythic map of our own journey. So to effect great personal transformation we can choose to bring the mythic map to the energetic level. We begin by moving our mesa center stones a quarter turn backwards, which in turn reverses our four sand paintings. This allows us to understand how we differentiated from what we had identified with, how we integrated it, and then how we transcended it by overriding our beliefs and becoming aware of our archetypal maps. Then we used other shamanic techniques to magnify and accelerate the transformation to a much greater level. Surrender would play a big part from here onwards, for we did not know how it would manifest in our physical lives until some time later.

Experiencing a Full Death

The *Death Rites* are the rites of death and the rites of life; they are great transformation rites. They are done either to release a person's soul after physical death or after a major transition in life. Our energy body is held to the physical body by two primary components. One of them is the *electromagnetic field*, which surrounds the physical body. It is produced by the electrical activity in the nervous system, and runs up and down the body. When electrical activity ceases the electromagnetic field collapses. Then only the *chakras* are left to hold the energy body to the physical body. Chakras are energy portals found along the spine and on the top of the head. They are the link between the physical nervous system in the human body and the energy present in the Universe. Chakras allow the physical body to carry energy through the nervous system, which can be used to help the body's natural healing process.

One of the shamanic groups I studied with believes the soul remains close to the body for about 40 hours after death, seeking to come to completion; other traditions believe it is 72 hours or more. Regardless most of them believe cremation helps the energy body release much more rapidly after physical death.

The shamanic rites done after someone dies involve *unscrewing* the chakras in the deceased and then sealing their physical body; since the electrical activity in the nervous system has ceased, undoing the chakras releases the last hold of the energy body on the physical body. In this way the soul doesn't get trapped in the physical body. The Inka believe that nine out of ten people have their energy field rise naturally to the Heavens. About one of ten deaths needs support in metabolizing heavy energies that may have arisen, either from not dying consciously (i.e. coma or medicated due to terminal illness), from dying tragically, or from not having made peace with loved ones and said their 'I love you' to everyone. It is important to know that even after we die we remain connected energetically to our loved ones and to those we interacted closely with on Earth. So leaving peacefully helps us connect with our incarnated loved ones in a much more refined way and with greater wisdom.

The *Death Rites* are a sacred process and the shaman must be in perfect ayni to perform them. If the person is still conscious it is essential for them to go through a *recapitulation process* where they remember the major events in their life. It may or may not involve the rest of the family being present, and it is based on the wishes of the departing soul. Then we proceed to cleanse the seven chakras in the energy body. This lightens the energy body and prepares it for the most significant flight of all: the journey *Home*. Once the person exhales their last breath we begin to disengage the chakras. It is important to start with the heart chakra for it is the axis of the energy body. We proceed by spiraling the other six chakras in a synchronized pattern. Then we rattle around the energy body to further loosen the energy field's hold on the physical body. It is imperative that we do not to touch the person's physical body during the *Death Rites*.

As a shaman it is important to map the landscape of the Upper World while still alive, so that we can be ready for our own *death flight*. This allows us to become familiar with it so that when the time comes we can die consciously and travel upward smoothly. This wisdom exists outside of time, so we must become familiar with it while still alive. As with all other rites and experiences the shaman will undergo the process of *death* herself before doing the rites on someone else. In the West we merely separate the energy body from the physical body, like an out of body or near-death experience. We travel only to the first level of the Upper World, the

Stone domain. In the East, however, we go to *Heaven* and return to our essential Self. We fully leave and cannot take any dense energy with us. Here we enter the domain of Spirit in the Upper World (the Human level), which is the fourth level.

What do we encounter after our death? What is the landscape like? I imagine it is a different experience for each soul. The following is my own experience.

Words seem poor to describe the experience of Death, but suffice it to say it is one of my favorite experiences in this life. We had a 'practice run' before the full process was carried on. I left my body after just a few chakras were undone, and for a split second saw myself flying through darkness. Immediately after I began to see mountains and the sunrise right in front of me. The colors all around were extremely vivid—blue, green, yellow, orange. Then I saw a spiral and felt I was being held in space by ether. All of a sudden I heard, "Come back." I thought I had just left. My group said I was out of my physical body at least two to three minutes, although it seemed like mere seconds. It was so beautiful and felt so natural that I did not want to come back!

Then came the real Death experience. Our teacher had told us before starting the Death Rites that some of us might be able to meet the 'gate keeper.' I translated this to mean 'I will meet the gate keeper' and set my intent to do so. First I went through my life's recapitulation in a small group and then we paired off to do rapid cleansing of the seven chakras. After that was finished we came back to our small group. We assigned roles of loved ones to each person in order to simulate a real death; this included assigning one of them as my shaman. I picked Ariel to be my shaman while other people played the role of my mother, my father, each of my two brothers, and one of my greatest loves.

After crying while saying my good-byes I left easily. I saw a tunnel, but with an aura of light, like an eclipse of the sun. As

I headed towards the tunnel, deceased family members began to approach as well as my beautiful pets. Suddenly one of the figures of light got much closer. I recognized her as one of my close and dear friends who had passed in the mid 1990s. She said, "I'm glad you're here to play. The work you're doing is excellent, but you must know it's not your time to leave."

I said, "This is beautiful. I want to meet the gatekeeper this time." Right at that time a huge white dove appeared. I related it to the Holy Spirit. I jumped on it and headed to a place beyond the sun. Then I reached a space that was gold and silver, yet transparent at the same time. Here I met what I felt was an older gentleman in like an outline form, but somehow I felt I knew him. He told me he was the gatekeeper and said, "Hello. You wanted to meet me, yet you have met me many times before. Don't you remember? However it is not your time yet. You are only half way through this life; you must go back soon. Bask in the light and then go back so you don't damage your physical vessel."

Just then I heard Ariel say, "Come back." Although reluctant and somewhat upset, I came back. It took some time to move fully into my physical body. The feeling I had from the experience was one of absolute freedom and lightness.

Once I came back to my daily life after this amazing experience I began to release many dramas—as well as people with dramas; I also released defense mechanisms that I had developed to deal with life. Soon thereafter I began to simplify everything in my life. I was satisfied with much less and became more aware of the beauty around me, gratitude permeating my every waking moment. The realization that we have everything we need to live in ecstasy every moment of every day invaded me, and the external and material worlds lost their appeal. My nature became one of living from within. Relating to the outside world and its inherent dramas took quite a bit of effort, and it still does.

Our whole planet is undergoing great transformation into a New Earth at this time, in essence having its own *Death Rites*. The Old Earth model we had been using no longer works. This is the same message the Inka elders gave us in Peru in 2002. For example the current way of healing has been based on imposing the will of man on the will of evolution. Western medicine is being surpassed in importance by Energy medicine, shifting the emphasis from reactive to preventive; instead of handing over the responsibility of our healing to someone else, we are taking responsibility for our own healing.

With this shift comes a generation willing to take responsibility for ourselves ... for our thoughts, our beliefs, our interactions with others and with the Earth ... in the process discovering the eternal and wise soul within. This acknowledges a Universe of inclusion and leaves behind the model of separation. We are not heading towards self-destruction, as many of the fear models want us to believe. Rather, it is as though we have a blank sheet of paper and must manifest what we want the new world to be, to look like. We dream this New Earth into reality through our conscious intent, actions and visualizations. The shaman acts as the explorer of this energy world, agreeing to delve into consciousness in order to discover the paradigms of the New Earth.

Liberating a Deceased Ancestor

Another part of our shamanic training involves learning a very healing and honoring process to assist our ancestors. We journey to the Upper World and track to see if we find an ancestor that may be trapped and has not reached Heaven. More than likely they will be in one of the first two levels of the Upper World, which are equivalent to what some call *purgatory*. It doesn't matter how much time has passed because the Upper World is void of space and time. Once we find them we observe, and then we return to ordinary reality and begin the process.

For our ancestors to be fully free and elevate we must combust their energies. Helping an ancestor heal is a hard undertaking for we feel their pain; we are still too empathetic while in a human body. This is why we must work through a surrogate, and this surrogate must also be a medicine person. As soon as we return from the Upper World we relate to the surrogate who our ancestor is and where we found them, with as many details as possible. The surrogate then journeys to the Upper World and tracks, letting us know when they find our ancestor. That is our cue to proceed to rapidly cleanse our ancestors seven chakras, working about one foot above the surrogate's physical body. It is important to be one foot above the surrogate so that we don't affect their physical and energy bodies. We finish by doing the death rites on the surrogate. At this time the lineage appears and assists the ancestor, setting them free. Our ancestors may feel us, but the key is to **not** engage emotionally; if you do so you cannot help them heal.

My experience with helping an ancestor was surprising; I did not expect to find the ancestor I did. I began my journey to the Upper World. The Stone level had lots of people there, all reaching out aggressively. The Plant domain was gentler yet with an edge of potential menace. I did not know if this was due to the fact that my intention was to liberate an ancestor trapped in the lower levels of the Upper World. Then I went to the Animal level and felt my power animals all around me, protecting me fiercely. I moved onto the fourth or Spirit domain, and my maternal great grandfather was waiting. He looked softly at me, and then held me with so much love and tenderness. He asked me to help his daughter—my grandmother, and said, "I tried to contact you to tell you. I am so glad you are doing this work and we can communicate now. Please go back to the Plant domain and help your grandmother be free. I know you can do it."

I asked, "Why can't you help her?"

He replied, "Because I have already passed on to the Spirit world, while you can move between the spirit and human worlds. I will do what I can to help you." I went back to that level and found her almost right away. She was sitting on top of a giant leaf, her skin very yellow. A few days after this experience my grandmother visited me during one of my meditations. She thanked me profusely and then embraced me lovingly. I remembered how sweet she was with me while alive. She was my favorite grandparent! One week after releasing her my mom called to tell me she was so excited that she had finally dreamt about her mother. She had passed at least a decade before and she had not visited my mom in her dreams. When I inquired what she died of my mom responded that it was liver related. That explained the yellow skin!

According to the Maya and Inka prophecies the Middle World—the one we now live in—will turn into the Lower World. The Middle World has become a place for transmuting heavy energies, which was usually done in the Lower World. Then the Upper World will become the Middle World. So we will be living in two worlds simultaneously: the Middle World and the Upper World. This coincides with many native civilizations that have said we will be living *'in Heaven while on Earth.'*

In order to help us anchor in the Upper World we received star transmissions. They are associated first with the Sun and then with the Pleiades. These would help us source ourselves from the place of our becoming, so that we are able to bring Universal energies of transformation into Earth. The *Star Rites* awaken extraordinary neurological capabilities that inform everything around us. They help us remember an age of wisdom before the arrival of human beings. While receiving these rites I became aware that the star I was born under was Venus; after the rites I consciously acquired a new configuration from the Heavens that would guide my destiny: Orion.

The Work of the East was a journey beyond time, to my original face. It was a full circle that returned me to my essential Self, where awareness helps me participate in dreaming a light filled New Earth into reality. *Now I strive to consciously dwell in the center of the Medicine Wheel!*

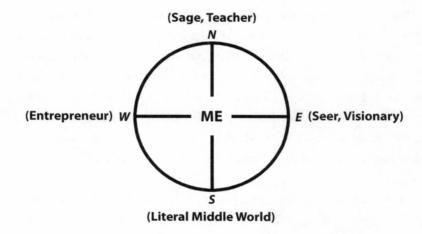

A Mystery School is Born

"The most beautiful thing we can experience is the mysterious."
—Albert Einstein

AROUND 1997, WHILE ON A BUSINESS TRIP WITH A colleague, a question was asked. My own answer left me quite surprised. She said, "If you could see ten years ahead, what do you *feel* you will be doing?" I took a couple of deep breaths and closing my eyes said, "Probably teaching women. I don't know what, but that is what I feel."

"Do you like teaching?" she inquired. "Something inside of me tells me I would love it," I nodded. "Have you ever done it before?" she queried further.

"Not in the literal sense," I said, "but I have always taught people around me what I know, even in Corporate America." She gave me a puzzled look.

A couple of years after that conversation I had a spontaneous journey of flying atop an eagle and going high above the mountains and lakes, thinking, "Isn't this a beautiful view of the Earth?" Suddenly the eagle took a dive into a magnificent room filled with luminous windows. There I saw myself on a stage, lecturing to several hundred women. Perplexed I looked at my eagle, knowing it could read my mind. "This is what you came to do," she said, "and it is big. Do you remember now?" After my heart skipped a beat, I began to remember!

From the age of five until about 12, I would run everyday to my mom, asking: "I know I came to do something really big, but I don't remember what anymore. Do you remember?"

She would look at me lovingly and respond, "No, I don't remember. But if I do I will let you know." Now I knew, yet *what* I was lecturing about remained a mystery ….

Several years passed and I continued my 'double life,' one foot in the spiritual world and the other in the business world. In late 2001, while doing a Medicine Wheel, I began to have visions of my mission. I knew energy healing was part of it as I had been doing it for many years. But what about the part related to teaching or lecturing to women? The business world, which had once thrilled and challenged me, had become tedious … a struggle. The spiritual world, on the other hand, showed me so much magic and so many miracles that it was hard to pull myself away from it.

When my business schedule permitted I would take a couple of weeks every month to immerse in spiritual stuff. This went on for most of 2002, which included my two-week shamanic pilgrimage to the highlands of Peru where I traveled with the Inka Q'ero people. Every chance I got I would embark on spiritual excursions to magnificent power places. As I felt major shifts coming unexpected fears crept up, especially those related to finances, to my identity, and to knowing *what's next*. For someone that had been so involved in strategic planning for multi-national corporations, always certain of the *next steps*, having a blank piece of paper filled with uncertainty was a little intimidating. However, as each month passed I noticed how *joyful* and *whole* the spiritual side made me feel, and how constrained and unnatural the business consulting world had become. The scales were certainly tipping!

In late 2002 my *spiritual sight* became much clearer and I began to have visions during my meditations. I saw a spiritual school for women developing, both in Latin America and in the United States. The concept was exciting and made me feel so alive that any financial concerns about leaving the world of business consulting were losing their power. My entire being was passionate about this mystical subject even though my training in this lifetime had been related to starting new business ventures. That internal excitement sparked more of my energy to travel towards the vision rather than towards business; in time details began to unravel.

Why women? I knew that spiritual awakening had to do with one's personal experience yet the soul is genderless. My spiritual quest these last two decades had taught me that I must accept what comes, many times without having an understanding or an explanation. When the question about *why women* arose during my workshops, all I would say was, "This is what I was shown. If I tried to explain it then my mind and potentially my ego would be involved, and this vision comes from my soul." Later I would come to understand that a critical mass of women was needed in order to begin the shift in consciousness through the path of the feminine; the school would soon include men. The path of the feminine was the journey within, and it was beginning to gather full force. The search for balance was obvious in everything within and around me.

Letting go of my ***identity*** was another significant challenge I was facing as I pondered giving up on my seventeen-year corporate career. Family lineage ('the daughter of …'), schooling up to the graduate level from the prestigious universities, successful fast-track management career at Fortune 100 companies, *'Corporate Executive'* since age 28, *'Executive Consultant'* to Fortune 200 companies for the last seven years of my business life, nice home in a nice neighborhood, financially independent … it all read like the typical over-achiever and it was the definition of 'success' that most of my generation had grown up with. However, like many other incarnated souls, I had realized that all those things ***did not make me happy … the void was still there.*** So who was I now? Certainly not what 'I did!' It had once been very comfortable letting my achievements define me.

My solar plexus chakra had been hurting and pulling for some time, even after one of my fellow medicine women had done a healing on it. I still felt that 'pull' as I delivered my first spiritual lecture, and a friend in the audience said I mentioned the third chakra several times throughout my talk. It was time to take a trip to see a close friend who was also a medicine woman. She proceeded to open the third chakra and do a healing on it, but it still didn't let go; this time it would require more. She journeyed and saw me in a cave with a group of people. It was a previous life. Something outside the cave was calling for me to follow my path, but I was torn because I did not want to leave my family, my group, the established. I felt guilty for leaving them in order to pursue my mission … my calling. Then the imagery changed completely and she saw a blind shepherd walking forward in an endless prairie, trusting the unfolding of his path. He was just moving forward without a need to 'see' where he was going. The image from the cave symbolized the 'expected path … the known road,' while the shepherd represented following my heart, the unknown.

My friend said she took out webs of toxic energy from my third chakra with her crystal; a lion cub had come to help her transmute the energy. The chakra relaxed. What was the issue, you wonder? The 'loss of my identity' … how I had defined myself up to now!

While I was still engaged in the business world, I had seen some clients who would return to heal issues we had addressed almost a year before. When I inquired they would invariable say, "It is so hard to change behaviors when you have been doing them all of your life. You should teach us how to complete the changes." In addition many of my friends had commented about how joyful and peaceful I seemed to be in my life, in spite of still having a very hectic business schedule. They suggested I teach other people how to feel at peace wherever they were, based on my own experience. With these shared insights, *I realized that the journey towards reaching* **stillness** *would be at the center of my teachings.*

The visions continued until one day, as I was waking up, I intuitively knew that *energy management* would be a central theme to the spiritual school. I knew shamanism and energy medicine were topics that I had selected for my own spiritual path, but they may not necessarily be the 'calling' for others. Therefore I would focus on topics that had made my life more joyful and peaceful, as well as on energetic practices that would help people shed their past and face their fears. This would help them effectively initiate change in those behaviors that were limiting them.

The last pieces of the puzzle would come in early 2003 with two very interesting experiences. The first one happened while I was conducting an all-day strategic planning meeting for a client. As soon as we began to discuss the product offering I became aware of thoughts that were not mine. I paid attention and realized I was seeing the thoughts of the executives I was speaking to, and most of them were not pleasant. They had to do with personal agendas and with how they could sabotage another executive. Although at a subconscious level I probably knew it was rampant in Corporate America, this was all too clear to ignore.

In the second experience, during a presentation to about fifty people from another corporation, I became the witness of a conversation between my soul and my human. It was as though I was a third person in the equation, an observer. The soul asked my human, "Is what you are doing here helping humanity?" "No," responded my human part. "Is what you are doing here helping Mother Earth?" the soul probed further. "No," responded my human again, seemingly concerned. "Then what are you doing here?" said the soul. That is when I got it: the time to move on had come!

In February of 2003 I spoke to my business associate and told her I would be leaving the business world later that year. She had been witnessing my spiritual evolution and was not surprised. She asked if I had any intentions of finishing the year, and I said I would like to do some part time work from August to December. One week per month would help me pay my bills, I thought, while allowing me to work on developing the concept of the spiritual school more fully. She agreed, relieved it seemed, and we went on to discuss the business at hand. In August of 2003, for many different reasons, I was thrust into the spiritual arena full force. The Universe would not have me compromise my mission by staying part time in the business world ... in ordinary reality. I left my business-consulting career at the end of July, ready to start my 'life.'

Awakening the Soul was born in late August of 2003, a mystery school intended to help women find their own wisdom and the freedom within ... their *stillness*. A mystery school is a learning place where we study the sacred. The name, you wonder? I had been getting the message, 'A Woman, A Soul' over and over in my journeys, and thought it was the title of this soon to be written book. It turned out that my spiritual 'hearing' was a little off and what the light beings were really saying to me was, **'Awakening the Soul.'** "There goes the title of my book," I thought.

The translation of **Awakening the Soul** into Spanish is 'Despertando el Alma,' and I felt it was breathtaking. Since I was to teach in the Americas the name had to be amazing in both English and Spanish. I worked diligently for a couple of months and by mid-October of 2003 had the logo, brochures, business cards, website, legal and accounting issues resolved, pinpointed target countries and audience, developed the initial building blocks for a school, and the general themes to teach. Oh how well the business world had trained me! Now it was time to develop the specific topics for each workshop and for lecturing. Teaching would begin in January of 2004!

The Urgency to Awaken …

It all began with many days of shamanic journeying. My intent was to discover *how to help people find that inner guidance and wisdom in the sweetest and most profound way.* There was an element of urgency in the Earth, for we needed to awaken many people to their true Divinity before we could create a mass shift in consciousness. Haven't we all dreamt of a beautiful and colorful world, filled with lush forests and greenery, all the varieties of animals and plants possible, that radiates absolute peace and unconditional love?

I used to think that was only a dream and that it would stay in dreamland. Yet as I embrace the whole Divinity, of which I am a part, I know with full certainty that it is possible. Have I seen it as a possibility? Have I journeyed to it? Did I live in a place like that before? The answer to all these questions is a resounding, *"Yes,"* but it is also a deep vision that I know will germinate if enough of us can see it. Dreaming the world into being? You bet! So the first giant step was to awaken as many women as possible, so that there would be a large enough mass to help create that shift in consciousness … the shift towards that beautiful and Divine world.

The Maya people talked about the 2012 prophecies, where the Katun ended and the Fifth Sun began (Katun is a twenty-year period, and the last one before 2012 had started in 1992). This particular Katun has been called the *cycle of transition and transformation* by the Maya, for many things would need to evolve for us to get to what they had envisioned the Fifth Sun would be. The Maya Cosmovision described the Fifth Sun as a new era of absolute light ... an unprecedented time in the history of the Earth according to the Elders.

In 2012 Venus would make a giant cross in the sky, coinciding with the intersection between the Milky Way and the Universe. Venus was the guiding star of the Maya people, and they had journeyed forward in time to devise a perfect calendar ... one that would also help them navigate their spiritual path while on Earth.

The Inka spoke about 2012 as an era where we would come back to basics. There would be massive changes in all those areas that no longer addressed our Spirit, so that we could come Home to our Divinity. Inka elders had shared that their prophecies told of 'systems' that had become cumbersome and inefficient at addressing the needs of the population and of the Earth, and they would disappear or change dramatically. These systems had to be modified or replaced by others that would facilitate people's awakening ... that would address the needs of spiritual people and children, and would increase the vibration of love and peace. The world would become a place for people who lived from their soul. They envisioned a world of barter and counter-trade, where services offered would enhance a person's wellbeing and that of Mother Earth and its inhabitants.

The *new children* who began arriving to this Earth school since the end of the last century have also been demanding a change and a massive awakening of the adult population. We have had the ***Indigo Children*** coming since the 1980s in large groups ... warriors demanding changes in every branch of the economy and in our treatment of the environment; then the ***Crystal Children*** started appearing in the 1990s, wanting an improvement in how we treated each other and all that lives on Earth; the ***Rainbow Children*** followed in the early 2000s, beautiful beings with an amazing balance of feminine and masculine; and then the ***Blue***

Ray Children and many other advanced souls, intergalactic and multidimensional light beings seeking to learn from and contribute to a planet in ascension.

These are all special children that need us to make huge changes in our perception, in our thoughts, in how we communicate amongst ourselves and with them, in our approach to the Earth and all its inhabitants, and in our acceptance of our innate God-given abilities. They need a lot of 'light and love' to live and even to survive, and we are the generation who agreed to create this change for them to thrive. So the urgency to awaken people was and still is tremendous. *The children of light are here! Do we need more proof that this world is spiraling into a beautiful and light-filled dimension?*

The School Framework Unfolds

This sense of urgency, plus the clear intent to awaken people in the softest and most loving way, led to the development of *teaching modules*. These would become successive seminars facilitating each step of spiritual awakening. The completion of the five modules would take between 12 to 16 months, with time available between workshops for students to integrate what they had learned into their daily lives.

For us to incorporate new learnings into our life—or re-learning if viewed from the soul's perspective, we need time to practice them. Experience is **key** to developing a spiritual discipline you can own. In addition, homework to assist each person in continuing in that space of peace and freedom they had felt during the seminar would need to be developed. A few months between the modules seemed ideal for training, discipline, and integration.

The next question was how long was appropriate for each module? As people were just beginning to commit to their spiritual quest, more than a couple of days might be too intense. However, one day would not be enough to get them out of their daily routines and mindsets. After some informal research, two to three days seemed perfect and could be done over a weekend. Aside from the workshop we would also have an evening dedicated to a sacred ceremony or a rite of passage. This would unite us with Mother Earth and the Cosmos simultaneously, allowing everyone to experience the union between Spirit and human, which all of us search for within ourselves.

The practice of celebrating our spirituality through genuine ritual has been largely lost. Shamanic practitioners around the world are one of the groups conspiring to bring it back. There are other spiritual disciplines that learn and celebrate through sacred ceremonies, and all of these practices are part of the fabric being woven for us to remember our roots and Divinity through ritual.

Another important part of the modules would be the use of energetic practices such as shamanic journeying and guided meditations, which would help accelerate healing at the 'energetic level.' There would be many guided journeys by the end of the five modules; this would help participants to ease into shapeshifting. Some of the topics to explore, during journeying, would be: discovering personal totem or power animal, finding inner peace, feeling safe in our own sacred garden, cleansing of the seven chakras, shedding limiting emotions … among others. Journeys are incredible in that one is able to bypass time and space, and thus communicate freely with the subconscious—the voice of the soul. In this way healing is profound and fast. Since it is at the energetic level it helps heal the energy body first, and then moves gradually to the other three: emotional, mental and physical bodies.

As the modules progress and the ability of students to meditate greatly improves, more guided meditations would be included in a single seminar. Healing and awakening would be accelerated with each subsequent workshop. This creates the holding of new life patterns and teachings. And so the basis for the coursework and format of the school unfolded.

The following is a description on how this whole framework came to be. I wish there was a lengthier explanation about how it all ensued, but everything unfolded naturally. The development of the five modules was a part of this magic, as one flowed perfectly to the next. The intention after completing all the modules is for students to have a roadmap for living peacefully, with stillness at the core. This will help them participate in the magic of everyday life!

Energy Management and the Steps to Spiritual Awakening

Initially students learn about general energy management concepts. This evolved from the questions that I continuously heard from clients:

- How do we lose energy?
- How do we gain energy?
- How can I learn to manage my energy better?
- How can I maintain a level of energy that makes me happy and healthy?
- I don't have enough energy to start new ideas. Can you help me?

So I began to ponder what the steps in my spiritual path had been. Spirituality is more about personal experience than about someone else's story. So I had to devise a way in which students could experience as many of the steps as possible, on an appropriate introductory level. Exercises were developed to accomplish this, which would also give students a roadmap to know what to look for in their own paths. Following energy management, students would have a taste of how a spiritual awakening path may unfold:

- What were the steps to awakening?
- How would we know where we are in our own spiritual path?
- How could we remain on the path?

Honesty and transparency were important to me, and I wanted students to be aware of what it took to move into the spiritual arena. This would help dissipate a few of the myths about embarking on a spiritual quest. Sometimes people believe that when they commit to a spiritual life the Universe conspires to remove all life obstacles and hardships, and in essence take care of them. This is a beautiful concept, but not what I had experienced.

When we first awaken we enter a world I call, *la-la-land.* It is light, magical and beautiful. However, in order to remain in that peaceful world on a daily basis, we must have the courage to: ***get rid of our ghosts, let go of our past*** and *face our fears.* We must also be aware of and manage our day-to-day thoughts and experiences with the greatest purity of intention and impeccability. Only then are we allowed into an eternal inner garden of beauty and wisdom ... one that holds the keys to Heaven and to the mystery of being alive!

Spiritual awakening doesn't mean we leave this world and float away, or that everything in our path will be easy and free of pain; rather, it means that we are better able to face the world we live in, understanding its lessons and moving forward fearlessly for the learning of our soul, choosing ***how*** we want to live. It also has to do with the realization that the Universe is benevolent and that we have a lot of help in the form of ethereal beings of light who collaborate to support and love us. And lastly, with the liberating truth that 'we are responsible for our own life and experiences,' we begin to chart our own course. This would be a monumental task for one module yet an exhilarating challenge for me!

Shamans and Tibetan Buddhists use mandalas or sand paintings for many different reasons. There is always an intention behind the creation of a mandala, whether it is peace, healing or gaining understanding. In shamanism a sand painting is a mythical tool that we can use to make changes in our lives, to heal, to regain energy, or to resolve situations that no longer serve us, amongst other things. They mirror back to us the condition of our issues, challenges or situations. They are an exercise of expression, not of perfection. In addition creating life changes through a mandala is easier than through the literal world. As we shift objects in the mandala, our lives shift as well. The most important aspect of sand paintings is that our mind cannot manipulate them for they are beyond its grip. Mandalas must be felt with the soul, not our ego. So students will be taught how to patiently *read* their mandala and communicate with it.

Participants will also be introduced to shamanic journeying, or as they are most commonly known 'guided meditations.' Changes are easier to implement at the energetic level even though they eventually manifest at the physical level. This module would offer a taste of what it's like to finally 'come Home!'

The Energy Body and the Chakra System

After learning about energy management, students will begin an in-depth look at their own Energy Body and their responsibility at keeping it healthy:

- What is the Energy Body?
- Why should I care about it?
- How will knowing about it help me feel better about my life and myself?

These were some of the questions I was hearing all the time. Aside from learning about the Energy Body, students will do exercises to *sense* their Energy Body and observe how it reacts to their thoughts and feelings. Most people expressed awe and a sense of reverence after this experience. One of my teachers would tell us over and over, "98% of our interactions are energetic, and only 2% are matter. Which world do you want to learn to live in?" Amazingly enough the majority of the population on Earth still lives in the 2% world!

Next students will learn about the Chakra System. This takes you deeper into the main organs of the Energy Body, where you realize how taking care of those main organs positively affect your three other bodies (physical, mental, and emotional) and therefore your overall health. Chakras are disks or wheels within our Energy Body that drink and distribute the life force basic for our wellbeing. They contain our history, our wounds, our emotions, and our spiritual Truths. Chakras are critical in the management of the energetic world, and thoroughly understanding them provides a roadmap for your spiritual awakening path.

Students are then taught how to test the chakras, determining how issues or situations affected them and others. We examine questions pertaining to each energy center, which in turn allows understanding to why you react in certain ways. In closing discussions we expand on how to heal the chakras, plus exercises to help students heal their own energetic and physical bodies. This module will lay a solid foundation and provide participants with their first taste of a clean energy body, and the massive realization that this is what fuels our dreams and life!

Balancing Feminine + Masculine Energies, and Shedding the Past, Part 1

The two first modules would be largely introductory and somewhat 'rational' within the context of the spiritual world. The time to kick into high gear and enter the realm of the intangible and the irrational had come. *What weighs us down the most when wanting to take spiritual flight … when wanting to enter the realm of peace?* Our past and our fears! First we must recover enough energy from our past and boost our courage. All that baggage from the past is heavy and leads us to repeat situations in our lives that were not necessarily positive. Our history need not define who we are. Learning to let go of the past does not mean that we forget our memories. Rather it is about learning the lessons from those events and changing perceptions to hold them in a more positive light. Once those memories no longer hold us captive we walk through life feeling free and light. We live the Present for what it is instead of judging it through the lens of what has been. Shedding our past is an act of power and of love. So letting go of it is an important component to this module.

Another topic that helped me obtain a greater perspective in my own spiritual path related to balancing male and female energies within. Many people perceive that because of the gender we pick to incarnate in, we are either all male or all female. However, like everything else in the Universe (i.e. planets, plants, energy), we must develop a balance of both energies. In order to have balance in our lives we need to achieve internal balance first. Our external world (relationships, work, family, etc.) would then mirror our inner balance. The first steps would be to define male energies and female energies, thereby minimizing cultural and social barriers. Teaching students how to balance these energies internally would be the second step. By now students are adept at moving into natural altered states, thus removing the barrier of the conscious or ego mind, and accelerating their own healing tremendously.

The flow of awakening dictated the introduction of an ancient spiritual tool. Students are now ready to learn about the Maya Tzolkin Calendar and the Maya Cosmovision. The calendar is an amazingly powerful instrument to navigate daily life. It was developed over 5,000 years ago and is still a great way to deal with the world of illusion. By the completion of this third module the perception of reality for most participants had started to shift to a more nurturing one. In addition they would become conscious that they are the drivers of their everyday experience!

Shedding the Past, Part ll, and Dreaming Your Future

The fourth module is a continuation of the massive topic of shedding the past, providing more tools for students to continue releasing throughout their lives. An important piece still to be addressed involved taking a deeper look at our shadows and facing them. Many of these are unconscious, but we must learn to release the terrorist within to create peace and beauty in our relationships and in our external environment. Once we let go of the most important traumas, thoughts and attitudes that were adversely affecting us, we have returned enough energy into our system so we can start learning how to manifest our future. By now students have become aware that they are the stewards of their own lives. But before embarking on creation it is necessary to learn the difference between living in the World of Love vs the World of Fear; we want to concentrate on participating in and creating only from the former. We also needed to differentiate between dreams and fantasies, so that we manifest that which our soul desires rather than have our ego explode an illusion in our faces.

For students' intentions to have the greatest opportunity of manifesting, they had to learn how to obtain assistance and tools from non-ordinary reality. Journeys to the future and to meet other spirit guides would be part of this crucial process, giving each person a full spectrum of their possibilities. It is essential for the wisdom and guidance to come from within rather than seeking it outside. Each one of us has the power to create from that piece of the Creator, which resides inside. By the end of this module students will realize how to bring forth a world that has magic and miracles everywhere ... and which they can now see and feel!

Facing our Fears and Spirituality in Every Day Life

Facing our fears is an intimidating topic, yet it is a large piece in the path to feeling free, light and peaceful. Fears have to do with possible events in our future, most of which have not manifested.

FEAR = False Evidence Appearing Real

Some of these fears mirror events in our past while others are learned from our culture and environment. An example of a collective fear is the *lack of safety,* and we must visit it in order to release it from ourselves and from humanity. Some fears stem from this lifetime while others come forth from past lives. When you ask people what they want in their future many begin by telling you what they don't want. However, this releases energy into the creation of those thoughts.

Most fears paralyze us and hold us back from venturing fully into the endless possibilities within our grasp. Facing them allows us to have a choice in how we react to them, rather than instinctively feeding something that may not even happen. In addition it frees us from an old paradigm, allowing us to pay attention to the moment and to our intuition. One of the key learnings in this module is that living in the present makes most of our fears disappear. As we turn our attention to the *now* we realize that all is well, and that our fears were unfounded.

The last piece would be how to integrate our spiritual selves with our daily lives. As Carolyn Myss says, "We are in a time of Spiritual Madness, where we pursue an inner spiritual life yet must live and work in an external world." It is about becoming *ego less*, while at the same time *getting to know the ego in order to become free of it.* So adapting what has been learned spiritually into every day life would be extremely helpful.

This was the final major topic for the fifth module, culminating over a year of intense study, dedication and tremendous transformation. The intention at the end of all this hard work was to emerge with stillness at the core ... on the inside. Only then would we be able to experience life fully and live in the Present Moment.

Mastery Level Teachings

A couple of years after the formation of **Awakening the Soul**, graduates of the modules' program began to request a deepening of their spirituality. They would ask me, "What's next? What are you going to teach us next?" As I mentioned initially my intention was to teach people how to find that stillness ... to make them aware that not only is it possible to find peace amongst the chaos in this world, it is our only choice! In the development of the five-module framework I drew largely from my own experience and daily practice. It was once again time to request the assistance and contribution of the greater wisdom of the Universe, and it all began to manifest magically. So where to now?

"We can only teach what we are," the master teachers have said through the ages. Requesting help from the Universe and my Higher Self, I journeyed with the intention of creating a new platform for those seeking to deepen their spiritual awakening into more mystical teachings. It became clear that the next chapter would be less of a general teaching about how to live life peacefully and more of a committed path into a spiritual discipline to which students needed to feel called. Shamanism was my choice of spiritual discipline, how I opted to live and breathe my every day life. I remember feeling the deep calling when I dedicated to this path. It is not just something you decide to 'learn more about' or dabble in. It is a committed spiritual practice in how we relate to ourselves, to each other, to the world, and to the Universe. So I would do my best to transmit my understanding and experiences of Shamanism to a group of seekers that had completed the five modules, allowing them to *feel* if it was their calling.

In teaching Shamanism to students, the first requirement would be to successfully complete the initial Modules and to commit to follow the path of the Medicine Wheel, engaging in a path of self-healing and spiritual enlightenment. The Medicine Wheel consists of four directions. The duration of each class would be expanded to several days, allowing students to enter a different realm void of space and time. Given my own practice and experience, my intention was to combine Native American, Inka and Maya shamanism as much as possible. Students would learn to enter altered states of consciousness spontaneously as well as become familiar with the landscape of different dimensions and realities, so that they could effect a positive change in this ordinary reality. It would involve an engagement with our natural environment and an innate knowing that we can speak directly to the Great Spirit. The right use of power would be at the center of the teachings, for shamanism can lead us to command the laws of nature through the power of intent. By the end of the four directions students would join the collective in creating the future world for our children's children. They would also be ready to spread their light in as many places and realities as they chose to.

Energy Medicine goes hand in hand with Shamanism and would be part of the Mastery Level teachings. While significant self-healing would take place during the shamanism portion, students were encouraged to help other people heal. We know we must heal ourselves in order to contribute to the light of the Universe, but we also have the responsibility to help others heal … particularly as major changes for our humanity are upon us. *We cannot waste any more time; the massive changes in Mother Earth are imminent.*

Venues and Their Personalities

Several of my friends and clients insisted I consider the cities they lived in as my first teaching locations. Since they were volunteering to provide the legwork at the local level this meant that the countries to visit initially would be Panama and Mexico ... Brazil eventually. This was the 'plan.' But the Universe had other ideas and I was engaged in Panama, Guatemala, Maryland/DC and Ft. Lauderdale. The rest of the United States and Latin America were soon to follow. Teachings would be in English and in Spanish, as audience appropriate.

Surrender would be an important lesson for me from the onset. In each city the typical questions would arise: How many people will register? How do we get the word out to let others that want to awaken know? Are there enough people interested in these topics? But this was a different arena than I was used to and questions would fall away once I understood that all was in Divine and Perfect Order. I was merely the one delivering the energy that was to pass through me, so I learned to become an observer and not take myself seriously. The number of attendees was not as important as their commitment and willingness to embark upon their spiritual path.

Each new day brought another request for either a speaking engagement or the set of five modules in a different city and country. Men began asking to participate, as well as teenagers. Those attending wanted their partners, children and friends to attend. The word spread quickly and **Awakening the Soul** expanded faster than I ever anticipated. The Universe always provides to those that are ready.

Attendees came from many diverse backgrounds: lawyers, writers, artists, teachers of all types and levels, investment bankers, corporate managers and executives, small business owners, homemakers, real estate agents, entrepreneurs, landscape designers, advertising executives, psychologists, psychiatrists, insurance brokers, nurses, physiotherapists, and healers … among many others. They each brought a unique perspective to the group they participated in, and great lessons and awareness to me. Different cities also had their personalities, each one unique and interesting in different ways. Thus I had to be aware and versatile in my module presentations to address the needs of the students.

Awakening the Soul was launched on February of 2004. The initial approach was to have a maximum of twenty women in each group, so that I would be able to engage one-on-one with each one. The Fort Lauderdale participants were the first group in the history of **Awakening the Soul**, and one that seemed to have been gathered by angels. The women were powerful, yet gentle; driven, but peaceful. The shift from the first module to the last was dramatic in all participants. Throughout the entire journey I witnessed them hold each other with love as deep changes took place, being supportive and always available. Many were diligent in their homework assignments and moved assertively into their spiritual path. These were all amazing women! There was a soul family amongst us, and as we moved forward in our lives there was anticipation of how our paths would continue to cross each other's.

Guatemala was a *coming home* for me as many of the participants were childhood friends or classmates that I had not seen for many years; others were related to someone whose family was friends with my family. Nonetheless it was one of the most courageous and committed groups to their personal growth. Interestingly I always felt as though family surrounded me. The setting was in Antigua Guatemala, a beautiful location amidst three majestic volcanoes and a place that I visited regularly while growing up. In addition I had the privilege of my mother attending the two-day workshops before her passing. What a joy to travel this path with one of my closest soul companions! A major side benefit in Guatemala was that I got to spend more time with my parents and dear friends. It was also part of my reciprocity to a land that had given me so much!

Panama was a younger group than any other city and a very inquisitive one. An interesting story regarding recognition of souls developed there. Sofia and Lucy met during the first module. Sofia was 29 years old, married and a schoolteacher by vocation. Lucy was in her mid-40s, a lawyer, with a teenage daughter. Sofia *sensed* while Lucy could *see*. After one particular class Sofia said to me, "I cannot take my eyes off of Lucy yet I'm scared to engage with her. There is something about her that calls me; she is so familiar." Lucy hadn't quite fallen into the spell of soul recognition yet.

By the second module Sofia described to me a recurrent dream she had of a prairie with a giant tree in it. When I asked her to share her story with the class, Lucy jumped up and excitedly said, "Is it like this landscape I have drawn in my notebook? Come and see." Sofia approached and let out a gasp. It was the exact same one. Although Lucy had begun to recognize Sofia, she was still not sure where the source of this familiarity lay. Sofia, on the other hand, continued resisting getting closer to Lucy; it was as though something was making her stay back. By the third module the group had their first past life regression. Sofia described sensing flowers in her prairie. Lucy had a full vision of a past life with Sofia, and the story finally began to unfold. She explained to Sofia what the path to the house was like, filled with fragrant flowers. She then shared the vision of the house, pillars and all.

The story unfolded to reveal that Lucy was Sofia's mother in that past life, which happened to be right before this one. Sofia was a young girl then, maybe six or seven years old. The setting was the 1950s. Lucy's husband in that lifetime was her father in this one. While traveling by car Lucy and her husband got into a heated argument; Sofia was in the back seat. The husband lost control of the car and they had a fatal crash, where Lucy and her husband died. It was not clear what happened to Sofia, but my feeling was she lived. In this lifetime Sofia refused to get close to Lucy because she felt abandoned in that previous lifetime. Lucy had told me that she hardly ever felt afraid in life until her daughter was born. Was it cellular memory that she could leave her daughter again, as in the previous life? I don't know, yet it seemed that way. By the third day of this third module Sofia and Lucy sat next to each other for the first time. Their energy fields were one, joined as only those of soul family can. This was a miracle and a privilege to witness!

The fourth group was in Maryland and participants seemed more aware of the spiritual and energetic worlds. They had reached out to many spiritual resources available to them and every person brought interesting wisdom to share in each session. There was also a wider age range, from 25 to 87. They were eclectic and had the most diverse personalities. I always looked forward to traveling north and exchanging energies with this beautiful group!

In Gratitude

After many years of teaching the five-module system and the Mastery level classes, it has been an honor to witness the most amazing transformations. Most students have begun to see their true Selves, and a roadmap to peace and wellbeing has become part of their energetic makeup. They have a greater awareness that choices create reality, and that thoughts are great contributors to that reality. They also have an intangible world that they now engage with and that brings beauty into their every day life. Uncertainty is seen as the field of all possibilities and embraced without reservation. Changes are the signposts of an even better life to come, no longer a place of fear or frustration. Death leads to rebirth, and places of darkness are now filled with light. As each one of us commits to our path of spiritual awakening we become an example to all those still pondering how to live their lives in a more peaceful and meaningful way, thereby adding our little grain to the massive shift in consciousness occurring at this time. To all the brave souls who embark on a spiritual journey, my congratulations and a big bow. There is no other way to live life than consciously!

I truly believe all the students have and continue to teach me more than I could ever teach them. I have felt privileged and humbled by their presence and their hard work. To each and every one of you, my most heartfelt gratitude and appreciation. Thank you for touching my life in such a special way!

Metamorphosis
in Process

"Faith is the strength by which a shattered world
shall emerge into the Light."
—Helen Keller

The Deepest Transformation

MY DREAMS AND MEDITATIONS COLLIDED WITH ABSOLUTE precision. Large, long roots lifting and walking North. "Oh no," I thought, "I am moving away from here." At the time I was living in South Florida, but long roots lifting meant a big move was imminent. The visions continued for one week. The following week, amidst the stillness in my Florida house, Blue Mountains began to appear. I only knew one set of Blue Mountains, and those are in North Carolina and Virginia: the Blue Ridge Mountains. I had never considered this part of the country, yet this time was not about what I thought, rather about following Divine guidance. So I told my spirit guides to be clearer, more precise. On my next three international trips different people from North Carolina sat next to me. 'This is odd,' I thought, 'I have never sat next to anyone from North Carolina before.' So the location was clear yet my mind got in the way. Given the fact that I was already teaching spiritual subjects going into the heart of the Bible Belt would be challenging. So again I asked my spirit guides for more clarity. Within a few days I got inundated with postcards from Asheville realtors; in addition my shamanic journeys were invaded by Asheville written in many different ways.

My dogs were used to the sunny, hot days of Florida. A move to the Blue Mountains would mean winter, and at their age I didn't think they would like it. In an attempt to find out we drove North in March, at the tail end of the winter. They ran in the forests, splashed in the waterfalls, and relished in nature. They both loved it! During our visit I had my first levitation experience. I had just begun a shamanic journey when I suddenly left my physical body and traveled in flight. I set my intent to 'see our future house' and was taken to a place of absolute beauty. From a giant window inside a house I could see endless ranges of mountains. Very few houses, not a lot of construction, but many trees and forests. An enchanting place!

Upon my return to Florida I put our house on the market. The search for the enchanting place in the mountains began. I wrote down the attributes of the ideal house and began to energize them with my thoughts, visualizations and emotions. It took one trip to the beautiful mountain town to find our sanctuary, and as soon as I walked into our house I knew it. I asked the realtor to cancel all other appointments and prepare to make an offer. By the end of June we were on our way north.

Close friends and family asked me why I was moving. How do you explain Divine Guidance? You don't ... you just follow it. Today I realize that the amazing energy of this place has helped me go much deeper into forever, and it holds me—oh so sweetly. The blessings of this exquisite location have been infinite; I could never have imagined such magnificence! Surrender and follow Divine Guidance. Beauty ensues ....

Our first trip to the Blue Ridge Mountains was breathtaking and the feeling of being held was more than confirmation for the journey ahead. I was excited to return to mountains and forests, and felt this magical place would help me deepen my connection to that wiser part of me. After setting up house in June of 2006, the girls and I began exploring our surroundings. The *girls* were my two constant companions, Tracy and Samantha. They were black miniature schnauzers, each with a giant personality. As I moved out of the ordinary world and fully into my spiritual path they did too. They played when it was time to play and they meditated when I meditated. They loved nature, especially the beach. Tracy was the guardian and brave one, while Samantha was a more spiritual puppy. Tracy was my intellect and courage, and Samantha was my heart and compassion.

Samantha could discern light energies from dense ones, especially in people. As loving as she was, if someone came in the house that had dense energies she would go to the opposite corner and stay there until they were gone. They never complained and were always ready for adventure. Whether I worked, read, did yoga, meditated, or just chilled, they were right next to me. In hard times they held me and gave me so much love, I knew I healed faster. I learned to cut the etheric cords between us, so that they didn't absorb any dense energies or feelings from me when I was going through hard times or when I was doing healing work. As I got deeper into my spiritual path and journeyed to previous lives, both of them appeared continuously. They will forever continue to be my faithful companions, and me theirs.

By the second week of July we had begun to explore our magical surroundings. The trails, the mesmerizing vistas, the beckoning mountains were exquisite. Although the girls were twelve and thirteen years old, they were elated to be in nature amidst such beautiful vibrations! It was as though we were being held and guided from the moment we arrived. As August came around I began preparing to teach a shamanism seminar. It was the second direction of the Medicine Wheel for a group of international participants, and Asheville would become a special place for them. The high vibrations of the area allowed them to go very deep, and their healings and realizations were extremely powerful. This began the wheels of motion for my life as well. After all what we teach is part of our own weaving, and we participate in the shifts with our students. It always made me wonder who the student was!

A few days after completing the seminar I received a call from my mom. She wanted to come visit and see where I had moved. We spoke every couple of days or so, and she could hear my excitement about the area. She planned her trip to coincide with one of my travels to Guatemala so that she could return to Asheville with me. In late September, after teaching several classes and having consults with clients, we boarded a direct flight from Guatemala to North Carolina. She would soon experience the magic of the Blue Ridge Mountains!

From the moment she got here I could see her taking deep breaths as she looked upon the breathtaking vistas. Our first journey down the Blue Ridge Parkway left her in awe. We always had a wonderful time together and this would be no different. We walked the trails with the girls, picnicked amongst the forests and mountains, shared endlessly until late hours of the evening, and even went hot air ballooning. After about a week, while we were having breakfast, she said to me, "This is the closest to Heaven I have ever felt! Your house is always so peaceful for me, like a retreat. These mountains are very special. Now I understand why you moved."

We always had shared a very special connection, and with her being the closest soul to me on this Earth it meant a lot that she had felt so deeply for my new home. But something about her comment made me ponder if there wasn't more to her words, almost as if her soul were reaching out to me with a deeper meaning. A few days after as we were sitting in the living room overlooking the spectacular mountain ranges, something gigantic and white flew across, level with the porch railing. She was used to me looking away to see even the most minuscule movement in nature and said, "Go see what it is. I know you saw something."

So I got up and walked out onto the porch, then turned left. The house was completely surrounded by trees, being almost the last house atop a lush mountain. As I glanced towards the higher branches of the trees my jaw dropped! A gigantic white owl was perched high on a maple tree, looking straight at me. It didn't move for a long time. 'Hmmm,' I thought. 'Owl is about death and rebirth. This is about my mom.' Just then I remembered a story she had told me about her own mother going to visit her for 30 days before dying. The realization hit me like a bullet train! She was coming to say good-bye to me! After taking a couple of deep breaths to center myself I returned to the present moment. I had just had a glimpse into future possibilities, and I needed to live in the moment as though I did not know what the future could bring. The owl seemed to know it had delivered its message and flew away. It was so big I doubted it was real.

At the end of October I took my mom back home to Guatemala. We had both had a wonderful time in the land of magic, even celebrating my 45th birthday together. After teaching and spending time with my parents in Guatemala I returned to Asheville. The girls were elated to see me!

At the beginning of April 2007 my father called and said my mom had had an emergency and gone into the hospital for septicemia (a blood infection, generally life threatening). She had given me a blanket permission to help her with emergencies. I began doing a remote healing on her, but something was different in her energy body. I felt her presence in my house; she asked me to cleanse her whole energy body, not just the affected chakras. A chill went down my spine and my neck started sweating.

When I finished doing the healing I called their home in Guatemala. At the same time the hospital was calling on the other phone line to let them know my mom had died. She had had a heart attack as they were trying to help her with the septicemia. I took a deep breath and then tears started flowing down my cheeks. I got up and headed to my meditation room to connect with her. I felt her embrace. Tracy and Samantha came and lay right next to me. They knew what was going on. I centered myself and began to do the *Death Rites* on my mom, helping her release easily and peacefully. Within a day I would fly to Guatemala for her funeral, mostly to accompany my father. I did not believe in the long-established funeral traditions of my birth religion and country, yet I respected them for my dad. It was the hardest week of my life to date! After organizing what I could in my parents' house and helping with as much matters of the heart as possible, I told my dad I would come back in a couple of weeks. I needed to grieve the departure of my closest soul companion in my own way.

One of the many gifts of the spiritual life is that you listen to the depths of your soul, learning to take care of healing yourself first so that you can then be present for others. My heart and soul were broken in a million pieces, and I needed to tend to them! I was so very grateful to my soul for the spiritual path we had traveled in this lifetime, for I had the tools to begin my healing journey.

The first few days I hiked for several hours. Merging with nature made me feel held and nurtured. I could feel the trees speaking their wisdom to me, reminding me that *All Was in Divine and Perfect Order.* Even if I did not understand it given the pain I was feeling, I could surrender to the innate knowing that all was as it was meant to be. I also knew deep inside that my mom had chosen her departure with the blessing and help of Great Spirit, and never gave it a second thought that something could have or should have been done to save her. Then I called a close soul friend and asked her to do a soul retrieval on me. Part of my essence had definitely exited with my mom's departure, and with it were gifts of resilience and stillness. She returned several soul pieces to me, and with each day the integration process allowed me to stand in the center of my being.

I returned to Guatemala as often as I could to help my dad in his grieving process. I recognized he had lost a big part of his soul. They were about to have their 50th wedding anniversary and had deeply loved each other. Even before my mom's death he had so many health issues that he could not travel to Asheville to visit me. He had medical care 24/7 and could barely leave his house. In one of those trips I got an emergency call from the girls' pet sitter in Asheville. Tracy had had a pulmonary embolism and was in critical condition. She had been in perfect health when I left, as was Samantha. I spoke to Tracy inside my heart and asked her to wait for my return; I would begin the trip back to Asheville the next day. Their vet was my friend and she agreed to meet me at the house as soon as I returned that night. Tracy died in my arms a few minutes after I made it home, shortly after we saw deeply into each other's soul through our eyes. It was almost two months to the date of my mom's death. I didn't know my heart could break any more! I turned to Samantha and held her close to me, asking her to be strong and courageous. We would get through this together. But Samantha would not look into my eyes. She would look away and seemed lost. Within a couple of days she stopped eating. I took one more trip to Guatemala, bringing her along with me. She withered away and started to whimper. I decided to bring her back to Asheville three days later, and after taking her in for a checkup, found out she had suddenly developed spleen cancer. I felt like a zombie, living in an in-between world. I held her all night, whispering to her how much I loved her. The next morning I met my vet friend at Samantha's favorite park, and holding her in my arms, put her to sleep.

Oh, my God, how my heart broke over and over again! It had only been eighteen days from Tracy's death. All the spiritual work

I had done could not lessen the deep pain I felt. I was unable to meditate because the silence was breaking my spirit. It was as though I was inside a dark tunnel and all the tools I had gathered these past fourteen years were not helping. The three pillars of my life had all left in just over two months! At the soul level I knew I had agreed to the script. *"All is in Divine and Perfect Order,"* I kept telling myself. But how could my soul believe that my human had the strength to endure so much continuing trauma? I had to believe in the depths of my core that I would have assistance from the spirit world even if I could not feel it at this time.

My soul family began to arrange coming to take care of my soul essence, without my participation. For the next seven weeks friends from different parts of the country and the world would come stay with me, all in perfect coordination. They didn't know or speak to each other, but it was all perfectly orchestrated. I knew my mom was helping me from above, yet the pain inside was so intense that I could not connect with her. It was as though the spiritual gifts I had worked so hard to hone were gone! There was nothing to hold on to, for every last strand of strength had been yanked away with the departure of my loved ones. I was definitely inside the *Dark Night of the Soul*, a deep existential crisis where all you can do is just be.

After Samantha's death I had four days alone before my soul family would come and be with me. The seconds were eternal and the silence in my house was deafening. Deep in sorrow I felt myself come apart, piece-by-piece. I would force myself to walk the forests, begging Mother Earth and the trees to hold me. When I returned home no one was there to accompany me, or so I thought. I implored the Universe for help!

The day after Samantha died I had one of the most amazing experiences of my life. Sitting on the couch with a lost gaze, I heard a whisper, "You know we are with you, don't you?" I turned and saw Jesus coming towards me. Just as I had seen him after the Shapeshifting workshop, his were eyes soft and loving, his energy so deeply peaceful. I allowed myself to be held in his all-encompassing energy. Within a few minutes he began telling me stories about his life, about how he had had to renounce to what he wanted in order to fulfill what he had agreed to come do while on Earth. He went into many detailed accounts of how much he had hurt inside and asked me to be strong.

He promised to be by my side every second of every day, and instructed me to try and put my attention on the fleeting moments of peace I may experience. Soon the moments of peace began to expand and those of sorrow got shorter. He also asked me to write about what I was grateful for in my passage of life with my mom and the girls, and to read it out loud as often as I could. After a couple of days a small ray of light began to shine deep inside my heart. I knew it would take patience, but the process was beginning.

My physical body was still having a hard time reassembling itself after all the shocks. I was having trouble with tingling sensations in my legs, and despite all the walking and hiking I was doing, they felt foreign to me. My lower back was in tremendous pain. It was clear my physical support system had been seriously challenged. I also did not feel hungry, and my solar plexus had developed a ball under the diaphragm. It was time to tend to my physical body. While searching for seminar locations right after my mom's death I had met a very powerful woman. Leslie offered a beautiful place for rent that seemed perfect for the shamanism workshops. After briefly getting to know her I learned she did massage work. So I called her and asked for an appointment, relaying a bit of what was happening to me. She agreed to see me the next day. It would prove to be a tremendous turning point in my healing process, and for that I will always be eternally grateful to her.

My shoulders, neck and lower back felt broken as I drove to my massage appointment with Leslie. The room was setup up and she was waiting for me. Within minutes what started as a massage shifted to energetic work, with Spirit guiding her in my transformation. She asked me to stand up as she stood behind me looking at my lower back. "Do you see anything?" I asked her.

"No, and that is the problem. There is nothing ... it is void of energy," Leslie said to me. "This happens with people ready to leave this world," she continued. Then she asked, "Beatriz, do you have a connection with Peru?"

And I answered, "Why?"

She said, "There is a shaman from Peru here, standing in the corner."

"What does he want?" I asked her.

She said, "He is here to help you. He says this is about discernment, about looking in the fine spaces. Do you know what that means?"

"No," I responded.

"He is standing silent now, his second and fourth chakra spinning with lots of energy," she told me. She then proceeded to put her hands over my lower back and I felt a lot of energy being sent into my second chakra. She moved away from my body, but the pressure in my back continued, as though someone was still working on me. This went on for a few minutes. Then Leslie returned and said, "He tells me there is something you lost that you must get back."

So I asked her, "Is this something another person needs to get for me or do I need to get it myself?"

She responded, "It is something only you can get, so search for it carefully."

Then I saw the image of a tall tree. In its base was a hole, like a tunnel. There was an object shining inside and I innately knew it belonged to me. "It is a part of your emotional body that you have lost. But you cannot survive without it," Leslie told me. "Let me know when you find it."

Several seconds passed and suddenly I said, "I found it."

I described to her where it was and she said, "Where is it in relation to this room?" I told her, and as she headed over to that spot the object jumped into her hand. She applied it to my back, around the second chakra. "Is it complete or is there more left?" she asked.

"There is a piece left," I answered automatically. She stretched her hand and the piece allowed her to grab it. She placed this piece on my upper back, behind my heart.

"It is scared," Leslie told me. "It wants to know that you will not allow it to leave again."

"I can't guarantee that," I responded. Of course I'm thinking, 'How can I guarantee anything if I don't know what will happen tomorrow?'

"What can you promise it?" Leslie asked.

"That I will love it," I said.

"That seems to be enough," she said. Leslie then checked my chakras. "Your chakras from third up are well, but the base and navel chakras are not spinning," she said.

In that moment I felt a shiver throughout my body. It was as thought my energy body was leaving. I knew this was the precise moment for me to decide if I was staying or exiting. Something very profound in me made the decision, and with an unknown power emerging I tried to tie a cord from Mother Earth to my base chakra. I visualized the red color of that chakra, vibrating and spinning. Then I mentally moved to my second chakra, trying to see the orange color that corresponded to it. After a few minutes Leslie said to me, "OK, they are spinning now." When she glanced at the clock an hour has passed. "We have been in a time warp," she said. It seemed as though only a few minutes had gone by.

My body still face down, she moved to my neck. "There are rows and rows of people, as far as I can see. They come for you, to honor you," Leslie continued, "I have never seen anything like this." Unexpectedly she began to sob. "They are telling me … 'don't just put oil on her, anoint her.' This is what was done to Jesus! Beatriz, who are you?" Leslie asked. "Why are so many beings of light here to honor you?"

I did not know. I could not answer her. I had asked myself the same question, especially then. Who was I to agree to such intense challenges? What kind of Being would think they could withstand, confront a situation like this? Who was I? I could not answer those questions, not yet … maybe some day.

Then Leslie moved to my feet. She started pressing the center of each sole. At that moment I asked myself, 'Who could keep going with all this pain? I don't know if it is worth continuing. Is this my sign to exit and go to Heaven?' Within seconds of this last question, Leslie exclaimed, "You must stay! You must stay! There are people waiting for you. They will benefit from what you are learning." Something in me shifted, as though I remembered a soul agreement. I also recalled the conversation with Jesus in my living room the day before. So in that moment I decided to stay. Leslie finished, exhausted. She blew the candles. "Take your time," she said. I did, and as I exited the massage room I felt much better, specially energetically. My physical body still felt pain, but not as penetrating as before. Without a doubt I needed energetic work first. That evening I thanked the Universe for putting Leslie in my path. They had heard my plea for help!

A day later my soul friends started arriving. Little by little I began to be put back together. The first soul sister that arrived did an immediate healing and soul retrieval on me. The piece that came back was related to Samantha. No doubt it was the last straw that was holding me together, and within a few days I felt some of my energy return. Then another dear friend came and did another soul retrieval for me. This one had more pieces I had lost after my mom's death. My physical body was not yet fully healed, but the energy and emotional bodies were starting to revive.

Eighteen days after my last dog's departure was my mom's birthday. I decided I was ready to go to Mt Mitchell—the highest peak east of the Mississippi, to do ceremony and release the ashes of my mom and the girls. I had split my mom's ashes into several containers so that I could give my dad and brothers each a portion. That way we could each carry out her wishes of where to spread them. I drove to the Mt. Mitchell State Park entrance off the Blue Ridge Parkway, and then went up to the top parking lot. I asked Great Spirit to guide me to the perfect place for their ashes to be honored and set free.

Soon thereafter I saw a sign of a hiking path that was closed and something inside told me this was our starting point. With one of my close friends at my side we began the hike. After about a half a mile of walking through an enchanted forest we found a large overhanging rock that housed deep crevices and hidden rock formations. Warmth spread inside my solar plexus and I knew this was the place. The fact that the pathway was closed meant we could do ceremony without being interrupted. After opening sacred space and setting my intention of liberating the ashes of my most loved beings, I connected with the spirit of the mountain. I honored it and then asked permission for what I was about to do. A strong wind blew from out of nowhere and the energy of the place shifted. I took that to be the sign I was waiting for.

The ceremony began, and one by one the ashes of each were liberated. The honoring took a couple of hours, and then something magical began to happen. I started connecting with my mom in a very clear way, as though she was standing right next to me. My perception shifted to the Energetic and I felt the merging of our energies. In my altered state I felt her tell me that I could always find her in my heart, in that small compartment where eternity resides. She then showed me how to access it and said: "It will all be well. You will emerge stronger, more peaceful and much more loving. Be patient with yourself. We are all working from this side to help you feel whole again."

The person that had hiked up to do ceremony was a completely different person than the one that had descended and exited the park. It was as though the last chapter of my lifetime had just finished being written, the book cover closed and a new and empty canvas was waiting to be painted, one moment at a time.

The moment I got home the last surprise of an amazing day was about to be revealed. The message light in my answering machine was blinking so I pushed play. The voice of a woman came forth, saying: "I know your heart is broken. I have a ten-week old, black female miniature schnauzer. Do you want her?" I did not know this woman and she did not know me. I wasn't looking for a dog yet, for I felt I was not ready to take care of a little creature. But it was my mom's birthday and I had a feeling about what could be going on. I called the lady and made an appointment to see the puppy that evening.

As soon as I held the little being in my hand and looked deep into her eyes I saw Tracy's soul! The little puppy grabbed onto my shirt and would not let go. "Unbelievable," I said to my friend accompanying me. She came back, exactly eighteen days after Samantha's departure and on my mom's birthday! "I'll definitely take her," I told the lady. "Thank you for this amazing gift on such a special day." Her new name is Anty Marie, and to this day she reminds me of the miraculous occurrences of that special date. I went home and sat in my meditation room for some time, thanking my mom and the Universe for this incredible set of synchronicities. My rebirth was imminent, a completely new life ahead!

From the very first moment I came to Asheville I knew the internal connection with my Higher Self would be further developed and strengthened. The levitation experience when we visited in

March of 2006 set the stage. The many open vortexes of energy, the fact that these are the oldest mountains in the world, and the many spiritual people in the area were all catalysts for my own growth. Little did I imagine what a massive transformation I would undergo in these beautiful mountains! I realized a few years after leaving the area how held I had been, and that if I had not listened to the message about moving to these magnificent mountains, my unbelievable healing and transmutation would not have happened as swiftly as it did. Undoubtedly the high vibration held me in a place where I did not dwell in the literal, the details. It was as though all of it helped me remain in the mythic and the energetic perceptual states, where the deepest healing takes place. Many years later I have only awe and gratitude for Asheville and the Blue Ridge Mountains!

In Closing

I was born under the Mayan sign symbolizing 'changes,' and somehow I always knew I would have to hold on tight for the ride of this lifetime! There have been lots of changes, many of them having to do with groups (corporations, friends, learning groups) and others with family. But mostly changes have had to do with my life: my career and now my path; my focus and interests; things that passionately excite me; beautiful consequences of rebelling against that which doesn't ring true and doesn't feel right; shedding layers of beliefs and illusions that have brought me to today, but don't define who I am nor who I want to be; the emergence of my true Self. Understanding the lessons I wrote for myself and my soul's mission; realizing I can dream my world into reality; cherishing my Divine connection above anything else; remembering unconditional love and compassion; recognizing my 'soul family;' and trusting ... ah, that is a big one! As I embark on yet another change in my life, I look back and am surprised at how the pieces fit perfectly together. I am amazed at my soul's wisdom in meticulously planning every little step and experience I've had, weaving an intricate poem of life.

And the story unfolds ....

Acknowledgements

Few words can express my gratitude to all the people that made this book a reality. To my dear friends that insisted I write about my experiences and path, as well as those that read through the first manuscripts, my heartfelt appreciation. To my Aunt Cristina who insisted that books have energy and I needed to move forward so that the original intention would not be dissipated. To my original mentor, my Mom, for giving me all the love and encouragement to always dream my life. Thank you also to my editor Roberta Binder, not only for making this arduous process so light and easy, but also for her tremendous encouragement. To the numerous teachers and writers that inspired me: Carlos Castaneda for introducing me to shamanism and a different way of looking at life since I was a teenager; Carolyn Myss for her deep yet simple teachings on managing energies; Jean Houston for her impeccability, clarity and insistence that we reach for the greatest possibility; Alberto Villoldo for introducing me to an amazing approach to shamanism and to dreaming our world. And finally, thank you to all the people that have believed in me and encouraged me throughout my education and corporate life.

About the Author

Beatriz M. Orive was born and raised in Guatemala and educated in the United States. As a youth, with her parents and siblings, she spent many happy weekends and vacations visiting Mayan villages and learning their customs and ceremonies. In later life, she would see this time as the original awakening of her Shamanic journey.

Beatriz is a multi-cultural and trilingual entrepreneur, obtaining an MBA from Northwestern's Kellogg Graduate School of Management. This background immediately opened the doors to an extremely successful corporate career in Strategic Planning and Strategic Marketing for seventeen years. Her highest professional placement was as Vice President and General Manager for the Latin American Division of a Fortune 50 corporation. At age 34 she left the rigors of the desk in the corner office, to open her own Consulting Firm and work for multiple Fortune 100 companies. This set-up provided her the versatility to pursue, on a more structured level, studies in diverse Spiritual Disciplines.

Since the late 1980s, Beatriz has been fully immersed in studying multiple Spiritual Disciplines as part of her personal quest to find that 'something missing.' In 1995 she decided to delve deeper into Shamanism and Energy Medicine, eventually making it her own spiritual discipline! A few years later she settled into serious full time study with a noted Shamanic Mentor/Teacher. With memories of her youthful experiences with the Maya, it was no surprise that this would be her calling. In 2003, Beatriz transitioned completely into the arena of Spiritual Teaching and Healing, founding a Mystery School, **Awakening the Soul,** where she continues to teach and lecture throughout the United States and Latin America. *A Return to Ancient Wisdom* is her first book.

For information about Class Schedules, Events, and ordering additional copies of this Book: **www.AwakeningTheSoul.net.**